MANAGEMENT-ORIENTED
MANAGEMENT INFORMATION
SYSTEMS

MANAGEMENT-ORIENTED
MANAGEMENT
INFORMATION SYSTEMS

JEROME KANTER

Honeywell Information Systems

Prentice-Hall, Inc., Englewood Cliffs, New Jersey

ISBN: 0-13-548727-7
Library of Congress Catalog Card No. 74-37663

Printed in the United States of America

PRENTICE-HALL INTERNATIONAL, INC., *London*
PRENTICE-HALL OF AUSTRALIA, PTY. LTD., *Sydney*
PRENTICE-HALL OF CANADA, LTD., *Toronto*
PRENTICE-HALL OF INDIA PRIVATE LIMITED, *New Delhi*
PRENTICE-HALL OF JAPAN, INC., *Tokyo*

FOREWORD

Management information systems provided the "wish fulfillment syndrome" of the sixties. The "wish fulfillment syndrome" works this way: when one has a serious problem and an approach develops that is only partially understood, but appears to bear some relation to the problem, this approach, regardless of its direct applicability, tends to become the solution. However, in the late sixties, a MIS backlash developed—writings on the subject took on negative and apologetic tones, attendance at courses on MIS dwindled, and computer books on MIS dropped from the best seller lists. This backlash has tended to obscure the role of MIS in the seventies.

I believe that MIS, if properly defined and understood, has untapped potential for business—indeed it may prove to be the only way to maintain a competitive industry posture. The purpose of this book is to put MIS in proper perspective so that business managers can understand what such systems can do and—equally as important—understand what they cannot do.

A major problem in the sixties has been the proliferation of books and magazine articles that purportedly deal with MIS. The term "management information system" has been used to describe systems which range from the preparation of an inventory report showing updated ending balances to the simulation of how new products will fare in complex marketing environments. The most rudimentary systems books, many devoted solely to describing the input, output, and processing characteristics of computers, have borne the title of management information systems. In another vein, the businessman thinks of MIS as being synonymous with the total systems concept where one grandiose system is designed to encompass the entire operation of a company, providing meaningful and timely reports upon which managers can base immediate decision and action. This is hard for the businessman to swallow, since he wonders how a computer is going to quantify the data which he knows is subjective and psychological in nature and which is often as important as the quantitative type of information.

Also implicit in management information systems is the idea that such a system assists management at all levels in the organization, including top management. MIS has come to mean automated board rooms where corporate executives can obtain the daily profit-and-loss picture, the current sales situation, or the instantaneous cash flow position by pushing a button on a graphical display console.

Thus, MIS has meant, on the one hand, something as basic as a simple order-processing or payroll system, and on the other hand, has been used to refer to advanced simulation applications and direct board room interaction with the computer. It's confusing to say the least.

This book is intended for the technically oriented, non-EDP manager who seeks a meaningful explanation of what a MIS is and what it can do for management. The manager with no EDP or technical background might find chapters 3, 4, and 5 a bit heavy going and may wish to read them last. The book should also prove meaningful for use as a text for a basic course in MIS or the design of MIS at the college or graduate level. It is not intended for the experienced EDP manager except as an introduction to MIS for the EDP manager whose experience has been limited to basic accounting and administrative applications.

The book opens by defining MIS and develops the framework that will be used throughout the book. Each word in the term MIS is explored and classified. Lack of such a framework has been the cause of the current confusion and misconceptions concerning MIS. Chapter 1 distinguishes two system dimensions—the first dimension being functional subsystems which cut across departmental boundaries within a company. These systems are called the horizontal dimension and include the major information systems of a company: for example, sales order processing and inventory control. The second dimension represents the logical process which each of the functional subsystems goes through in order to be computerized and thus become a viable information system. This is termed the vertical dimension and includes the steps of design, analysis, synthesis, and implementation. After a look at the state of the art in management information systems and several examples of successful MIS in Chapter 2, Chapter 3 covers the horizontal system dimension, while Chapter 4 covers the vertical dimension.

Chapter 5 discusses the technological factors that are required to implement the various forms of MIS. Although MIS need not be powered by computers and related technology, the computer in all but the most rare instances represents the *sine qua non* of medium and large scale MIS. The software and application dimensions are studied in addition to the hardware technology since, in many cases, it has been the software and application tools that have lagged behind the hardware. Communications, data management software systems, large scale direct access storage devices, management-oriented computer languages, and management science application aids such as simulation and linear programming are discussed.

Chapters 6 and 7 focus on the management aspects of MIS and are very much management oriented. Chapter 6 describes the impact of MIS on management and contrasts the extreme positions of the complete extinction of middle management and the viewpoint that MIS will have minimal effect on middle and upper levels of management. The framework described in Chapter 1 makes this discussion more meaningful. Chapter 7 is the corollary to Chapter 6 and discusses the role that managers should adopt to avail themselves of the benefits of MIS. One of the statements that managers commonly hear these days is that they must get involved and be educated in EDP. While managers have come to accept this statement, the focus is now on the question of *how* should they get involved and *what* should they learn about computers and EDP.

Chapter 8 summarizes the trends and direction of future EDP systems, placing them in perspective to the prior generations of computer processing. The major developments needed for implementation of advanced management information systems are explored. A practical forecast is made in contrast to the rather "blue sky" predictions that abound in today's literature. The blue sky camp fails to take into account the general economic basis of business and the psychological elements in the make-up of management, workers, and consumers that establish the bounds of technological advancement.

Throughout the book, study guide lines have been provided for the use of instructors and students who will be employing the book as a text. Each chapter concludes with a number of study "casettes" or short cases which can be used as a foundation for classroom assignments and discussion. The casettes elaborate on major issues discussed in the chapter and are based on actual company experiences. Pertinent questions are appended to each "casette" to stimulate analysis and discussion.

A bibliography is appended to each chapter. In addition, Chapter 4 concludes with a longer comprehensive case study which can be used to stress the principles of system design, system trade offs, and the analysis of an application subsystem and its role in MIS. A study guide which divides the material into five individual assignments, as well as sample solutions, are presented. Individual case histories and company experiences are embedded in each chapter.

The book is not an exhaustive treatise of management information systems. It presents a framework for those seeking understanding of MIS as well as for those responsible for the planning and implementation of MIS within a business environment. Guidelines are presented for successful employment of MIS concepts. The book explores MIS from the management and business viewpoint. The thesis of the book is that this is the correct viewpoint. While the framework established is heavily influenced by the efforts of Anthony, Deardon, and Churchill of the Harvard Business School, Simon of Carnegie-Mellon University, and Forester and Carroll of MIT, I have not followed the typical scholarly approach in writing the book. I think I share with other businessmen the discouragement of trying to wade through a book that is filled with references, footnotes, quotations, and critiques of other people's works. With this in mind, I have emphasized readability and understanding. The book is intended for the business manager, not the scholar, and therefore refrains from the "wordsmanship" and "quotesmanship" that I think characterizes many of today's business books. In this light, a systems taxonomist is called a person who classifies systems, and an information technology methodologist is a systems man.

Tackling a subject like MIS is an ambitious undertaking. The goal of the book is to make a contribution to the basic understanding and employment of business oriented management information systems. My viewpoint on MIS emanates from the following background:

- Manager of an EDP department in a large manufacturing and distribution company.
- Assistant controller in charge of accounting and financial control operations in a manufacturing company.
- Assistant to the plant manager of a manufacturing company in developing organizational and informational systems to improve plant operations.
- Experience in designing and implementing applications, including management information systems, for use by companies in several industries.
- Manager of a planning department using the output of computers to aid marketing and planning functions.
- Knowledge of surveys and studies of information systems and direct contact with EDP professionals and practitioners.
- Instructor and lecturer in computer sciences at Babson College; Amos Tuck Business School, Dartmouth; Northeastern University; and the Harvard Business School.

In undertaking a book on MIS, the most important credential I possess is an emotional involvement in using, developing, and installing MIS and portions of MIS in various companies.

I gratefully acknowledge the continued encouragement and cooperation of the management of Honeywell Information Systems, particularly Christopher J. Lynch, Vice President of Marketing, and Richard E. Weber, Director of Marketing Support. I have had the pleasure of working very closely with these two gentlemen over the period of the time it has taken me to write the book.

I wish to express a deep debt of gratitude to Veronica Cannell, who also was an invaluable contributor to my last book. She has added her intelligence and insight to the myriad of administrative and technical matters that are so essential in completeing a task of this magnitude. I can't imagine reaching the publication stage without her.

JEROME KANTER

CONTENTS

MANAGEMENT-ORIENTED MANAGEMENT INFORMATION SYSTEMS

Chapter 1

MIS—AN ANALYTICAL FRAMEWORK

The objective of this chapter is to build an analytical framework in order to facilitate a meaningful discussion of management information systems. Recently I
read a provocative *Harvard Business Review* article having as its thesis the idea
that management had not been affected by computerized information systems and
that it was doubtful that it would be in the next five years. A long rebuttal was
printed several issues later, pointing out example after example of how management has been affected by the computer. In carefully reviewing both the article
and the rebuttal, it became clear that the two authors were talking about completely different levels of management, and I had the feeling that there would be
a surprisingly high level of agreement between the two writers if the semantic barrier were removed. Thus I think it is well worth the effort to define terms and to
establish a generalized framework from which to view the often misinterpreted
management information system concept.

Before dissecting each term in management information system, I will
present a definition. A MIS is a system that aids management in making, carrying
out, and controlling decisions. Decision making, including the process leading up
to the decision, can be termed planning, and management can be defined as the
planning and control of the physical and personnel resources of the company in
order to reach company objectives. This definition of management differs from
other descriptions—one of which is getting things done through people—but I feel
it is more definitive. Getting things done through people, plus the selecting, training,
and motivating of people, is assumed part of the control function, for implementing and controlling the decisions made will obviously require the motivation
of people. Referring back to the MIS definition, we can simplify it by saying that
MIS is a system that aids management in performing its job. Later chapters will

1

analyze the manager's job in greater detail and will indicate in which areas computerized management information systems can make the greatest impact and in which areas its impact is doubtful, even in the future. The following analysis should aid this discussion.

ELEMENTS OF A MANAGEMENT INFORMATION SYSTEM

Exploration of the problem begins by looking at the basic elements or ingredients of a management information system. The term MIS is a well-conceived one in that if one understands the three words or parts that comprise it, one can obtain a basic understanding of the whole. This point may seem obvious, but it is not true of certain other technical terms or the so-called buzz words that form the argot of a new industry.

LEVELS OF MANAGEMENT

The first term to define is management. Figure 1.1 presents the organization chart of a manufacturing company. Company organization charts generally have considerably more detail than the one shown in the figure. However, this chart has enough detail to illustrate the distinction between the different levels of management. There are several ways to describe the various management levels. Although lines of demarcation are not absolute, one can distinguish certain layers of management within the organization.

TOP MANAGEMENT

The executive committee, consisting of the president and the heads of the major departments of the company, constitutes what is usually referred to as top management (the cross–hatched boxes). If the company has diversified manufacturing operations, a higher–level corporate executive committee will consist of the vice-president/general manager of each manufacturing division and the vice-presidents of the staff departments that operate at the corporate level. For purposes of discussion, it will be assumed that there is a single division and that top management is the executive committee of that division.

When serving in this capacity, the members of the committee determine the short– and long–range objectives of the company, the physical, monetary, and personnel resources to realize these objectives, and the policies and strategies that best utilize the resources. This activity can be called strategic planning. Although the final decisions are the province of the executive committee, a good deal of the study of market conditions, the analysis of competition and business opportunities, and the development of alternate product plans and strategies is accomplished by staff groups, either at the divisional or the departmental level. In the organizational

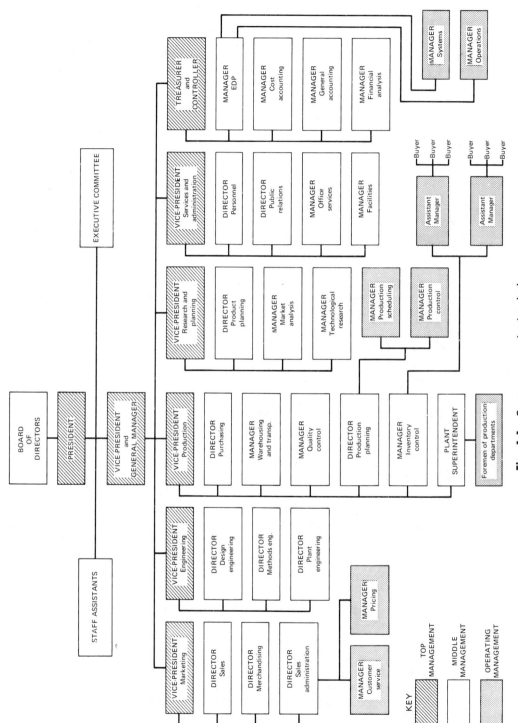

Fig. 1.1 Company organizational chart

3

illustration used here, the staff work would be accomplished in the research and planning department.

In their capacity as department heads, the members of the executive committee have the responsibility of implementing and controlling the decisions made. This activity differs materially from their strategic planning role. The major challenge of top management is to wear these two hats effectively. The department heads direct functions that can be classified as either line or staff. The line departments are concerned with those functions related to producing and delivering a product to a customer physically. The basic line departments illustrated in Figure 1.1 are marketing and production, although both line and staff subfunctions are found within the departments.

On the other hand, departments that perform a supporting service not directly concerned with the physical flow of goods are considered staff departments. The staff departments listed in the figure are engineering, research and planning, services and administration, and the treasurer and controller's department. Depending on the nature of a particular business, line and staff departments have relative degrees of importance. Similarly, areas within the line and staff departments have relative degrees of importance. For example, in a company with a rapidly changing, highly stylized product, the engineering department has more significance than it does in a company with a more stable product line. It is possible that only certain department heads will be members of the executive committee. For instance, the engineering department of a food processor or bicycle manufacturer may not have the same importance as, say, the production department, so the vice-president in charge of engineering would not attend regular meetings of the executive committee. This would not be true in the case of a computer manufacturer or a supplier to the national space program, the activities of both requiring high technical and engineering content.

MIDDLE MANAGEMENT

The managers reporting to the department heads are considered middle management (unshaded boxes in Figure 1.1). Middle management, therefore, includes such people as the director of sales, the director of design engineering, the director of purchasing, and the director of personnel. As with department heads, members of middle management have relative degrees of significance— degrees often reflected in the titles of people reporting to the same vice-president. For example, the head purchasing man has a director's title and the head quality control man has a manager's title, yet both report to the vice-president in charge of production.

Although elements of planning and control exist at all levels of management, control is the predominant element in the middle manager's job. Top management has established the overall goals and objectives of the company. It is middle management's job to acquire and control the necessary resources in order to implement these objectives. A prime measurement of a middle manager's job is how efficiently he accomplishes his objectives—that is, how optimally he processes the various inputs with which he works into the required output. It is recognized that optimal is a relative term in that one rarely knows if the particular process utilized is optimal; optimal usually refers to some predetermined yardstick, such as a production standard within a standard cost system.

OPERATING MANAGEMENT

The managers or supervisors who report to middle management constitute the operating level of management. Figure 1.1 is abbreviated in that it does not list all such people. Examples of the operating management levels listed are the managers of customer service and pricing, who report to the director of sales administration, and the managers of production scheduling and production control, who report to the director of production planning. There is less planning in the operating level than in either middle or top management. If middle management is concerned with the overall aggregate of functions and activities, then operating management is concerned with more finite and specific activities. Examples of such activities are buying 25 barrels of flour or producing a lot of 50 rear wheel assemblies. These are specific tasks that are performed within the context of a set of fairly well prescribed rules and procedures.

There are problems in attempting to distinguish three layers of management. One problem is that it is difficult to stick to only three levels when most companies have an organizational hierarchy consisting of six or more levels; that is, some managers are six levels or more removed from the company president. Thus, in maintaining this three-level category, some managers are in the same category as the managers to whom they report. Although only three levels are shown in Figure 1.1, it is quite probable that there are managers who report to the operational-level managers. For example, the assistant managers of inventory control may have head buyers who supervise other buyers. In this case, both the head buyer and the assistant manager of inventory control are considered operating management. It is possible to distinguish additional sublevels within each of the three levels; thus there could be a high level, middle level, and lower level of operating management. This further breakdown may have some usefulness because in many instances where computer experts have pointed to the impact of computers on management, they have been referring to operating management, and even lower levels of operating management rather than top management.

Another problem is the distinction between levels of management. Top management's responsibilities have been categorized as determining the overall goals and objectives of the business, whereas middle management is concerned with implementing these objectives. Operating management and the people who work for them perform finite and specific tasks, the results of which enable middle management to carry out its portion of top-management objectives. A fine line distinguishes these levels. Generally the distinction cannot be made by reviewing the organization chart and the reporting structure of the company. As businessmen are aware, both a formal and an informal organization exist within a company. Despite these problems, it is useful, for the purpose of establishing an analytical framework for MIS, to view management as consisting of three levels.

Figure 1.2 summarizes the interaction of the three levels. Top management

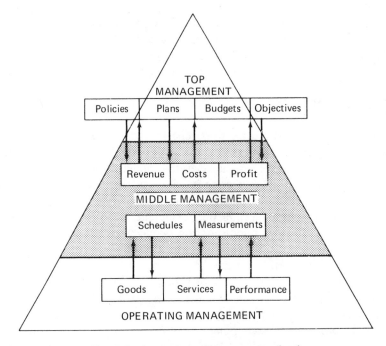

Fig. 1.2 Interaction of management levels

establishes the policies, plans, and objectives of the company, as well as a general budget framework under which the various departments will operate. These factors are promulgated and passed down to middle management, where they are translated into specific revenue, cost, and profit goals, particularly if each department works under a cost or profit center concept. These are reviewed, analyzed, and modified in accordance with the overall plans and policies until agreement is reached. Middle management then issues the specific schedules and measurement yardsticks to operating management. The latter level has the job of producing the goods and services required to meet the revenue and profit goals, which in turn will enable the company to reach its overall plans and objectives.

DISTINCTION BETWEEN MANAGEMENT LEVELS

It is significant to compare the job content of the three levels of management. Figure 1.3 contrasts the levels by reference to 12 characteristics. As has been stated, the first two characteristics represent the essence of management. There is a heavy planning content in top management with less at the middle-management level and a minimum at the operating level. Control is focused on implementation, so that there is a heavy control content at the middle and operating levels but only a moderate amount at the top. In reality, planning and control take place at all levels of management, for it is difficult to separate one activity from the other. Every management job is a microcosm of the total organization to some extent. Top management can never define company objectives to the point where there

Characteristic	Top management	Middle management	Operating management
1. Focus on planning	Heavy	Moderate	Minimum
2. Focus on control	Moderate	Heavy	Heavy
3. Time frame	One to five years	Up to a year	Day to Day
4. Scope of activity	Extremely broad	Entire functional area	Single subfunction or subtask
5. Nature of activity	Relatively instructured	Moderately structured	Highly structured
6. Level of complexity	Very complex, many variables	Less complex, better defined variables	Straightforward
7. Job measurement	Difficult	Less difficult	Relatively easy
8. Result of activity	Plans, policies and strategies	Implementation schedules, performance yardsticks	End product
9. Type of information utilized	External	Internal, more accurate	Internal historical, high level of accuracy
10. Mental attributes	Creative, innovative	Responsible, persuasive, administrative	Efficient, effective
11. Number of people involved	Few	Moderate number	Many
12. Department/divisional interaction	Intra-division	Intra-department	Inter-department

Fig. 1.3 Job content of management levels

7

is no room for interpretation. Therefore it is necessary for lower levels of management to plan as well, although they may do so in a more restricted environment. Within each department and subdepartment, there are usually counterparts to the executive committee who meet periodically to plan the activity for the next time period and to review techniques for implementing the plans. The individual departments have their own equivalent of top, middle, and operating management.

Top management deals with activity that has a time dimension of 1 to 5 years. This is not to say that they ignore shorter–term problems; rather, it indicates that the focus of the executive committee's attention is on the future. In some cases, the span is greater than 5 years. Middle management must project activity a year to enable the development of the annual operation plan, but normally the focus is on weeks or months. The key questions raised at meetings of middle management is how the prior period, whether a week, 2 weeks, or a month, compared to plan and, if below plan, how they can take remedial action. Middle management deals with plans and performance against plans. Operating management's time frame is on a day-to-day basis. They have specific tasks to accomplish and they can measure these accomplishments on a short-term basis. A week usually constitutes the time span.

The next three characteristics apply to the overall nature of the activity. It is already clear that the scope of top management's responsibilities is extremely broad, whereas middle management is concerned with major functional areas, such as production planning or quality control. Operating management's attention is focused on individual subfunctions, the elements of which enable a function to be accomplished. The nature of activity runs from an unstructured framework at the top to a highly structured one at the bottom. Top management is dealing with such factors as the marketplace, the products and services to offer the marketplace, the competitive factors, and the timing of product introductions. Although some companies have succeeded in building a statistical market model that helps in the structuring of the outside world, much of the data on which the model feeds is qualitative and subjective in nature and has a varying probability quotient. As a result, top management's job is complex and involves numerous variables, many of which are difficult to measure. The variables at the middle-management level are better defined, for they deal with events and activities that take place within the operating environment of the company. Although some people would say that the world at the operating level is not as straightforward as indicated on the chart, it is when compared to higher-management levels. A foreman may consider the reassignment of workers to expedite a rush order as a difficult task, especially if there are union restrictions on assignments. However, this activity does not approach the complexity of forecasting the profitability and impact on company operations of the introduction of a new product line.

The result or output of top management's activity consists of the plans, procedures, and strategies that the company will follow over the next year, plans that are consistent with the longer-range thinking of the company. Middle management produces, as their output, the schedules and performance measurements to accomplish the plan, while the result of operating management's activity is the end product itself. Thus the objective of a business enterprise is to evolve broad-gauged and somewhat intangible directives and plans into progressively more detailed and tangible work plans that eventually result in the tangible production of a product. As will be discussed in the next section, top management deals primarily in external information, whereas middle and operating management deal with internal and historical information. There is a greater degree of accuracy and validity in the internal brand of information.

The last three characteristics cover personal attributes of the job content. Top-management's job requires creativity, innovation, and the ability to make decisions under varying degrees of uncertainty. Middle-management's job entails a persuasiveness and motivational element that can get the job done. While top management can be regarded as the navigator and architect of the ship, the middle manager is the captain who barks the orders and sustains the people effort to reach the destination. Operating management must employ efficient and effective techniques that will accomplish the job. The number-of-people characteristic reflects the hierarchal pyramid of company organization with few people at the top and many at the bottom. Finally, each management level has interaction paths with other management levels. Top management must deal at the division level to ensure that their plans are consistent with corporate goals and objectives. Middle managers of one department must interact with management of other departments because of he interdependence of one department to another. For example, an important customer needs a rush order by a certain date. This is a case where the sales department influences the production department and vice versa. Operating management's interaction can usually be confined to the department in which it operates.

I feel it was important to delve as deeply as I have into the nature of the activity at different management levels. Too many system practitioners have designed (some have even implemented or attempted to implement) so-called management information systems without an understanding of the management process. The result of such efforts has either been abortive and costly systems that missed their mark or systems under the guise of MIS that really were aimed at the lower-management levels—sometimes at the operating management but often at clerical levels below the operating-management level. Thus it is important to understand the management process and to determine the focus of MIS. I have mentioned that every management job is a microcosm of the total organization. This point is true with the electronic-data-processing manager's job as it appears on the organizational chart in Figure 1.1. The planning element of the EDP manager's job is to ascertain the activities and responsibilities of management and to develop with them an information system that assists them in carrying out their responsibilities. Too often a hasty and haphazard planning job precedes a premature plunge into the implementation phase. An understanding of the management process is a necessary prerequisite to a management information system. As will be pointed out later, difficulties remain in successfully designing and implementing an information system even when the management process is understood; without such an understanding, however, there is no chance of success. It will also be pointed out that MISs have been more successful when directed at the operating level of management.

TYPES OF MANAGEMENT INFORMATION

Information is the second element in the term management information system. Information has come to be recognized as an increasingly valuable commodity required by management in order to plan and control business operations effectively. Many consider information to be as significant a resource as the traditional four m's of men, machines, material, and money.

Information is the "stuff" of paper-work systems just as material is the "stuff" of production systems. For purposes of definition, this analogy is shown in Figure 1.4. Data is defined as raw material and may enter the processing system in the form of a punched card, punched paper tape, writings on the back of envelopes, and so on. Processed data is called information and is in a form to assist management and other users. Concerning the use of the word "data," although I realize that the word data is plural, with the singular being datum, I have never felt comfortable in the use of the plural and therefore will use data in the singular sense throughout the book.

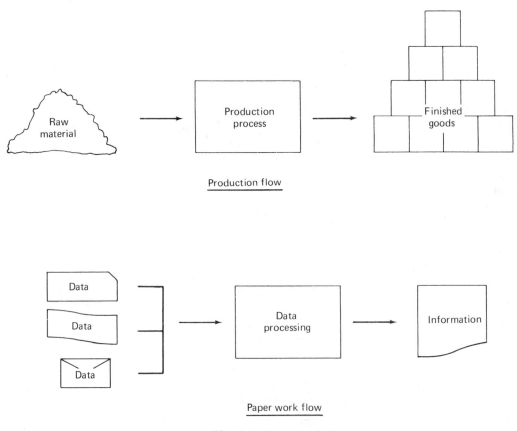

Production flow

Paper work flow

Fig. 1.4 Paper work flow

BUSINESS DIMENSION OF INFORMATION

It has already been stated that different levels of management utilize different types of information. There are a variety of ways to classify information. Figure 1.5 contrasts the business dimension of information over a continuum with top management at one end and operating management at the other. Middle management, as always, falls in between, having elements of both.

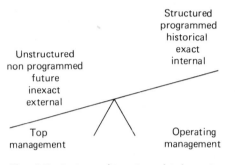

Fig. 1.5 Business dimension of information

The factors shown in the figure obviously are related. For example, information that is unstructured is difficult to program. Structured information tends to be rhythmic in that it follows a repetitive pattern which occurs at prescribed time periods. Thus the foreman has the monthly production schedule for a particular product, which indicates that 50 units are scheduled for each of the next ten days. He will want to review the information that indicates the material cost, labor cost, and expenses incurred on a day-to-day basis to see if the schedule is being met and if it is being met efficiently. Because the information is structured, it can be programmed. Rules and procedures can be established to develop schedules and measurements that will be most efficient for the known operating conditions. This is the reason that there are more computerized information systems programmed to assist operating management than there are systems assisting top management. The nature of top management's responsibilities revolves around strategic planning, where the nature of information is unstructured and therefore difficult to program. For example, it is difficult to determine with exactness the market share of a company's products or the particular penetration in a specific market segment.

Information for planning purposes stresses the future and thus is inexact when compared to information required at the operating level. This is not to say that top management is not interested in past history and in operating results. However, past results must be viewed in light of external conditions and the marketplace in which the company competes. The focus of top management is on future plans and policies. The matrix shown in Figure 1.6 focuses on the difference between internal and external information.

Internal information is a by-product of the normal operations of a business. For example, a recording of inventory usage for the past week is typical internal

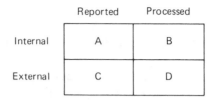

Fig. 1.6   Information matrix

information. Internal information generally is historical or static in nature; it is after the fact data. This point is true at least in category A when the information is reported but not statistically processed. In the case of inventory usage, if the information is limited to prior history and no attempt is made statistically to sample or draw meaningful correlations from the data, this represents internally reported data. However, if inventory usage is statistically plotted to project future usage patterns, which are used to set optimum inventory levels, it represents an example of category B or statistically processed internal information.

External information is data whose source is outside the operations of the company. An example is population growth in the market served by a company or the changes in ethnic makeup of the market. Category C reports the data but makes no attempt to analyze it statistically, and category D uses various mathematical techniques to analyze and correlate the data. A sales forecast that projects the future based on historical sales movement would be category B information, whereas a sales forecast that also includes external market statistics and trends would be a combination of B and D. The relative use of the various forms of information by a computer system is consistent with the alphabetic sequence; that is, A is found in a computer system more often than B, B is found more often than C, and C is found more often than D.

TECHNICAL DIMENSION OF INFORMATION

The concept of a data base that is so important to a management information system will be described in more detail in later chapters. Simply stated, the data base is a unified collection of data that is utilized by the various information systems. The form, capacity, and degree of integration of the data depend on the needs to which the data is put, plus cost considerations. The technical dimensions of the data base are such elements as response time, capacity, interrelationships of data elements, security, and validity. The cost considerations involve the summation of the following three costs:

1. Cost to acquire data

2. Cost to maintain data

3. Cost to access data

Figure 1.7 describes the data base concept and the relationship of the originators/users of the data/information and the information or system specialists.

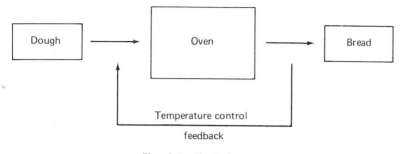

Fig. 1.9 Physical system

The dough is the principal input and enters the oven. Automatic controls continually monitor the temperature and humidity, actuating certain remedial functions if the elements fall above or below specific predetermined tolerances. This is an example of a process control system or a closed-loop industrial process. It is a physical system. For the most part, information systems try to achieve the same level of control over physical processes that are not as receptive to the closed-loop type of treatment. An example is a discrete manufacturing company as compared to a continuous process manufacturer. In discrete manufacturing, there are a number of individual work stations where raw material is fabricated and assembled into various in-process stages until a prescribed finished-goods item is produced. This differs from the process type of manufacturing, like cement plants, petroleum companies, or bakeries, where there is a continuous process of feeding raw material in one end and obtaining a finished item at the other. An information system for a discrete manufacturer would be a production scheduling system that takes orders for particular items for a particular period of time and develops a work schedule to produce them. The information system is based on the physical facilities that are available. It has been stated that the job of the system analyst is not to initiate changes in organizational structure or the information requirements of management, although he can point out the benefits of so doing. Similarly, it is not his job to initiate changes in the physical systems that exist within a company. The physical systems are the givens; system analysis should concentrate on improving management control over the existing facilities and materials.

A management information system encompasses both physical and information systems. An information system can be designed to enable management to obtain a clearer view of the company's use or misue of its facilities. It can suggest alternatives and test the potential consequences of these alternatives to improve the use of facilities. The ramifications of adding a warehouse or increasing production capacity by an additional assembly line can be better ascertained through the use of a properly designed information system. The point is not that information systems and physical systems are unrelated activities that can and should be tackled separately. Rather, the distinction is made to differentiate the role of management from the role of the system analyst.

The definition of a system has been given and the distinction made between a physical system and an information system. Referring now to the information system, I would like to distinguish two dimensions of information systems, the first being the horizontal dimension, which looks at a system from the point of view of its place or function in a company's operation. The other dimension is the vertical one, representing the phases that each subsystem goes through on its way to implementation. The implementation need not include a computer—this point is obvious—but, for purposes of this discussion, it will be assumed that the information problem is large enough and has the characteristics to put its solution into the realm of electronic data processing.

FUNCTIONAL SYSTEMS—
THE HORIZONTAL DIMENSION

Figure 1.10 illustrates the horizontal system dimension of a manufacturing company. This is a highly simplified schematic that will serve our purposes here. [The functional or horizontal systems will be described in greater detail in Chapter 3.] The boldface arrows on the bottom of Figure 1.10 follow the physical flow of material through the factory. Raw material, piece parts, and supplies originate from a variety of vendors and flow into the factory. Within the factory, the materials are stocked in finished stores, semifinished stores, or raw material, depending on classification and physical storage facilities. Material is then requisitioned from the inventory-holding areas to the fabrication and assembly operations necessary to turn the materials into finished products. Inspection stations at selected points in the operation check for both quantity and quality of product. Finished goods are stored in inventory areas within the main factory or in finished-goods warehouses at various locations throughout the country. As orders are received, the goods are released from the factory or warehouse and transported to the required sales outlet. Sales outlets range from large distributors to direct shipment to individual consumers.

The heavily outlined blocks (vendor, factory, sales outlet, and business economy) indicate physical entities as contrasted to the other blocks, which represent information systems to control the physical flow of goods from the vendor through the factory and into the hands of the consumer. The prime business objective of a manufacturer is to facilitate this material flow in the most economical manner and still satisfy customer demand to the extent that the incoming sales cash stream exceeds the outgoing cash stream. The resultant profit must produce a return on investment that meets the business goals of the company.

Turning now to the information systems that control the physical flow, the order processing system fits in at the front end. This system provides the direct contact with the sales outlets, handles the flow of orders into the factory, expedites orders, and facilitates customer payment for goods shipped. The order processing system is linked directly to the material control system. The job of material control is to ensure that there is a balanced finished-goods inventory to satisfy customer demand in the required time frame. Material control is also indirectly related to the production planning and control system. It establishes when production orders must be initiated to replenish stock levels. In addition to finished-goods inventory, the material control system controls piece parts, assemblies, raw material, and other in-process inventories. Moreover, material control is directly linked to the vendor. Items that are not manufactured must be requisitioned from outside sup-

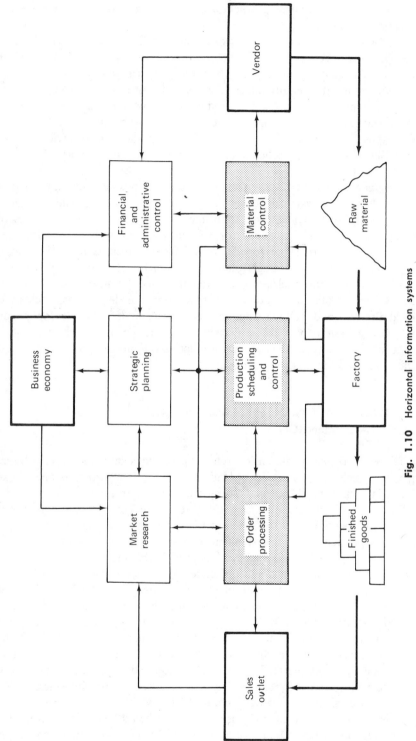

Fig. 1.10 Horizontal information systems

17

pliers; therefore the purchasing function is an important part of the material control system.

Production scheduling and control is undoubtedly the most significant system at the operating level. It is here that orders and forecasts for orders, which together form the gross manufacturing requirements, are screened against available stock to determine net requirements (the amount that must be produced to satisfy customer demand). Scheduling the production of net requirements while making the most economical use of the manpower, machines, and material at the company's disposal is the job of production scheduling and control. The arrows indicate a tie-in of production scheduling and control with the factory. This link is a most important one.

The market research system analyzes sales trends and provides both long- and short-range forecasts for the strategic planning system. The financial and administrative control system is responsible for the accounting statements of the company and plots cash positions for various time intervals. The administrative control system is responsible for the most efficient utilization of the company's personnel resources. The strategic planning system receives summary reports from the other systems, particularly market research and financial and administrative control, combines this information with that from outside sources, such as Gross National Product and political factors, and assists in making the top policy decisions for the company. These decisions include profit and budget planning, resource and capacity analysis, new product development, and general business objectives, both short and long range.

DESIGN AND ANALYSIS OF SYSTEMS— THE VERTICAL DIMENSION

The vertical system dimension refers to the steps that transform a horizontal system or a piece of it into an operational reality. The cross–hatched boxes of Figure 1.10 represent functional subsystems that are relevant to middle- and operating-management levels. These subsystems are geared to handle the information requirements of job functions at that level. The unshaded boxes represent functional subsystems that are significant to the strategic area of operations, or mainly top management. These subsystems provide the information resources necessary to chart the overall plans and objectives of the company.

Figure 1.11 illustrates the steps of design and analysis in the form of an iceberg. It may appear at first that the most complex, time-consuming part of the system job is the programming portion, which is represented by the upper part of the iceberg— that portion above water. This is where the individual computer instructions are written and translated into a computer program to be executed on the machine. In reality, this is the most well-defined part of the job and can be accomplished within a reasonable time frame. System design is a broader category in which the system is analyzed in detail prior to programming. It is this phase that describes the input, output, and processing steps and ensures that all blend together to meet the system specifications. High-quality system design accomplishes this process in the most economical fashion consistent with system conventions and standards. Be-

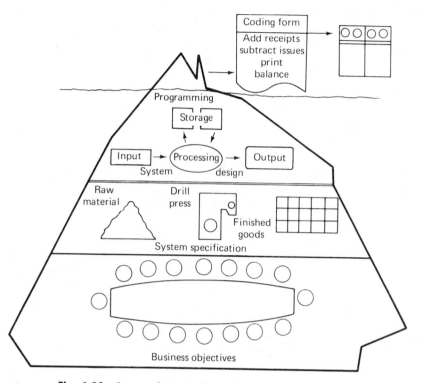

Fig. 1.11 System design and analysis—the vertical dimension

cause many systems utilize common data files and common source data, a requisite of good system design is the avoidance of redundancy and duplication.

System specification is the stage preceding system design where the purpose and objectives of the system are stated. This stage involves the overall review of the operation being systematized to determine exactly what information is needed for the best control of the operation. This phase of the job is obviously of extreme importance because it is the sole reason for conducting system analysis in the first place.

Business objectives form the base of the iceberg. The system that is analyzed may be but a small portion of the overall business operation but it must be consistent with the company's business objectives.

There is a purpose in using an iceberg to illustrate the stages of system development. One should be able to observe that proceeding from the top of the iceberg to the base requires a proportionately higher level of management involvement. Also, the time required to complete the various phases in system development is in direct proportion to the area each represents within the iceberg. This point may seem surprising, but because more people and departments are involved as one proceeds from top to bottom, the elapsed time for that phase is greater. For example, the determination of system specifications for a forecasting system requires a thorough analysis, review, and agreement by each of the departments utilizing the system. Once the detailed specs are agreed to, it is a fairly straight-forward and precise effort to get the system running on a computer. This will be more apparent after studying the elements of each phase of system development in a later chapter. Like an iceberg, the vast proportion of the mass lies beneath the surface.

TOTAL SYSTEMS AND INTEGRATED SYSTEMS

The term management information system can be viewed in totality now that we have defined the three words that make up the term. The definition at the beginning of the chapter stated that MIS is a system that aids management in performing its job. Since management was defined as the planning and control of company resources to reach company objectives, MIS aids the management process. However, this is too broad a definition, which is the reason for the various categorizations of management, information, and systems made in this chapter. Too often MIS is used synonymously with the terms "total system" and "integrated system." Although it is possible for a company to have a system that incorporates all three concepts, it is certainly possible to have one without the other two. A total system implies that all the functional systems have been designed and implemented. Although many companies can state that they have made inroads into the major functional areas, few would even boast that they have implemented all elements of each of the functional systems listed in Figure 1.10, not considering the functional systems that are not included. Studies of medium and large companies have shown that there is a relatively low saturation ratio of computerized applications—the saturation ratio being measured by dividing the computer time of operational applications by the running time of all existing and future applications, were they running on the computer. Survey after survey indicates that many companies have not yet tackled complete functional system areas, like market research, or major subsystems of other functional areas, like production scheduling and control. If a prerequisite of a MIS is a total system, then there is substantiation for the disillusionment with MIS that exists in many quarters today. However, MIS is not synonymous with a total system. Although it is may be a long-run goal to establish a total system or at least to aim in that direction, MIS can be directed at specific functional areas with very impressive results. It is certainly not an all or nothing proposition.

An integrated system implies that all the functional systems are linked together into one entity. Individual systems may be designed to meet the needs of a restricted area of the company's operation but with the needs of the whole organization in mind. Functional areas are not tackled in isolation but only after realization of their relationship with the total system. This is a most desirable goal and represents a characteristic of MIS; however, an integrated system and a management information system are not synonymous. It is possible to develop an integrated system aimed not at the management level but at the clerical and operating levels. The result could be a completely integrated system, but not MIS.

MIS does not imply that it aids all levels of management. Frequently a computerized MIS is taken to mean a system that reacts instantaneously to top-management requests, pouring out data that shows the status of the company at 60-second intervals in graphic form on television screens. A company can employ

MIS concepts that focus on middle and operating management rather than top management. As will be shown in subsequent chapters, it is more feasible to approach MIS from this point of view. It will also become clear that top management operates in a longer-range and more-strategic framework, thus eliminating the need for real-time access to information.

CHARACTERISTICS OF MIS

It should be apparent that MIS is not an easy concept with which to deal. It can be viewed and analyzed from many sides. MIS has been both used and abused. The first step in understanding its potential impact on business operation is to break through the various semantic barriers that exist. Such is the objective of this chapter. This section will summarize the pertinent characteristics of MIS.

1. Management Oriented

This is the most significant characteristic of MIS. The system is designed from the top down. The "top down" approach does not imply that the system will be geared to providing information directly to top management; rather, the system development starts from an appraisal of management needs and overall business objectives. It is possible that middle management or operating management is the focus of the system, such that their needs are the cornerstone on which the system is built. To illustrate the point, a payroll system designed to process employee time cards and produce pay checks, deduction registers, payroll registers, and supporting material needed for government purposes is not a management-oriented system. It only satisfies administrative ends. However, a payroll system that supplies foremen with daily and weekly labor-cost variance reports and production management with monthly labor summaries showing the amount of overtime, idle time, labor variances, and labor cost trends is management oriented. It is geared to satisfying management needs, which, in this case, are to optimize the use of the labor force.

2. Management Directed

Because of the management orientation of MIS, it is imperative that management actively direct the system development efforts. Involvement is not enough. In the preceding examples, management must determine what labor standards should be established and what information is necessary to improve its control of labor costs. It is rare to find a MIS where the manager himself, or a high–level representative of his department, is not spending a good deal of time in system design. It is not a one–time involvement, for continued review and participation are necessary to ensure that the implemented system meets the specifications of the system that was designed. Therefore, management is responsible for setting system specifications, and it must play a major role in the subsequent trade-off decisions that inevitably occur in system development. An important element of effective system planning is the process for determining the priority of application development. Management must control this process if a management information system is to be objective. A company without a formal application approval cycle and a management steering committee to determine priorities will never develop a MIS.

3. Integrated

As mentioned earlier, although not synonymous with, the integrated concept is a necessary characteristic of management information systems. Integration is significant because of the ability to produce more meaningful management information. For example, in order to develop an effective production scheduling system, it is necessary to balance such factors as (a) setup costs, (b) work force, (c) overtime rates, (d) production capacity, (e) inventory levels, (f) capital requirements, and (g) customer service. A system that ignores one of these elements—inventory level, for example—is not providing management with an optimal schedule. The cost of carrying excess inventory may more than offset the other benefits of the system. Integration, in the sense intended here, means taking a comprehensive view or a complete picture look at the interlocking subsystems that operate within a company. One can start a MIS by attacking a specific subsystem, but unless its place in the total system is realized and properly reflected, serious shortcomings may result. Thus an integrated system that blends information from several operational areas is a necessary element of MIS.

4. Common Data Flows

Because of the integration concept of MIS, there is an opportunity to avoid duplication and redundancy in data gathering, storage, and dissemination. System designers are aware that a few key source documents account for much of the information flow and affect many functional areas. For example, customer orders are the basis for billing the customer for the goods ordered, setting up the accounts receivable, initiating production activity, sales analysis, sales forecasting, and so on. It is prudent to capture this data closest to the source where the event occurs and use it throughout the functional areas. It is also prudent to capture it once and thus avoid the duplicate entry of source data into several systems. This concept also holds in building and using master files and in providing reports. The common data flow concept supports several of the basic tenets of system analysis—avoiding duplication, combining similar functions, and simplifying operations wherever possible. The development of common data flows is an economically sound and logical concept, but it must be viewed in a practical and pragmatic light. Because of a company's method of operation and its internal procedures, it may be better to live with a little duplication in order to make the system acceptable and workable. MIS and integration are more important for their ability to blend the relationship of several functional areas of a business and to produce more meaningful management information, rather than for producing that information more economically.

Given the track record and experience to date, one should look closely at the degree of integration of common data flows. Although benefits exist, the degree of difficulty is high and many would-be implementers have failed because they underemphasized the complexity and amount of time or did not possess the necessary system design skills. What is being questioned is not the desirability of building the concept of common data flows into the system; rather, it is the degree to which the concept is used. Building a system that cannot operate unless *all* data springs from a common data path is usually an unwise design concept—as many companies have discovered to their detriment.

5. Heavy Planning Element

Management information systems do not occur overnight; they take from 3 to 5 years and longer to get established firmly within a company. Therefore a heavy planning element must be present in MIS development. Just as a civil engineer does not design a highway to handle today's traffic but to handle the traffic 5 to 10 years from now, so the MIS designer must have the future objectives and needs of the company firmly in mind. The designer must avoid the possibility of system obsolescence before the system gets into operation. Needless to say, sound system planning is an essential ingredient to successful MIS.

6. Subsystem Concept

In tackling a project as broad and complex in scope as a management information system, one must avoid losing sight of *both* the forest and the trees. Even though the system is viewed as a single entity, it must be broken down into digestible subsystems that can be implemented one at a time. A phasing plan must be developed. The breakdown of MIS into meaningful subsystems sets the stage for this phasing plan. Although the functional areas of sales-order processing, material control, and so on, as illustrated in Figure 1.10, have been referred to as systems, in reality they are subsystems that, in turn, can be broken down into additional subsystems. This subsystem analysis is essential for applying boundaries to the problem, thus enabling the designer to focus on manageable entities that can be assigned and computerized by selected systems and programming teams.

7. Central Data Base

As explained earlier, the data base is the mortar that holds the functional systems together. Each system requires access to a master file of data covering inventory, personnel, vendors, customers, general ledger, work in process, and so on. If the data is stored efficiently and with common usage in mind, one master file can provide the data needed by any of the functional systems. It seems logical to gather data once, properly validate it, and place it on a central storage medium that can be accessed by any system. However, it is not unusual to find a company with several data files, one serving one functional system and another serving another system. This is obviously not the most efficient way to operate. Thorough discussion of the central data base will take place in subsequent chapters. Although it is possible to achieve the basic objectives of MIS without a central data base, thus paying the price of duplicate storage and duplicate file updating, more often than not the central data base is a definite characteristic of management information systems.

8. Computerized

It is possible to have a MIS without being powered by a computer, but most people would agree that the computer is the *sine qua non* of medium- and large-scale information systems. The need for system throughput to handle a wide variety of applications and the quick response required by system users often make it mandatory for the data to be in electronic media and for the processing to be accomplished by a high-speed computer. Other necessary attributes of the computer to MIS are accuracy and consistency in processing data and the reduction of demand on the clerical staff. These needs in management information systems make the computer a prime requirement.

SUMMARY

In order to put the concept of management information system into proper context, this chapter has presented an analytical framework from which to view the subject. Each term in the word has been discussed, and various categorizations have been made. Three levels of management were distinguished, and the salient job characteristics and responsibilities of top, middle, and operating management were contrasted. Information was viewed from the business dimension and the technical dimension. The types of information required by the three management levels were discussed. A basic system module introduced the discussion of different types of systems. The distinction between a physical system and an information system was made with the statement that the system analyst is responsible for the information and not the physical system. Two system dimensions were illustrated: one being the horizontal dimension, which views a system from its function in company operations; and the other being the vertical dimension, which represents the phases that each horizontal system goes through in order to be computerized. Finally, MIS was compared to the total system and integrated system. Eight basic characteristics of MIS concluded the chapter.

This chapter is very pivotal to the remainder of the book. After a brief look in Chapter 2 at the state of the art in MIS and the computers that provide the power for such systems, Chapter 3 will delve deeper into the horizontal system dimension, while Chapter 4 will explore the vertical system dimension. Chapter 5 will analyze the technical demands of MIS, which will include elaboration on items 7 and 8 under the characteristics of MIS. Chapters 6 and 7 will elaborate on characteristics 1 and 2 and will be based on the definitions of management, information, and system in this chapter. Finally, Chapter 8 will take a look at the future for computerized management information systems. Because of the heavy dependence of subsequent chapters on this one, the reader should have a good understanding of the analytical framework for MIS described here before proceeding.

STUDY CASETTES

MIS BASED ON DYNAMIC DATA— NOT BIG COMPUTERS

[By Raymond A. Zack, Motorola, Inc. *Automation Magazine,* May 1969]

Usually, when a discussion of management information systems takes place, the conversationalists include the general accounting, finance, and reporting functions. Rarely does the viewpoint of operations management, the group for which management information systems hold the greatest potential, become a dominant voice. It is expected that the same people who applied the early computers to routine accounting problems can apply the computer to the operations activities of business. But general business administration computer specialists are not geared to the idea that effective *operating* management information systems are *dynamic* in nature. That is, financial or accounting functions are historical; operating functions are current. An effective system must be built around "real-time" information.

Furthermore, there is a stereotype that a management information system implies having a complex system with a large computer. General accounting-oriented practitioners are ill-equipped to recognize the full potential of the small data processor. The technical disciplines required to implement real-time systems are much more severe than those required to implement batch systems because emphasis must be placed on collecting data at its source. In this instance, the experience of the continuous processing industries provides valuable insight. The approaches they adopted differ completely from typical approaches attempted by business administration-oriented computer specialists for operating management systems.

New, self-contained hybrid packages which employ both computer control and analog disciplines appear to be the answer to the smaller unit of plant where about fifty functional loops are to be optimized. A large-scale computer might provide additional benefits, but these appear to be of marginal necessity in the face of the costs associated with the efficient use of the large computer.

The continuous process industries have shown how to collect and process data on a real-time basis by dividing the data into smaller, more manageable chunks. They have developed Management Information Systems techniques which are adaptable to discrete process operations.

Study Questions

1. Is it easier to control a physical process system than an information system?

2. Do you think the concept expressed here that discrete process operation can benefit from adopting continuous process techniques is a sound one?

3. Do you think MIS implies having a complex system and a large computer?

4. Contrast the use of one large computer with the use of multiple smaller or mini computers.

HONEYWELL RESIDENTIAL DIVISION

[From "An Integrated System for Manufacturer's," by T. R. Hughes, Published in Proceedings of the 1967 International Data Processing Conference]

The Residential Division of Honeywell is responsible for the design, manufacture, and marketing of automatic controls and systems used in the control of environmental conditions and appliances for the residential dwelling. These products are distributed in the United States through Original Equipment Manufacturers, heating wholesalers, and direct to retailer-users. They are sold to other Honeywell divisions for use in locations outside the United States, and for similar applications in the industrial and commercial markets.

Residential Division factory facilities are located in Minneapolis and in Gardena, California. There are sales offices in 50 locations, and these are organized into 23 branches within five regions, covering the entire 50 states. There are 7,000 employees. The product variety is great (over 10,000), and several thousand customer orders are processed each week.

Perhaps one of the most significant EDP programs the Residential Division has implemented is the "Service" program, which is not a computer program, but an "attitude" program designed to achieve a successful computer program. The total group of system analysts, programmers, and operations personnel has subscribed to this philosophy:

SERVICE

IT'S THE USERS' SYSTEM

THE USERS ARE OUR CUSTOMERS

WE'RE AS GOOD AS THE USERS THINK WE ARE

Very strong emphasis has been placed on point number one: "It's the user's system." Throughout the design, users have participated in all phases of the program operation, because only in this way can you achieve a system which will fill their needs.

The user must initiate the problem, maintain and guide the work on the project, and assume responsibility for the decisions through the stages of definition and investigation of the problem. No one is better suited for this responsibility, in terms of background, experience, and interest.

The EDP team contributes their knowledge and experience in the principles of problem analysis and solution, and in the methods of data processing. They advise, consult, investigate, analyze, caution, and make recommendations to the user.

The Residential Division has found that program "Service" is its greatest aid in maximizing payoff while minimizing pitfalls.

Study Questions

1. What do you think of Residential Division's Service Program?

2. How do you think a company should follow up such a program?

3. What are the potential positive and negative aspects to users of this program?

BIBLIOGRAPHY

ACKOFF, R. L., Management Misinformation Systems. *Management Science,* Vol. 14, #4, Dec., 1967, pp. B147–156.

ANTHONY, R. N., *Planning and Control Systems: A Framework for Analysis.* Division of Research, Graduate School of Business Administration, Harvard University, Cambridge, Massachusetts, 1965.

ARON, J. D., Information Systems in Perspective. *Computing Surveys,* Vol. 1, #4, Dec., 1969, pp. 213–236.

BLUMENTHOL, S. C., *Management Information Systems: A Framework for Planning and Development.* Prentice-Hall, Inc., Englewood Cliffs, N. J., 1969.

CANNING, R. G., What's The Status of MIS? *EDP Analyzer,* Vol. 7, #10 and #11, October–November, 1969.

CHURCHILL, N. C., J. H. KEMPSTER, and M. URETSKY, *Computer Based Information Systems for Management—A Survey.* National Association for Accountants, New York, 1968.

DEMING, R. H., *Characteristics of an Effective Management Control System in an Industrial Organization.* Division of Research, Graduate School of Business Administration, Harvard University, Cambridge, Mass., 1968.

HEAD, R. V., The Elusive MIS. *Datamation,* Sept. 1, 1970, pp. 22–27.

OPTNER, S. L., *Systems Analysis for Business Management,* 2nd ed. Prentice-Hall, Englewood Cliffs, New Jersey, 1968, 277 pp.

PRINCE, T. R., *Information Systems for Management Planning and Control,* Revised ed. Richard D. Irwin, Homewood, Illinois, 1970, 523 pp.

ROSS, J., *Management by Information System.* Prentice-Hall, Englewood Cliffs, New Jersey, 1970, 322 pp.

SANDERS, D. H., ed. *Computers and Management.* McGraw-Hill Book Company, New York, 1970, 458 pp.

Chapter 2

THE STATE OF THE ART;

COMPUTERS AND MIS

Computers have been on the industrial scene for two decades now. The first commercial machine, the Univac 1, manufactured by Remington Rand Corp., was installed in the Bureau of the Census in 1951. Today computer users find themselves at the threshold of a new decade of electronic data processing. Our numbering system has within it a mechanism for triggering much needed self-analysis, introspection, and a general stocktaking of the state of the nation. That mechanism is the even-number syndrome. Class reunions, major anniversaries, company conclaves, predictions of future events, government programs, and other events take place in even–numbered years that are divisible by either 5 or 10. Thus we have the tenth class reunion, the fiftieth year of company operation, and a prediction of how life will be in the year 2000. We have now entered the seventies—a special time for the computer industry, for it marks the third decade for commercial computers and affords an opportunity to look back and see where the first two decades have led us and to assess the general state of the nation as the 1970's unfold.

A QUANTITATIVE VIEW OF THE EDP INDUSTRY

Some general quantitative facts stand out in viewing the past two decades. Figure 2.1 portrays the dollar value of computers installed domestically for the 5-year periods from 1950 projected out to 1975. Several explanatory notes should be made concerning quantitative figures pertaining to the EDP industry. No common set of figures has been published by the government as in the case of other industries. Therefore there are two ways to gather statistics. One method is to survey the computer users themselves and add the value of computers on site to arrive at total installed value. Some organizations do so and update the data on an annual or semiannual basis. The other method is to gather shipment data from the computer manufacturers. Since most of the computer manufacturers are large, multidivisional, diversified-product-line companies, and since there is no federal requirement to report sales or shipments on a divisional or product line basis, the reported data is difficult to obtain with any assurance as to accuracy. Suffice to say, the figures are estimates and must be viewed within a tolerance of ±10%. Figure 2.1 is felt to represent as accurate a portrayal as can be obtained. It is derived from an extrapolation and correlation of published sources, such as A. D. Little, International Data Corporation, the Diebold Group, and Quantum Sciences. The derivation is also true for Figures 2.3 and 2.4. Figure 2.2 is drawn from a study made by Quantum Sciences.

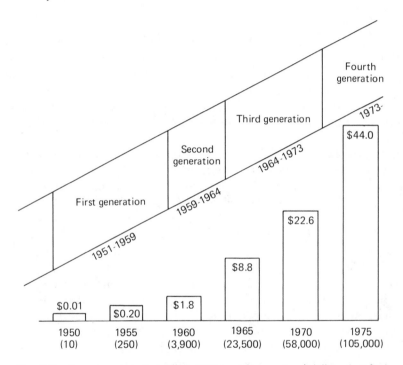

Fig. 2.1 Computers installed 1950–1975; purchase price $ billion (number)

Another factor to be considered is the definition of a computer. Figure 2.1 does not include the category of computers commonly referred to as "mini's" (computers selling for under $25,000). This category includes small scientific computers geared primarily for handling scientific computations, plus special-purpose computers that are aimed at process control applications or at specific communication subsystems of larger systems. Although, this category represents a fairly good number of computers, its dollar value in proportion to the total dollar value of all computers is less than 5 percent today. However, the mini's are expected to grow at a faster rate than the rest of the computer industry.

I feel that the installed figures give a better overall view of computer activity as opposed to yearly shipments. When shipments are considered, one must be clear as to whether the reference is to gross shipments (everything that leaves the manufacturer's shipping docks) or to net shipments (gross shipments less returns). In years of mass replacements, such as when IBM Series 360 replaced Series 1400, the gross shipment figure is misleading if one is looking for an index of how much additional computer dollars are being added to the economy. No commonly agreed-to definition of gross and net shipments exists; therefore the more meaningful figure is the value of computers installed by the composite list of users throughout the country. This figure represents the total computing value of machines in the economy. If a company replaces an IBM 1401 costing $175,000 with a 360/30 costing $250,000, the net added dollar value is $75,000. The dollar figures in Figure 2.1 are not adjusted for inflationary conditions or depreciation. They represent the value at time of purchase. If a machine is rented, it is converted to its equivalent purchase value.

It should also be noted that computer power per dollar expenditure has been increasing rather dramatically during the 20-year history of computers. Figure 2.1 and the figures that follow indicate dollar value of computers rather than computing power. While central processing power per dollar cost has been steadily rising, the performance-price ratios of peripherals, terminals, and communications equipment have not risen as fast. Unlike other industries where prices have risen for equal power and performance, this situation has not been true in the computer industry.

With these explanations, let us take a look at Figure 2.1. In 1950 only about ten computers were installed at a value of $10 million. By 1955 there was a twentyfold increase in dollar value, or $200 million. The next 5-year period produced a ninefold increase to $1.8 billion. The growth in numbers of computers outdistanced the dollar growth, thus indicating that smaller computers were being installed. The period from 1960 to 1965 saw a fivefold increase to $8.8 billion, while the period 1965 to 1970 saw a threefold increase in dollar value to $22.6 billion. The forecast for 1975 is a twofold increase to $44.3 billion.

The generations of computer hardware have been superimposed on the graph. The first generation, characterized by the vacuum tube as the principal electronic component, covered the period 1950 to 1959. The second generation, with transistors replacing vacuum tubes, began in 1959. The third generation, with the microcircuit coming to the fore, was introduced in 1964. The advent of the fourth generation is expected to occur somewhere around 1973 or 1974. Although the growth has been phenomenal over the past two decades, the rate is leveling off. But the leveling off is only relative because a doubling of the dollar value projected from 1970 to 1975 means a yearly increase of 15 percent. This figure will maintain the EDP industry as the fastest–growing major industry in the economy. There is no question that, quantitatively at least, computers have been a phenomenal success.

Expenditures for EDP can be viewed on an annual spending rate. Since the ratio of monthly rental to purchase price is about 48:1, the $22.6 billion dollars installed value in 1970 can be translated into a monthly rental of $470 million. Surveys indicate that the hardware cost of an EDP installation is only about 35 percent of the total cost (systems and programming salaries and operating expenses comprising the remaining 65 percent). Thus the total monthly expenditure for EDP services is in excess of $1 billion. We will be looking into what U.S.–

based companies are realizing from this expenditure shortly; needless to say, the monthly EDP bill is impressive.

THE CHANGING DIMENSIONS OF THE EDP INDUSTRY

Figure 2.2 shows the estimated revenue breakdown by segments of the EDP industry. During the 1950s the hardware element dominated, and one could calculate the total revenue by summing the total income of the eight major computer manufacturers. The software and support services were marketed under the hardware umbrella. The services rendered by independent software houses and service centers were a minor part of the total revenue. However, in the sixties, the computer or EDP industry became fragmented, and the rapidly expanding software and

Component	1970 revenue $ billions	% 1970 total	1975 revenue $ billions	% 1975 total
Hardware	$6.00	72%	$13.00	63%
Software	0.45	5	1.60	8
Network information services	0.34	4	1.80	9
Service Bureaus	0.65	8	1.00	5
Facilities management	0.29	3	1.50	7
Education services	0.10	1	0.60	3
Leasing	0.55	7	1.00	5
Total	$8.38	100%	$20.50	100%

Fig. 2.2 Information services industry (source: *Quantum Sciences*)

support activities created an information services industry of which computers represented only a segment. As can be seen in Figure 2.1, the hardware segment is expected to drop in percentage from 72 percent of the revenue in 1970 to 63 percent in 1975. The biggest increases can be noted in (a) network information services defined as on-line services provided by central agencies to remote sites that subscribe to the data processing facilities of an organization, and (b) facilities management where a service agency takes control of the entire data processing facility of an organization. Software and education services are growing during this 5-year period, while service bureaus and the leasing business are dropping in percentage of the total market. It should be noted that all segments are growing rapidly but that some are growing at a faster rate than others.

DIMENSIONING THE MARKET BY COMPUTER SIZE
AND INDUSTRY SHARE

Figures 2.3 and 2.4 show the allocation of computers installed by size and industry in 1970 and projected to 1975. The most dramatic shifts in computer-size allocation is that medium, large, and extra-large computers are expected to drop in share of market, while medium-large and extra-small computers will grow in percentage to the total number installed. This situation is caused by the continuing lowering of the entry price of a computer system such that the price tag falls into the range of more first-time users. It is also a reflection of the use of

Computor size	Average value $ million	1970 installed value $ billion	% 1970 total	1975 installed value $ billion	% 1975 total
Extra large	6.0	$ 2.5	11.1%	$ 3.6	8.0%
Large	1.6	5.9	26.1	7.2	17.0
Medium large	0.65	4.2	18.6	11.0	25.0
Medium	0.35	6.5	28.8	10.1	23.0
Small	0.12	3.1	13.7	6.3	14.0
Extra small	0.04	0.4	1.7	5.8	13.0
Total	—	$22.6	100.0%	$44.0	100.0%

Fig. 2.3   Installed value by computer size

smaller computers as remote communication processors tying in to a larger network of computers. Computer power per dollar is expected to increase to the point where medium-large computers in the purchase price range of $650,000 to $1 million will be made prevalent than the large or extra-large computers.

The industry split shows manufacturing as the leading user of computers with the greatest growth expected in the hospital/medical and education areas. The federal government, which at one time accounted for about 70 percent of all computer usage, will continue to drop in its share of market. The other industries will maintain their approximate position.

OTHER QUANTITATIVE INDICATORS

Several other quantitative facts are pertinent. When we view the market in regard to computer vendors, IBM has about 65 to 70 percent of the installed value,

Industry	1970 installed value $ billion	% of 1970 total	1975 installed value $ billion	% of 1975 total
Manufacturing	$ 7.47	33%	$15.0	34%
Distribution	0.64	3	1.4	3
Retailing	0.56	2	1.2	3
Insurance	1.66	7	3.0	7
Hospital/medical	0.24	1	1.4	3
Education	1.10	5	3.1	7
State and local govt.	1.24	5	2.4	5
Banking and finance	1.71	8	4.0	9
Utilities and business services	2.13	10	4.0	9
Federal government	2.74	12	3.4	8
Other	3.13	14	5.1	12
Total	$22.62	100%	$44.0	100%

Fig. 2.4 Installed computer value by industry segment

Honeywell Information Systems, Inc., and Univac have about 8 to 10 percent, while the following manufacturers share from 3 to 7 percent of the market: Control Data, NCR, and Burroughs. Xerox Data Systems and Digital Equipment Corp. complete the big eight list of manufacturers, each having about 1 percent of the market.

Another interesting statistic is the growth of the international market compared to the domestic market. About 67 percent of the shipments of American-based manufacturers go to the domestic market. Looking at it from the international point of view, one third of the shipments of domestically-based computer manufacturers go to the international market—and this has been increasing every year. This percentage is expected to be 40 percent by 1975.

One last statistic is the application of Pareto's law in the computer industry. Pareto's law or the 20/80 theory states that, in most situations, 20 percent of the transactions account for 80 percent of the activity. Thus, of the products produced by a particular company, 20 percent account for 80 percent of the volume. Similarly, in the computer industry, 20 percent of the companies account for about 80 percent of installed value. It is even more skewed at the top end, for about 200 companies (most from *Fortune*'s 500) or less than 1 percent of the companies in the United States account for 35 percent of the installed value of computers. These 200 companies collectively have about 2800 sites where computers are installed. Each site has an average of six computers. Thus the 200 companies have 16,800 computers installed worth $7.9 billion, an average of $470,000 per computer.

This, then, is the quantitative picture of computer usage broken down by installed value, number of computers, computer size, industry allocation, industry segment revenue, domestic-international split, computer vendor, and company size. Any way it is viewed, the growth has been phenomenal. Existing companies are investing 12 to 15 percent more each year in computer power and more and more small companies are becoming new computer users. Quantitatively, the information services industry has been a bonanza. Let us now take a look at the qualitative aspects of the industry.

QUALITATIVE VIEW OF EDP USAGE

While the quantitative picture reads growth, growth, and more growth, the qualitative picture is not as bullish. Periodic surveys point out the unmistakable fact that the management of companies using computers has not been completely satisfied with computer results. A survey of 900 companies by the Research Institute of America indicates that only about half the companies surveyed are happy with the results of their computer operation. A *Wall Street Journal* survey shows the predominance of accounting and basic clerical applications as compared to management-oriented applications, while an in-depth survey of 36 large manufacturing companies by McKinsey & Company concluded that, in terms of technical achievement, the computer revolution is far ahead of expectations, whereas, in terms of economic payoff, it is rapidly losing momentum.

Several things are clear concerning computer usage as we enter the early and mid-seventies. First, despite the highly publicized advanced applications being performed by a few, the vast majority of computer time is still devoted to routine administrative areas, such as accounting, payroll, and order processing. Secondly, companies have made only modest progress toward any type of system that could be termed a management information system. Systems in the 1960s have been aiding clerical and administrative personnel and lower supervisory levels but have made scant impact on middle and upper levels of management. Few managers have utilized computers to aid in decision making; for most, the job of management is still the same as it was in precomputer days. It is apparent that the sixties belonged to the technocrats—the engineers and support people representing the computer manufacturers—and the EDP systems and programming staffs of the computer users.

The focus of the computer manufacturer is changing, but the emphasis on product offerings in the sixties was influenced by factors other than a realistic assessment of what users really needed. What users really needed was not so much the quantitative proliferation of product offerings that engulfed the market but, rather, higher-quality and more reliable products. This is particularly true in the software area. The latter sixties were characterized by everyone trying to get into the act. As a result, there was a wide variety and assortment of hardware, software, and support offerings that promised to resolve the user's key data processing problems. What the user needed was something a little simpler, but something that worked. Several prognosticators have suggested that the best thing the various vendors could offer the user in the early 1970's is to refine, update, and bring up to original specification those hardware and software products delivered in the late sixties. This situation may not come to pass because in some instances the objectives of the vendors are not consistent with those of the user. For example, the timing of the introduction of a new generation of hardware that makes obsolete the previous generation may be influenced by factors other than whether the user is ready for such a change.

From the user's standpoint, the key decisions of what computer system to install and the priority and selection of applications to be implemented have rested with the technicians. In certain cases, the EDP management possessed the general business perspective to make wise decisions but, in more cases than not, the decisions were not based on sound economic and business principles. This is not to cast aspersions on EDP management, for they have labored long and hard in the implementation of computer applications. They are also knowledgeable and highly proficient in their technical skill. The problem has been that in many cases their general lack of overall business background has not permitted them to ask the right questions of the right people; and the right people, business management, have not taken the leadership and given the EDP people the guidance that they so desperately needed.

It is not surprising that very few comprehensive management information systems exist today. By definition, a MIS aids management in doing its *management* job. How can this step be accomplished without management involvement and participation in the system? There is a similar analogy in the development of accounting systems. The accounting profession has developed over the years as an outgrowth of the need to fulfill external requirements, such as those imposed by the government, security and exchange commissions, and stockholders. Profit-and-loss statements and balance sheets are a principal, result of the accounting system, and these follow fairly standard and well-understood procedures and regulations. The internal accounting or control system of a company is a completely different matter. There exists a whole host of different types of problems brought on by decentralization and the profit center concept. Companies have striven to maintain the entrepreneur concept within a large industrial complex—the feeling of individual responsibiilty over a prescribed operation and the motivation and rewarding of individual achievement based on results and performance. Accountants and controllers who have attempted to apply the same external accounting rules to internal operations have experienced severe disillusionment and failure. They discovered that systems which charge individual profit centers with overhead and burden over which the managers of the profit centers have no control are ineffectual. Thus internal accounting systems are really management systems and require managers to develop them. Computer systems that are aimed at the administrative, clerical, and primarily external requirements can be developed by EDP personnel. The assumption that management-oriented systems or systems directed at the prime operating (nonclerical) areas of a business can also be developed by EDP personnel is an invalid one.

Despite the rather bleak record for MIS in the 1960s, the success experienced by a few—the leading edge, as it were—indicates that MIS will be employed by an increasing number of companies in the 1970s. It represents a major trend in EDP usage. Two highly publicized examples of MIS in the last decade are the Pillsbury Company in Minneapolis and Honeywell's Micro Switch Division in Freeport, Ill. These two companies prove the point that it can be done and that there are considerable payoffs when it happens. Pillsbury's system has developed to the point where a data base is being built to represent the external marketplace in which Pillsbury operates, identifying the existing and potential users of various products. This external data base enables the market to be broken down by product, type of customer, time period, geographical location, and other classifications. The proper modeling of this file of data enables management to answer important questions, such as the potential effect of advertising programs, the forecast for existing products and new products not yet introduced, and the most effective manner of product distribution and sales coverage.

Micro Switch, on the other hand, in the 1960's concentrated on a MIS to control internal company operations. I have recorded in a previous book, *The Computer and the Executive,* how the Micro Switch Division, manufacturer of precision snap switches and mercury switches (12,000 finished-goods items in all), has dedicated their computer efforts toward a MIS. Their initial concentration has been on the main operating areas of the business—inventory control, sales forecasting, and production scheduling—wielding these systems into an integrated single entity serving management at all levels. This mainstream-integrated approach has reduced inventory over 30 percent during a period of rising sales volume, helped increase on-schedule deliveries from 80 to over 95 percent, and reduced production cost variances from 16 to 1 percent. It is interesting to note that both the Pillsbury and the Micro Switch systems were, as Pillsbury calls it, directed to serve value creation first and cost reduction later or, as Micro Switch terms it, profit-making applications versus cost-cutting ones. Also, both companies are characterized by a management fully committed to EDP and heavily involved in system development.

ENVIRONMENT FOR MIS DEVELOPMENT

It is interesting to look at Figure 2.4, which indicates an industry breakdown of installed computers, and analyze where MIS has achieved the strongest foothold. Although both Pillsbury and Honeywell Micro Switch fall into the manufacturing category, this is not the industry segment where MIS is strongest. The reason is not that MIS has the least potential here but rather that the complexities and interaction of information subsystems within a manufacturing company make it difficult to design and install one. For the most part, MIS has succeeded in manufacturing companies in those instances where management has studied and analyzed the entire system complex but has concentrated on one major subsystem. For example, in large durable-goods manufacturers where the product value is high and there is a need for careful analysis of customer orders because of ongoing maintenance, modification, add-on business, and repeat sales, management systems have been built around centralized data bases of customer-status files. Many departments use this file and continually demand a variety of statistical and analytical reports; in many instances the management by exception principle is utilized whereby the system itself triggers action and expedites reports when certain combinations or conditions are met. A good number of comprehensive MIS approaches have concentrated on a single but vital area of business operation. There are not as many examples of systems like Honeywell's Micro Switch Division which attack the entire information base of the company and require a high level of integration before payoffs can be attained.

MIS appears to be more prevalent in the insurance and banking fields. Here we have the single-file concept where the customer data base is vital to the entire operation. For example, the demand deposit file of a bank is a focal point for a major part of a bank's operation. In current systems, the savings account and loan account files have been combined into a single-file concept. However, even prior to this, the demand deposit file represented a prime source of management information and MIS has been built around this central data base of information. Typical of the use of MIS is the approach used by the Southern California First National Bank with headquarters in San Diego and over $600 million in assets. Their MIS, which was initiated in 1967, was geared to changing the outputs of 27 application areas already computerized and which covered demand deposit accounts, installment consumer loans, real estate loans, savings accounts, and so on, so that they could feed a new general ledger system. Important management reports emanate from the general ledger system, which is a summary of all business activity of the bank. The MIS takes into account the responsibility center concept employed by the bank and reports are geared to this breakdown.

In a like manner, the single-file concept exists in the insurance field where the major business systems center on the policyholder's file. The insurance company combines several types of policies into a central file similar to the bank's. A policyholder may hold several different types of policies with the company, just as a bank customer holds several types of banking accounts. The problems of MIS development between banks and insurance companies have much more in common than the problems of manufacturing companies do. Utility companies fall into the bank-insurance category as well. The point is not that all banks, insurance companies, and utility companies are similar in operation but that, when viewing them in light of MIS, they represent a distinct category as opposed to manufacturing companies. Elements in their method of operation make them more receptive to the employment of MIS. Besides the central file concept, the fact that banks and insurance companies are more structured in their way of doing business (because of federal and state laws and well-defined procedures) and because their main product is information and service, as opposed to a manufactured product, the development of MIS has proceeded at a faster pace. Banks, insurance companies, and utilities have been in data processing longer than manufacturers (distributors and retailers can be included in the same category as manufacturers for purposes of this discussion) and have tended to be more stable in organization and operation. These factors are important, for it usually takes from 3 to 5 years to design and install a MIS effectively.

Another industry area where MIS has made headway is in the federal government. Examples can be found in information-retrieval types of applications. Organizations like the National Institute of Health and the Department of Defense have installed what might be termed technical management information systems. For example, *Datamation Magazine* reported on a system developed by the Department of Defense in coordination with the National Aeronautical and Space Administration. The purpose of the system is to provide meaningful and timely access to various research and technology efforts. Each research effort is indexed, and a file of key elements concerning the effort is gathered and made a part of a central data base. The data base is so ordered and structured that it is extremely responsive to a wide assortment of management requests for information. This type of system has many of the elements of the banking or insurance operation, which make it an easier target for MIS than other industries. Added similarities are a stable organizational structure and fairly exacting procedures and regulations. Another element facilitating the employment of MIS is an environment that can ensure adherance to rather strict rules regulating input and update procedures regarding the central data base file. The older and better-established firms provide a more suitable environment for this required degree of regimentation.

The industries referred to have the working environment that is more suitable to MIS development. As mentioned, however, this does not lessen the potential that MIS has for such industries as manufacturing, distribution, and retailing. Although it may be more difficult to achieve, the payoffs and benefits of MIS are even more significant, as indicated by the Pillsbury and Micro Switch examples.

CASE STUDY OF A COMPUTER USER THROUGH THREE GENERATIONS

In concluding the qualitative look at the computer user of the past two decades, a case study is appropriate. Although the Forman Manufacturing Company does not represent any single company, but rather a composite picture of EDP usage, I feel that the case study is representative of a large class of users who have evolved through three generations of computer hardware.

Forman produces electrical components for the business equipment, computer, and aerospace industries. Their business has had a rapid growth from the $20-million sales volume in the midfifties to over $100 million in 1971. The growth has been a result of the rapid expansion of the markets being served by Forman. The 15–year period between 1955 and 1970 has been marked by a proliferation of new product offerings to keep pace with the changing nature of the electronics industry and the end users of Forman products. Plant and personnel expansion have been limited only by the time to acquire and build new facilities and the supply of skilled personnel. This is the background in which the internal data processing operation has developed.

In 1955 Forman had a large-scale punched-card installation that was producing sales orders, processing pay roll, and accomplishing a variety of accounting jobs. Forman was spending $48,000 per year on machine rental and $60,000 on salaries and operating expenses for a total data processing expense of $108,000. In 1958 the punched-card supervisor made a recommendation to install an IBM 650 computer, a first-generation system utilizing vacuum tubes and a drum memory. Magnetic tapes were later added to the system with the total hardware cost amounting to $72,000 per year, plus an additional $100,000 for programming and operating expenses, or a total of $172,000. The conversion was made pretty much on an "as is" basis; that is, most of the punched-card applications were converted to the 650 and took advantage of the greater processing speed, but basically they turned out the same reports and accomplished the job in the same manner in which they were performed previously. By this time sales volume had picked up, personnel had been added to the payroll, and new products had been introduced, so that the 650 was up to capacity shortly after it was installed.

A mild crisis in Forman's data processing history was faced in the years 1959 and 1960. The controller realized that the company was paying more for EDP but was not getting any more from it; in fact, he felt that the conversion set them back a notch. He noticed an increasing error rate in the reports they received following the conversion. He realized that the nature of their business was changing rapidly and wondered whether their current data processing had the flexibility to incorporate all the changes. It was significant that the general management of the company was not involved at all in EDP planning. Except for the complaints on reports they received, there were no requests for additional applications nor apparent concern for the status of the computer operation or its future. The controller thought this might be due to the rapid changes that were taking place within the company, including the organizational shakeups that occurred with periodic frequency.

The controller also began to realize the shortcomings of his tab supervisor, who had inherited a first-generation computer system to operate. He wondered whether the tab supervisor could cope with the increasing complexity of the job and the increasing managerial duties imposed by the addition of system analysts and programmers to his staff. Having no one with whom to discuss and analyze the problem, the controller decided to maintain the status quo and indeed approved the EDP manager's recommendation to install an IBM second-generation 1401 to replace the 650.

The system was installed in 1962; with the tape and disk peripherals and supporting ancillary equipment, the rental was $96,000 per year. Programming, systems, and operating expenses brought the total EDP annual expenditure to $225,000. The advent of disk processing and the conversion of the 650 programs to the language of the 1401 set back the Forman EDP operation once again. The controller recalls vividly the painful and prolonged conversion period. The 650s did not get replaced on schedule, and the company found itself paying two rentals for a longer period of time than they cared to remember. Accentuating the problem was the turnover of system analysts and programmers that had taken place over the past two years and the inability to obtain competent replacements. It was at this point that management became involved in EDP, but the involvement started on a negative note. EDP operations had reached a stage where reports were not getting out, customer billings and shipments were delayed, and company bills were not being paid on time.

A superhuman effort on the part of the controller, his newly hired EDP manager, and several key system analysts pulled the operation through this very tenuous period. By early 1964 the EDP operation was under new management and things were moving along at a good clip; in fact, some new applications found their way to the computer. However, the controller realized that they bore no resemblance to a long-range or even a short-range plan. This realization was a result of a memo he had received from the new general manager of the company.

The new general manager had different views on data processing and was concerned over some of the newer developments, such as management information systems and communications facilities, which would tie in Forman's burgeoning regional offices and plants. The controller was reflecting on the pressure from the general manager when IBM announced a new family of computers called System 360. The 1401 was already approaching capacity operation and he knew some type of change was necessary. Still, he wanted to avoid at all costs the traumatic conversion that they had gone through in changing from the 650 to the 1401. After months of discussions and feasibility studies, the decision was made to order an IBM 360/30 to replace the 1401. At the same time it was decided to form a management steering committee to fashion a longer-range plan that would begin to provide management with the information needed to make better and more timely decisions. In 1965 a solid plan for a MIS was formulated and the general manager, as well as the steering committee, was quite excited about the prospect.

The arrival of the third generation 360/30 in 1966 had a major impact on these plans. The conversion did not go smoothly and was blamed partly on Forman's lack of well-documented programs and shoddy system design (many of the programs being converted followed the same approach as the original 650 program; the controller could understand what was meant by running first-generation programs on third-generation equipment) and partly on the inability of the manufacturer's conversion aids to live up to expectation. In any event, the next two years were spent in getting older programs rewritten and running on the new hardware. A major training job was required to orientate existing personnel and train newly hired personnel on the new hardware and software systems. In the midst of the conversion, the EDP manager left Forman to take a job with a newly formed software company and the company was without effective EDP leadership for two months.

By 1970 a competent EDP manager had been hired and the installation was running smoothly again. New applications had been implemented and the initial steps toward a MIS had been taken. One of the larger field offices was sending and receiving data over communication lines and there were plans to tie in other field facilities on a phased program. A 370/135 had replaced the 360/30 and EDP expenditures were now $210,000 for hardware and $300,000 for supporting costs, for a total of $510,000 per year. This figure was considerably more than that for the 1401 installation, but volume had grown steadily, for the Forman sales and product line had expanded in the late sixties. Actual EDP expenditures per sales dollar had declined, and this fact gave some solace to the controller. The big question was the future direction of EDP. The controller knew that the MIS route was the way to go, but he also knew the difficulties of extending this concept in a company whose products and methods of doing business were changing so rapidly. In addition, the frequent management changes and personnel reorganizations added to the problem. Finally, there were rumblings of the introduction of a brand new fourth-generation line of computers. However, the controller tried to keep this last factor out of his thinking process.

SUMMARY OF FORMAN'S EXPERIENCE

Such is the picture of a company that has gone through three generations of computer hardware—four if you consider the conversion from manual methods to punched-card equipment as the first. The subject of a system approach more geared to servicing management has come up several times in the evolution through the three generations, but it has always received secondary priority because of the other technical and people problems. It is interesting to see that the EDP function still resides in the controller's bailiwick and has been rather immune from top management direction or involvement. This is the position that many companies find themselves in as they move into the 1970s. There has been considerable progress but also serious problems and roadblocks in achieving the real EDP potential. The computer as a management tool remains a relatively untapped concept. There are many reasons for this situation, but the Forman example pinpoints four major factors.

1. Lack of Management Involvement

Management involvement and commitment to a program that affects them is essential to the success of any program. It is particularly relevant in the EDP area. There are many reasons, such as frequent changes in top management organization, lack of understanding of what a computer can do for management, or preoccupation with the numerous operating problems facing a company. Nonetheless, the absence of top management guidance and control in the data processing activity is a major deterrent to the successful employment of EDP and MIS.

2. The EDP People Problem

As can be seen in the Forman case, there is a need for strong EDP leadership to direct the computer operation. There is also a need for a strong system and programming staff to implement the applications selected for computerization. Finding and keeping EDP personnel are a major challenge in an environment where demand exceeds the supply of competent people.

3. The Conversion Requirement

Whether conversion is considered a requirement or not, the rapid growth of EDP services and the continued improvement in cost-performance ratios of succeeding generations of computers places the decision of replacing computer systems squarely before EDP management. Many computer users would strongly agree that their computer operations would be in better shape today if they had concentrated more on system design and MIS than on changing computers every four or five years.

4. Absence of a Comprehensive EDP Plan

It is somewhat shocking to read surveys that indicate that about one out of every two users does not possess a 2-to-3 year EDP plan. Left to the day-to-day management by crisis method of operation, it is little wonder that computer users have been easy prey to those elements of the EDP community who want them to add computing power and replace their existing computer with a new one having more power and capacity. The existence of a plan enables the user to view hardware developments in relation to the growth and direction of his company's application development. In this way, one avoids changing hardware every few years and winding up with a system that is not totally consistent with the company's longer-range requirements. Lack of a comprehensive plan has been responsible for many a traumatic system conversion.

SUMMARY

This chapter has focused on the quantitative and qualitative aspects of the EDP industry and the use of computer systems. The quantitative factors, such as growth rate in the first two decades of computers, have been most impressive; however, the qualitative dimension is less impressive. Although computer users have employed the device to accomplish administrative and record-keeping types of jobs, the incidence of advanced applications and management-oriented systems is relatively low. However, the results of those who have tackled these areas have been impressive enough to warrant an optimistic outlook for the 1970's. The 1960's belonged to the technocrats, the 1970's belong to management. Computers and the people who run them have gone through a necessary learning curve. Mistakes were made and overcome, and much progress occurred, although not fast enough to suit management. The conditions are propitious for management to take over the direction of computer usage. As they do so, the computer will be redirected to serve their needs. This is the much needed impetus and catalyst for management information systems. The 1970's will see the term MIS return to popularity. No longer will MIS imply a unattainable panacea, a system concept that looks good to the theorist or academician but is impractical, if not impossible, to implement. The next decade will see the emphasis on management in information systems. This decade belongs to the manager.

STUDY CASETTES

MARKET OUTLOOK FOR THE SEVENTIES

[From "Market Outlook for the Seventies," by Heinz Nixdorf, *Computer Weekly International*, August 12, 1971]

I see future growth in demand for small computers coming from two very different types of business—the very large organization, which previously thought almost exclusively main frame, and the very small organization, which previously thought itself too small to own a computer.

The change in thinking in large organizations is particularly interesting. In the past the very existence of large computers encouraged users to think in terms of highly centralized units. However, the demand for rapid, accurate, and up-to-date information at operational level is causing companies to have a second look at their structures. Efficiency appears to demand a substantial measure of decentralization.

For centralization to work effectively man would have to live and work in units of 100,000 and more. In fact, he operates in groups of considerably less than 1000. Fortunately we now have computers that are small enough and cheap enough to service the needs of these smaller groups. If we add to this the capacity for the individual small computers to go on-line to a main frame computer, we begin to see computer networks capable of satisfying the demands for local operational information, and for centralized control and forecasting.

This move by large organizations toward the small computer is already well advanced in Europe, with banks, insurance companies, and retail and wholesale organizations installing increasing numbers of small computers. The basic common factor is that all these organizations have a large number of establishments or departments scattered over a very wide area, but each of necessity having to report to a central HQ.

We at Nixdorf are convinced that this move to decentralization, coupled with on-line capacity, is gathering momentum.

Playing a significant part in this type of situation will be the terminal which has itself been upgraded considerably. Intelligent terminals are now replacing their unsophisticated predecessors, or in some cases a small computer is used with on-line capabilities. The terminal market could possibly be one of the fastest growth sections of the computer industry and I expect this to more than double its size during the next two years. At the moment between 50 and 60 percent of small computers are purchased by the small-to-medium size business and 40 to 50 percent by the large organizations. However, as the larger companies realize the value of the small machines, these figures could change until the majority of these are purchased by large companies.

Just as the size of organizations using small computers is getting larger, so the size of companies able to benefit from the small computer is getting smaller. As wages and overheads rise throughout Europe, the number of employees required to justify the installation of a small business computer is becoming less. I used to say that every 21st employee should be a Nixdorf computer. I believe this should now be the 11th.

In the early days of computers, smaller businesses could not contemplate installing a computer because of their large size, their requirement for special air-conditioned rooms and their high price. Miniaturization and other technological advances have made possible the small computer with a high capacity in a small volume that is suitable for in-office use. The same technological changes have brought the price within the reach of all but the very smallest companies.

In the immediate future, the small computer will be required to carry out much the same functions as at present, so the education will be in the use of computers not in the tasks.

During the next few years, I see the basic small computer duties remaining in the payroll, invoicing and stock control fields, because of the requirement for information at the source. I do not believe that in the near future computers will be used on any large scale to solve sophisticated business problems—managements will still have to manage.

However, there are areas that are emerging as possible big growth areas for tomorrow. Process control, for which the computer is ideally suited, is still only in its infancy as a computer market, but could develop very rapidly with the introduction of highly sophisticated technical processes. Here again a number of small low-cost computers are likely to be more cost-effective than one large, centralized main frame computer. We have 100 small computers controlling the manufacture of our own computers.

The other major growth area I see is teaching. In this field there is already a shortage of teachers, and as subjects become more complex and people remain at teaching establishments longer, this shortage is going to become more acute. This area could eventually become the major growth and development area, and in the not-too-distant future I can see manufacturers selling more teaching machines than either industrial or business types.

Study Questions

1. Do you think Mr. Nixdorf is correct in his assessment of the growth of small computers?

2. Do you think that more small computers will be purchased by large companies than small companies in the future?

3. What areas of growth other than process control and education, as mentioned by Mr. Nixdorf, do you think are the growth areas for computers?

BIBLIOGRAPHY

Annual Reference Guide. Business Automation, September, 1970.

Datamation Industry Directory, Technical Publishing Company, 1971. 453 pp.

DEAN, N. J., and J. W. TAYLOR, Managing to Manage the Computer. *Harvard Business Review,* September–October, 1966.

EDP Almanac. Data Management, January, 1971.

GARRITY, J. T., Top Management and Computer Profits. *Harvard Business Review,* July–August, 1963.

Management and the Computer. A *Wall Street Journal* study of the management men responsible for their companies' purchases of computer equipment and services. Dow Jones & Co. Inc., 1969.

RUSCH, R., *Computers: Their History and How They Work.* Simon & Schuster, New York, 1969, 126 pp.

SAGE, D. M., Information Systems: A Brief Look Into History. *Datamation,* November, 1968.

SALAVERRY, E. C. (ed.), *Computers 70; A Census of Computer Installations and Directory of Computer Service Companies in the San Francisco Bay area.* KLH Associates, 1969, 200 pp.

SHORTER, EDWARD, *The Historian and the Computer.* Prentice-Hall, Inc., Englewood Cliffs, New Jersey, 1971.

*The International Directory of Computer and Information System Services—*1969. Europa Publications, London, 1969, 348 pp.

Chapter 3

FUNCTIONAL SUBSYSTEMS—
THE HORIZONTAL DIMENSION

This chapter will explore in more detail the horizontal system dimension described in Chapter 1. Figure 1.10 depicted the basic information subsystems that are the prerequisites of a management information system. We will now delve deeper into these subsystems, illustrating how they can be identified, classified, and placed in proper perspective to one another. The way to approach MIS development is to look at the broad road map first and then break it down into progressively finer and finer detail until individual milestones are established. In actual practice, the development involves working at the problem from both ends. It is similar to establishing an annual plan for a business operation. Theoretically, the best approach is to work from the top down with top management expressing the basic strategies and goals of the organization and then passing them down to lower levels of management for use as guidelines in establishing lower–level plans. In reality, the time pressures and the feedback requirements necessitate simultaneous work plans. These plans, which are worked both from the top down and the bottom up, are correlated at various stages in the planning cycle. Thus, while the general flow is top down, there are a series of iterative feedback loops prior to the finalization of the plan. This is true with management information systems. Although the approach suggested will be a sequential one where the establishment of management objectives, strategies, and goals is the first step, it becomes obvious that this approach cannot be achieved in practice. This fact should not detract from the basic requirement of MIS that it be management oriented. Perspective is required to determine at what point management's points of view are well enough known to be used as a basis for action. To wait for 100 percent clarity and certainty is unrealistic. The wise MIS developer is able to make this distinction, to proceed accordingly but to seek management feedback continually as a check and balance.

The easiest way to understand the horizontal dimension of management information systems is to use an example. The example is a typical company in the food-distribution business. The example or model could be a distributor of any type of product or group of products, a manufacturer, an insurance company, a bank, an educational or government operation, a hospital, or a service company. The type of company is relatively unimportant; the general principles of horizontal system analysis and classification, the methodology of looking at a company's information requirements as a series of interlocking subsystems is applicable and pertinent across industry lines.

HORIZONTAL INFORMATION SYSTEM MODEL

Our information system model will begin with the sales activity or sales subsystem. It has been often stated that "nothing begins until something is sold." This point is certainly true, and we will see that basic sales data is a primary information source from which flows a host of useful management reports and analyses. Each system will now be called a subsystem, for it will be but one part of a single integrated management information system. Figure 3.1 is the starting point of the integrated system.

It is obviously important to satisfy customer demand, for doing so is the principal reason for being in business. Management should continually strive to

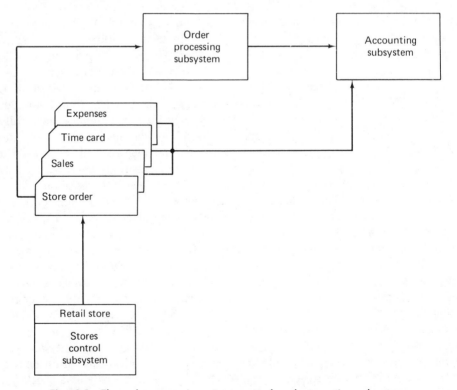

Fig. 3.1 The order processing, stores control and accounting subsystems

give the customer the best product at the best price and at the same time should realize a profit in line with the product being offered. The basic cycle starts here because what goes out of the store must be replaced. As the shelves in the store are depleted, certain store-order operations are put into play that result in the reorder of goods to replenish the shelves. The store will reorder goods on the basis of turnover and the lead time required to replenish the item. The store order is one of the basic source documents that initiates a long series of activities throughout many departments. This document enters the first of the subsystems— the order processing subsystem. This subsystem will screen the orders for errors in omission as well as commission and enure that the order is valid before it proceeds further into other subsystems. The connecting arrow to the accounting subsystem indicates that the order is the basis for setting up accounts receivable and eventually reconciling the cash payment for the goods.

Another source document is the record of sales or the movement of items from the store. This source document will eventually produce meaningful sales statistics and analyses as output from the accounting and marketing subsystems.

In addition to the store order and record of sales, it takes people to run a store, and they must be paid according to services rendered. A time card represents the medium for recording hours worked; in Figure 3.1 it is shown entering the accounting subsystem. Similarly, the expenses of store operation (heat, light, and maintenance) are recorded and entered into the accounting subsystem. This would be the case only if the company controlled its own stores (as in a chain operation).

The stores control subsystem has not been greatly affected by automated information systems. However, there are significant possibilities. Checkout counter devices can optically read imprinted prices and item numbers on products, automatically producing the customer sales total and recording as a by-product the item and quantity sold as input into the order processing subsystem. A simpler method is for the checkout clerk to key in the item number listed on the product for automatic entry into order processing. Another information system within the stores control system is the scheduling of checkout personnel based on a simulation of activity through the store as a reflection of historical sales patterns and known conditions. For example, a study can indicate the requirement for a Thursday and Friday when Saturday is a holiday; also, it is known that about 70 percent of the business for the week is done on Thursday, Friday, and Saturday. These factors can be reflected in a queuing model to assist in the scheduling of personnel.

Figure 3.2 adds the inventory control subsystem as well as the materials control and transportation subsystems. After the store order has been validated by the order processing subsystem, it moves to the inventory control subsystem where it must be screened against the current inventory in the warehouse. This process is indicated by the two-way arrow connecting the order processing and inventory control subsystems. If there is sufficient inventory on hand, the order processing subsystem produces a store-order picking document for the warehouse and an order invoice for the retail store. Since employee labor and operating expenses were recorded at the store level, so they must be recorded at the warehouse level. These items can be seen entering the accounting system in Figure 3.2. The blank card will be explained in Figure 3.3.

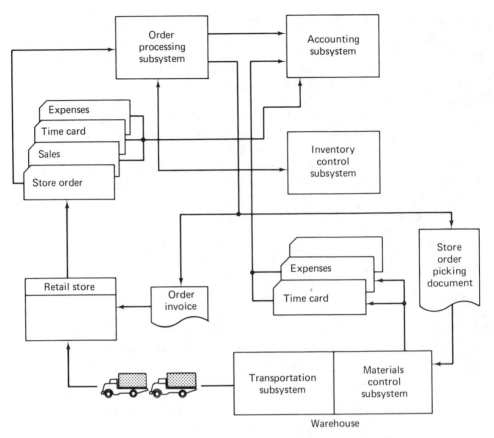

Fig. 3.2 Addition of inventory control, materials control, and transportation subsystems

The materials control and transportation subsystems are excellent examples of how an integrated system operates. For example, the basic information on orders and movement from the warehouse can be used to lay out warehouse space more efficiently. Similarly, the information on each order, such as the cubic content and weight of items comprising the order, can be used to load and route trucks. These valuable by-products can often be real payoff applications. Thus the same basic raw data is processed in a little different way to help effectively in the handling of another functional activity.

Figure 3.3 adds another subsystem to the overall integrated system—the purchasing subsystem. This subsystem is dependent on the strength of the inventory control subsystem. A well-conceived inventory control system provides for automatic ordering based on such considerations as customer service, economic order quantity, and lead time. Orders were screened against inventory records in Figure 3.2. When the inventory of particular items reaches a predetermined reorder point, the inventory control subsystem directs the purchasing system to write a purchase order, which can either be produced by computer or be done manually. The purchase order is made out and sent to the respective vendor or manufacturer. The vendor in turn fills the order, ships the product to the ware-

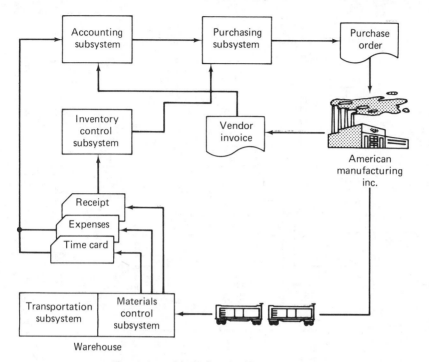

Fig. 3.3 Adding the purchasing subsystem

house, and submits his invoice for entry into the accounting subsystem. This process initiates Accounts Payable activity and the eventual reconciliation of cash payments. The arrow indicates the connection of the accounting and purchasing subsystems.

The blank card of Figure 3.2 can now be identified as a receipt card. This card enters the inventory control subsystem to update pertinent inventory records; it is also passed through to the accounting subsystem to form the basis for vendor payment.

Figure 3.4 brings together the subsystems that have been mentioned up to this point. Two additional arrows have been added to the illustration. The first connects the inventory control and accounting subsystems. This step is necessary because inventory data is a requirement of accounting reports. The second arrow shows the important output of the accounting subsystem. Accounting acts as the scorekeeper of all the subsystems mentioned thus far. It accumulates such data as store orders, cash sales, expenses, receipts, and vendor invoices, and from this basic source information produces a host of meaningful management reports. Three of these reports are noted in Figure 3.4—profit-and-loss statement, inventory statistics, and sales statistics. These reports might show, for example, profitability by region, by store, or by department; or they might show sales by salesman or item grouping. They might also indicate inventory turnover or return on inventory investment.

The subsystems discussed thus far are basic ones common to most businesses. They are fairly routine computer applications, but it is still uncommon to find a computer system built with the required open-ended integrated approach that has

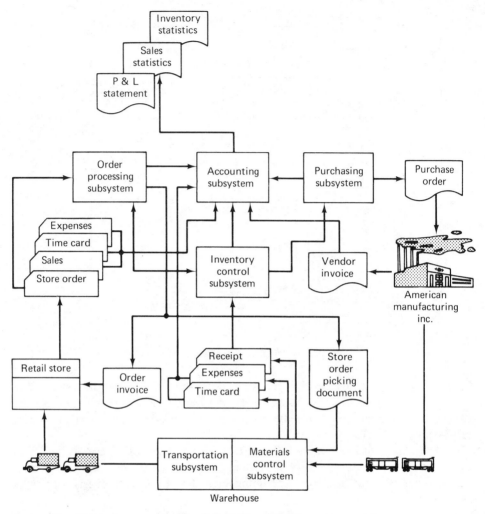

Fig. 3.4 Basic subsystems

incorporated all the subsystems and still has the capability of additional, more sophisticatd subsystems. Figure 3.5 shows more advanced subsystems that can build on the basic ones already described.

Marketing and strategic planning are the subsystems that produce the real payoffs from an integrated system. As a by-product of the basic subsystems, the marketing subsystem uses the basic source data that has been collected and filed. However, the data is processed in different ways to answer specific management questions—questions such as the effect of promotion on sales, the effect of pricing changes and product mix, the comparative advantages of a limited as compared to a full product line, the significance of store layout and shelf allocation on profit, and the desirability of introducing new items or product lines.

Another key output of the marketing subsystem is the sales forecast. The forecast is based on historical sales movement (information coming from the accounting system), as well as on projected external events (buying trends, economic factors, and so on). The sales forecast is significant to all aspects of the

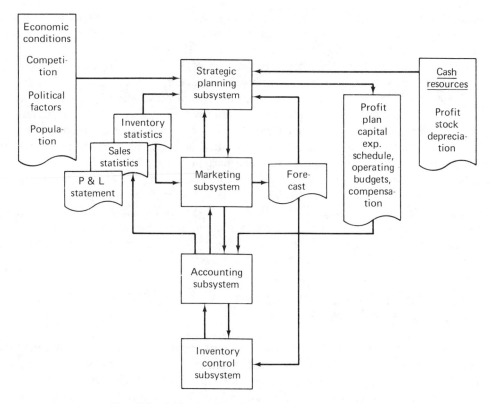

Fig. 3.5 Addition of marketing and strategic planning

business and is shown in Figure 3.4 as entering the inventory control system as a basis of establishing inventory policy and entering the strategic planning subsystem as a basis of influencing total company goals and objectives. The marketing subsystem has been all but neglected by today's computer systems. There are several reasons for this situation. The first is the absence of the integrated concept. The subsystems previously described were not built to collect and store data for other uses; they were built only for the immediate job, whether order processing or payroll. Therefore the basic data needed for more sophisticated analysis is not available; it has been captured but not retained. A second reason why the marketing subsystem is not often tackled is that the payoffs from this subsystem are not as tangible as from the other subsystems. It is easy to see the clerical savings from computerizing order processing, but it is more difficult to see how a change in advertising policy can improve profit margins. It is not that the potential benefits of the latter are insignificant; to the contrary, the benefits can be far more meaningful than computerizing order processing. The point is that conservative management is less convinced that the benefits can be attained.

The strategic planning subsystem is the core of the system model. It is here that the major company decisions are made. Reports produced by the accounting subsystem are digested, reviewed, and analyzed. Overall company policies are determined and promulgated. Sophisticated integrated systems employ business models and simulation to determine the effect of different management policies on the profitability of the company. A mathematical model is constructed that indicates the effect of particular management decisions on such factors as sales, costs, and profits. Thus it is possible to structure a paper world to react as the real world does and thereby project the results of management decisions before they are made. The model is built from data captured as part of the basic subsystems and the simulation is conducted using the same historical data. In addition to the historical or internal data, the management planning subsystem uses external data gathered from outside sources. On one side are the basic economic factors, such as trends in Gross National Product, political factors, and population growth, while on the other side are the available cash resources, such as profit plow-back, new stock issues, and depreciation. These factors are part of the mathematical model built to evaluate and determine management policy. The results of the strategic planning subsystem are marketing policies, as well as the profit plan, capital expenditure schedule, and operating budget. These figures enter the accounting subsystem to form the basis of measuring actual operation. They form the yardstick for measurement. The cycle is thus completed. Figure 3.6 presents the complete integrated system that we have been building in stages.

INFORMATION SYSTEM MODEL AND THE HORIZONTAL SUBSYSTEMS IN A MIS

Figure 3.6 represents the horizontal subsystems that comprise a management information system. Nine are represented, but they could probably be fanned out to 40 or 50. The nine are major subsystems, each one of which can be further subdivided into others. For example, the financial and accounting subsystem includes subsystems for accounts receivable, accounts payable, general ledger, payroll, cost accounting, and the like. A significant point to bear in mind in planning a MIS is to lay out the overall road map first. It is true that the initial focus may, for example, be on improving the sales-order processing subsystem; however, this should be undertaken in light of where that particular system fits into the whole. Middle and top management can understand a framework similar to that illustrated in Figure 3.6. Too often the first thing they are shown is a detailed flow chart of the order processing cycle. This is discouraging to them, for they are unaware of where order processing fits into the overall information network and what part it will play in a management information system. Although interested and vitally concerned with improving the order cycle, thereby improving inventory turnover and reducing capital requirements, they would like to get a "feel" of how the by-product data from this application can help them pinpoint unfavorable sales trends by product line and store location, plus suggesting action to improve the situation. Developing an information system model for your company in your industry is an important first step in developing and gaining the benefits of MIS.

INTEGRATION AND INTERRELATIONSHIP OF SUBSYSTEMS

At the beginning of the Industrial Revolution, business was run by individual entrepreneurs who did the planning, selling, producing, accounting, and other necessary jobs. The basic data and information needed to carry out these duties

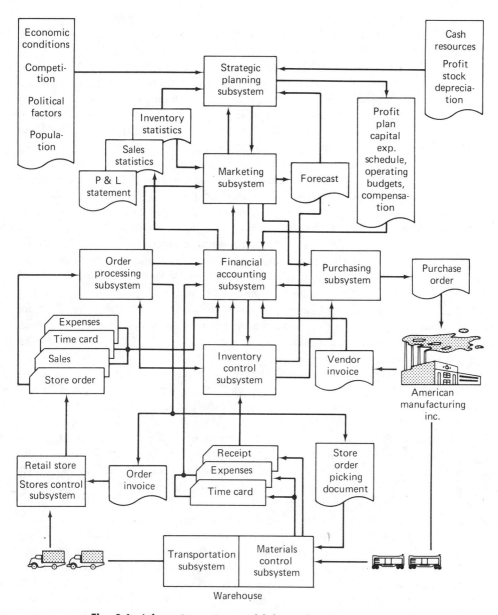

Fig. 3.6 Information system model for a distribution company

were filed in the entrepreneur's head. His data processing system was integrated because there was a central source of information from which sprung all policies, plans, and decisions. However, the tasks began to grow more complex until he could no longer handle all of them himself. He hired people to help him, and he set up functional responsibilities, such as accounting, production, and engineering, and assigned people to these various functions. In the beginning there was a good deal of overlap in the assignment of individuals to functions; functional specialization would be a later development. But as business evolved, the entrepreneur found he could not train people himself. Colleges and universities offered to assist in the task. As university curricula were developed, fences began to appear that were to become the functional boundaries within a business—the accounting profession was formed, the advertising profession, and so on.

This is not to say that these functional boundaries were logical in nature; it just happened to be the way they were recognized within a business organization. With the entrepreneur we had a natural integrated system, but the growth of functional boundaries determines the kind of data utilized by the various groups and tends to limit the scope of problems and the vision of individuals tackling these problems. This explains, to a great extent, why the majority of data processing systems are performing only accounting applications. The computer is under the control of the accounting department and the functional boundaries of accounting perpetuate applications like payroll, accounts receivable, and accounts payable.

This situation suggests a real challenge for management. The top executive must somehow get the various functional heads to coordinate their activities—to achieve the same effectiveness as the single entrepreneur. The integrated systems concept is a prime vehicle for accomplishing this step, emphasizing that although the whole is made up of parts, the parts must not be of such a specialized and unique character that their function as part of the whole is forgotten.

Obviously management cannot play a passive role in the design and development of an integrated system. Since the system crosses all functional boundaries, only top management can ensure that the computer will best serve the overall needs of the company and not be used for parochial interests.

Figure 3.6 enables the system analyst or business manager to see the interrelationships of subsystems. The tracing and interaction of key source data will illustrate the necessity and practical implications of designing systems that avoid redundancy and take advantage of common data flows. The sales forecast is a prime example. The forecast is a key strategic tool in the operation of any company. First of all, a sales forecast is crucial to the planning process. It is the basis of determining whether a new item should be introduced or whether an entirely new product line should be developed. It forms the rationale for establishing plant capacity and long-range facility needs. It is a key determinant for budget preparation and profitability projection. In the operational and control area, the sales forecast determines purchasing policies (how much to order, when to order), manufacturing policies, work levels, hiring, training, quota setting, machine loading, inventory levels, and the like. It would appear prudent to recognize the commonality and significance of the sales forecast and to take these elements into account in designing a management information system. It is common to have a variety of forecasting systems in use within a single enterprise, some of which are mutually inconsistent. Thus the manufacturing manager may be formulating his production schedule on forecast A while the materials control manager, who is responsible for supplying raw materials to enable forecast A to be met, may be ordering on the basis of forecast B. This situation seems a strange way to operate, but it is the method some companies employ. It is a classic example of the lack of system integration.

The preceding discussion does not imply that the same forecast should be used in every instance. Indeed, there may be logical reasons for using different forecasts. For example, it may be wise from an inventory standpoint to use a higher or more optimistic forecast, thus risking a chance of overstocking at a time when particular products are hard to procure. On the other hand, it may be logical to use a lower or more realistic forecast in setting sales and quota goals for salesmen lest their motivation and performance be adversely affected. The important point is that the concept of integration should be recognized; there should be a single function dedicated to sales forecasting. It should be accomplished by the group having access to the most current and meaningful data and having the ability to best process that data. All forecasts should emanate from the same quantitative data. If adjustments are desired to reflect various probabilities and risks, these adjustments should be made by the same group. Thus a forecast could consist of a most likely, most optimistic, and most pessimistic outlook. The various departments could then select the forecast that represented the level of risk and management judgment that they thought best under the circumstances. However, in no case should the situation arise where the manufacturing manager and the material manager use different forecasts—one second guessing the other. In this case, they should get together, jointly agree on a forecast, and proceed to provide the necessary resources to meet the forecast.

It is surprising, when reviewing an information system model, to discover that almost all the information needed emanates from a rather small number of common source documents. It is also surprising to see the interconnection of systems that were thought to be entities in themselves but that are really connected by a common flow of data. A prime example is a purchase requisition. This document initiates a long series of activities, starting with the writing of a purchase order by the accounting department, and includes the physical receipt of the goods, the quality control check, the paper-work updating of inventory records, the establishment of accounts payable and eventual vendor payment. Thus the purchase requisition affects the accounting, financial, quality control, receiving, purchasing, and inventory control functions. An integrated system approach recognizes rather than ignores these interrelationships. The system may begin with the automation of a specific function but only after the total picture is studied. Then subsystems can be added later with minimum effort and duplication.

IMPLEMENTATION CONSIDERATIONS

This subject will be discussed in more depth in the subsequent chapter. Several general concepts are in order at this point. Designers of a system (particularly a MIS) must have the foresight to ensure that the system is not obsolete before it is installed. Management information systems are long-term projects and demand a great deal more planning and foresight than conventional systems. In the same way an airport must be built to handle tomorrow's traffic, so must a MIS. It is true that many future events and activities are difficult to foresee. However, every effort should be made to build in the flexibilities to allow for the expected or unexpected. Thus just as it is good practice to build a four-lane highway with an option on the adjacent land so that additional lanes might be added in the future, so it is wise to develop a basic system design to incorporate readily added volume or the changing nature of future operations.

An example will help clarify this point. A data base is a prime requisite of a MIS, as we shall see. The data base holds relevant data about a company's operation and is usually organized around basic files, such as an employee file, a customer file, or an inventory file. Many systems are built on a data base that is very rigid in nature. I have known cases in which it has cost a company thousands of dollars to revise files and programs that access these files because the number of inventory items expanded to where the original four-digit identification number would not suffice. It seems prudent, especially in MIS design, to allow for this type of eventuality. Another example might be where a real payoff application is precluded because of lack of system flexibility. In a MIS for a distributor, it developed that an automatic dispatching system could aid materially in truck loading and order deliveries. This system involved an analysis of the cubic volume of the order as well as the weight. A group of orders were loaded onto trucks based on the total weight. While each truck has a weight limitation, an equally important facet is the cubic volume of the order. An order of light items, such as paper products, has a major impact on loading when compared to an order consisting mainly of heavy items (canned goods). It was decided to append a cubic volume field for each inventory item to facilitate truck loading and dispatching.

Allowance must be made in the inventory record and in the system design to allow for this type of flexibility. If not, considerable rework and effort are required. This is where the communications gap and credibility gap between operating and middle management and EDP management begin to widen. Management cannot understand why such a seemingly trivial change causes so much rework. The reason is that the system was designed without the necessary flexibility. One of the principal ground rules of MIS is that it should be designed open-ended to incorporate the inevitable changes as rapidly as today's traffic patterns. Initially, it takes more foresight and more planning time, but management must take a longer-range view and be more geared to life-cycle analysis.

RELATIONSHIP OF PHYSICAL SYSTEMS WITH INFORMATION SYSTEMS

It has been stated that it is very difficult to separate a physical system from an information system, but although difficult, it is important for the system designer to do so. There are several considerations in this regard that the distribution information model brings to light. A store's shelf alignment and general layout are predicated on what is convenient for the customer, what promotes the sale of specific items that are either particularly profitable or overstocked, and what maximizes the amount of goods sold. This situation is true in almost every retail operation. The store layout should take into account such factors as the fact that buyers tend to pay more attention to the right aisle than the left; thus it would seem prudent to put impulse items on the right side.

The store manager reorders items by walking down the aisle (as the shopper does) and jotting down what he is short of. The order catalog is in sequence by store layout. This, by the way, presupposes that all stores are physically organized in the same manner; if not, more than one type of catalog is required. On the other hand, the warehouse supplying the items is organized in a different way from the store layout. This fact is not surprising, for certain types of items lend themselves to particular types of storage facilities. Thus the drugs and sundry items are located where there are small bin areas with the required shelving. A system designer determines that he can reduce order processing time and computer equipment cost by laying out the warehouse in the same sequence as the store. Doing so precludes the need to sort the orders into warehouse sequence prior to sending picking slips to the warehouse. Furthermore, it facilitates the unloading of orders from the truck directly onto the shelves, since the orders would be picked and loaded by store location.

We have a situation here that shows the close interrelationship between a physical system and an information system. In many actual cases, the information system overrules the physical system, and indeed physical layouts have been changed to facilitate system design. This is a case of the tail wagging the dog. Although the system designer can point out areas such as the preceding ones, plus the pros and cons of the alternatives, management must make the final decision. When management is not involved in system design, the EDP staff exerts major leverage on system decisions. The decisions may be sound ones, but when the EDP staff is short on business perspective, the decision can have serious consequences for a company.

Another example of the relationship between physical and information systems is where a system designer develops a strategy whereby the stores of two adjacent divisions are served by a common warehouse. This idea is certainly valid, and there is nothing wrong in proposing and supporting the concept with a transportation and inventory model that shows the costs and customer service of one warehouse versus two. However, for the most part, the physical facilities and operating strategies (e.g., profit centers) are the givens of system design; the information system should build from these factors and should not get bogged down in analyzing a host of problems and considerations beyond the scope of EDP and MIS.

PRIORITY ANALYSIS IN SELECTION OF SUBSYSTEMS

In viewing Figure 3.6, it is clear that a distributor could not hope to accomplish a good portion of the MIS in a short period of time. It is equally clear that starting points must be established, as well as a priority and sequence of information subsystems implementation. The following list shows possible criteria to use in selecting subsystems for implementation.

- Degree of difficulty in implementing
- Time and cost in implementing
- Operational problem areas
- Potential high tangible payoff
- Potential high intangible payoff
- What other companies have done

- Potential competitive impact
- Where your capability lies
- Degree of stability of operational area
- User acceptance

The first two criteria have probably been overused as a reason for not tackling certain applications. Because the EDP manager frequently makes the final selection, he tends to steer away from those areas that are difficult and time consuming. This situation is desirable to some degree, but he must bear in mind that the potential impact (cost savings and benefits) on the organization is a more significant determinant. Sometimes it is appropriate to look for applications that can materially improve a problem area of a company; for example, it takes 72 hours to fill an order and even then a third of the items are out of stock. Tangible and intangible benefits are most significant selection criteria. A computerized system can show tangible benefits, such as cutting clerical costs or reducing inventory, but it can also produce intangible benefits, such as improved customer service, which is most significant although difficult to measure.

The sixth criterion should be used only as a guide. Companies of about the same size in the same industry may be similar in operation, but they are not identical. What is good for the industry may not be good for you. A system that can give a company a major competitive edge should be ranked fairly high in the priority list.

The next three criteria take into account the capabilities of the people responsible for system development, the environment of the operational area utilizing the system, and the degree or probability of acceptance by the end user. Thus the initial thrust of MIS might be steered away from the warehousing department if the personnel have continually resisted any form of automation. As in other system decisions, there are competing and conflicting elements such that a relative weighing of the selection criteria is necessary.

Another set of ground rules in giving priority to computer subsystems is the relative computerization quotient of each application area. Computer development can usually be justified when several or all of the following conditions are met:

- High volume of transactions
- Repetitive nature of transactions
- Quick response time
- Sizable mathematical computations
- Source data has multiple uses

Therefore it is possible that although a real problem area exists within a company and the payoffs are there if the problem can be resolved, it still may not meet the computerization criteria listed above. This is not to say that the problem should go unresolved; it does say that computerization and MIS may not be the best way to solve it.

Surveys have shown that a key to profitable MIS is the application selection and approval cycle used by a company. Where a joint advisory board of EDP people and management review, analyze, and decide computerization priority, the company's EDP operations were more successful than when the selection of computer application was left to the EDP personnel. Methods of giving priority to and selecting computer applications will be discussed in more depth in the next chapter.

TIME FRAME AND PHASING PLAN

The foregoing discussion leads quite naturally to the establishment of a time frame and phasing plan for MIS development. An initial question is: On what level of management should MIS be focused? Although essential to get top management's backing, support, and participation in the system, it is not wise to focus MIS initially at top management. As has been stated, the planning nature of the executive's job and the complexity of the decision process at that level make it a difficult area to computerize. Also, it is true that many of the strategic and planning decisions emanate from data captured within other information subsystems. Thus the basic subsystems are necessary prerequisites for planning and strategic subsystems. The most realistic focus is on middle management recognizing at the outset that the system will probably have greatest impact on operating management and the people who work for operating management. It is wise to focus the system design at one level above the area of greatest impact. Doing so will ensure proper management participation and involvement and will also place pressure on system flexibility, thereby enabling extensions of the system with minor modification.

A phasing plan suggested for a distributor is as follows:

Phase 1	Order processing
	Inventory control
	Portions of accounting
Phase 2	Transportation
	Materials control
	Purchasing
	Stores control
	Other portions of accounting
Phase 3	Financial
	Marketing
	Strategic planning

This phasing plan is a rather conservative one, but it does reflect the normal learning curve employed by companies just embarking on MIS. If the design is developed on an open-ended basis and reflects the eventual integration of information subsystems per the information system MIS model, the EDP staff can move into phase 2 applications immediately after phase 1 is completed. Thus practical MIS envisions a philosophy that is top management oriented or "top down" in design, but conceivably operating management or "bottoms up" in implementation. Problems in MIS have arisen from systems being both designed and implemented from the bottom up.

For companies who want to move faster into MIS and who are willing to make the necessary expenditure, a parallel effort can be directed at top management and the strategic planning information subsystems. A small team of management science or operations research experts can be exploring techniques for aiding management decision making. This activity should be closely dovetailed with the basic MIS development to ensure that the necessary historical data will be available as a system by-product and in a form suitable for incorporating into the strategic systems. An Operations Research (OR) group could, for example, be studying the warehouse location situation with a view toward optimizing the number and location of division warehouses. They could also be developing a model that aids in the selection of store sites based on traffic patterns, population composition, shopping center complexes, and the like. This parallel program of two groups concentrating on two levels of management is a most desirable mode of operation.

CENTRAL DATA BASE REQUIREMENTS

The development of the integrated system illustrates the need for gathering basic information from key source documents and using this information throughout the system. Similarly, it is equally important to develop basic master files, which are used in common by the various subsystems. These common master files are normally referred to as a central data base.

The central data base holds all relevant information about a company's operation in one readily accessible file. The file is arranged so that duplication and redundancy are avoided. Information concerning on-going activities is captured once, validated, and entered into the proper location in the data base. Normally the central data base is subdivided into the major information subsets needed to run a business. These subsets are (a) customer and sales file, (b) vendor file, (c) personnel file, (d) inventory file, and (e) general ledger accounting file. The various subsystems use information from the same file. The key element in a data base concept is that each subsystem utilizes the same data base in satisfying its information needs. Duplicate files or subsets of the central data base are eliminated.

Figure 3.7 illustrates the central data base concept in the form of a bucket or bowl of facts. It is so designed that different levels of management—in this case, marketing, accounting, and various members of top and operating management—can dip into and sift off the information that is relevant to their particular sphere of operation. For example, marketing management would be interested primarily in the customer/sales file, accounting management would be interested in information emanating from the general ledger file, while top management would want a summary statement off the top of the bowl. Thus the needs and function of management determine how deeply they dip into the bowl.

Figure 3.8 lists the basic data files, the type of data contained in each file, and the various time demands on information emanating from the files. Some applications or uses of the file require fast response, defined as from a few seconds to an hour; others require medium response time, defined as from several hours to one day, while still others require only slow response, defined as several days

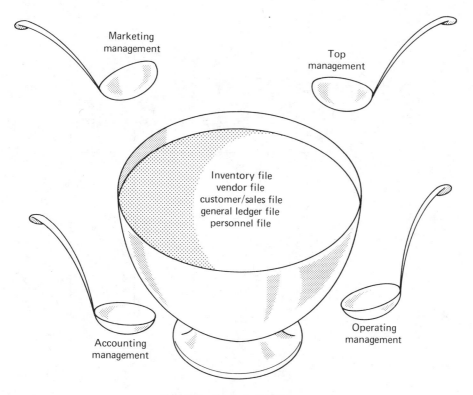

Marketing
management

Top
management

Inventory file
vendor file
customer/sales file
general ledger file
personnel file

Accounting
management

Operating
management

Fig. 3.7 Central data base

to a week or even a month in some cases. This type of analysis is necessary to select the type of electronic storage media best suited to the MIS requirements. To use the customer file as an example, it may be desirable to make a credit check at the check-cashing booth of a supermarket. This step could be done by inserting the customer's credit card into a device that is linked via a communication line into a computer storage device. Similarly, it may be necessary to deliver an emergency order to a store within an hour if the store is out of a special sale item. This is not to say that complex computerized on-line systems are necessary to effect fast response time. For example, a daily listing in credit card sequence of customers with credit problems might suffice in this instance. A chart similar to Figure 3.8 does help to establish the necessary computerized storage hierarchy. The use of the word hierarchy implies that all data need not be accessible in the same amount of time; certain data (possibly entire files) can be stored on sequential, slow-access (but cheap) magnetic tape, while other data can be stored on high-capacity, high-speed random access devices. The data base concept is a most logical approach to the paper-work explosion that has hit many business areas. However, management should not overlook some important considerations in developing the data base as part of an integrated system.

A fairly obvious problem is the fact that erroneously entered data has an immediate influence on other subsystems and departments utilizing the data. Of course, this can be a desirable factor in that the errors will be noticed more quickly

Data base element	Type of data	Fast response time	Medium response time	Slow response time
Customer file	Name Address Credit information Contract terms	Credit check Emergency orders	Normal order processing	Accounts receivable Cash collection Check reconciliation AR aging
Inventory file	Price, cost, weight Status and location of inventory items	Stock position in/out	Order processing Order point analysis Truck loading	Inventory status Obsolete inv. report Inventory value analysis Turnover ratio
Personnel file	Name, address, Wage rate Personnel status Deductions of all employees	Paychecks for bankers and part time people	Job accounting Labor analysis Overtime report	Weekly/monthly payroll Payroll register Internal revenue reports
General ledger file	Debits and credits Status of each account in general ledger	No requirements	Proforma - profit and loss and balance sheet	Profit and loss state- ment Balance sheet Account status
Sales history file	Units and dollars sold by region by division by store	No requirements	Forecast	Sales analysis Trend analysis Budget comparisions
Vendor file	Name, address Status, amount owed, Vendor rating Open orders for each vendor	No requirements	Purchase order	Vendor analysis Accounts payable Cash payments Check reconciliation

Fig. 3.8 Data base requirements

and that feedback should help purify the data and ensure that necessary input controls are established and adhered to.

Another problem in building a single central file is the interdepartment co-operation needed to arrive at the pertinent data elements in the file. One department may need a degree of detail that may burden the reporting source such that the quality of all input suffers. The solution to these problems normally means discussions, meetings, and eventual compromise if the implementation time frame is to be met.

An interesting organizational phenomenon is often encountered during the development of the data base. This phenomenon can be called the "geometric organizational syndrome." It stems from the fact that joint decisions are needed to reach compromises related to the central file content. This does not seem a formidable task until one realizes that the interaction pathways of four people are more than double that of two people. The progression is more of a geometric than an arithmetic nature. Thus there is one communication path with 2 people, three with 3 people, six with 4 people, ten with 5 people, etc. Consequently, adding a fifth communicating party increases the communication pathways not by 25 percent but by 67 percent. The "geometric organizational syndrome" is probably even more accentuated by the psychological and political blocks that individuals bring with them to the situation.

Another problem in developing a central data base is information security. When individual departments maintain their own data files, security of file information is not a problem. They know that other departments will not have access to confidential facts about their operation. In a highly centralized organization, the confidential nature of the central data base is not of primary concern, but in a highly decentralized organization where divisions are autonomous, the centralization of data in one central file can represent a serious obstacle. The divisions are skeptical about the information they submit; they wonder how it is going to be used. They do not want their performance figures to be known by other divisions.

The suspicion generated by the security aspects of the central data base can have a significant effect on the validity of what is supplied by the various users. It is true that certain quantitative data can be checked for obvious errors, but there is little or no check on the qualitative data—and this data can be extremely significant in the planning and analysis functions. Qualitative data can take the form of how the customer is currently using the product or how he plans to use it in the future. It also takes the form of information on customer complaints and problems in an effort to improve the product and service. The real measure of the success of the data base concept is the input going into the system. The psychological considerations of submitting confidential data must be carefully considered.

Problems might also arise from the fact that there is a time dimension as well as a content dimension to information. For example, in a particular situation, it might take 2 to 3 months from the time an order is placed by a customer to validate the terms of the order officially. From the point of view of the sales office, the sales effort for this particular order is completed. They would like to see the results reflected in the particular period in which the customer placed the order. Their thinking is that in 90 percent of the cases, the contractual negotiations are a formality and do not change the basic terms of the order. This may not be the feeling of the production or accounting departments. Each of these departments has a different date at which they would like to see the order reflected as part of the customer and sales data base supplying reports to their departments.

Unless the new system satisfied the requirements of each user, the user is compelled to maintain his own system, which of course, defeats the purpose of the central data base concept. The longer the user runs his old system in parallel, the more difficult it is to get him to supply accurate data to a new system that is not serving his needs.

Instituting an integrated system built around a central data base system brings to light deep-rooted management problems, problems that would continue to grow if left unattended. These are the "quiet problems," the problems of company communication, organization, and control. The development of the data base acts as the catalyst in bringing the "quiet problems" to the surface.

MANUFACTURING INFORMATION SYSTEM MODEL

Figure 3.9 adds six subsystems to the distribution system model to produce a manufacturing model. Since all manufacturers perform the distribution function, the major difference between the two operations is that the distributor orders all manufactured items from a vendor while the manufacturer produces the items himself and orders only raw materials, assemblies, and price parts. The physical facilities now include a factory as well as a warehouse.

The manufacturing model adds the engineering and research subsystem (E & R), which is a vital one to a manufacturing operation. The engineers design the products the company produces and develop bill-of-material and routing sheet information. Basically, the bill of material indicates the components and assemblies (and quantities of each) required to build an end item, whereas the routing sheet indicates the type and sequence of production operations necessary to transform the raw material and components into finished goods. The E & R subsystem is also responsible for establishing requirements and standards for quality control and machine maintenance.

Figure 3.9 indicates the interrelationship of the E & R subsystem with quality control, maintenance, production scheduling, and requirements generation. Let us see how these subsystems are tied together with the distribution subsystems described earlier.

The requirements generation subsystem takes finished-goods requirements (sales forecast, plus sales orders, minus finished-goods inventory) from the inventory control subsystem and, utilizing the bill of material information from the E & R subsystem, determines the requirements for subassemblies, piece parts, and raw material by multiplying the number of finished-goods items by the components that constitute each end item. The total for each subunit is then measured against inventory records to produce net requirements.

This netting process is direct input into the production scheduling subsystem. The routing data, also supplied by the E & R subsystem, is combined with the net requirements to produce a production schedule. The production control subsystem deals with the day-to-day implementation of the production plan by issuing

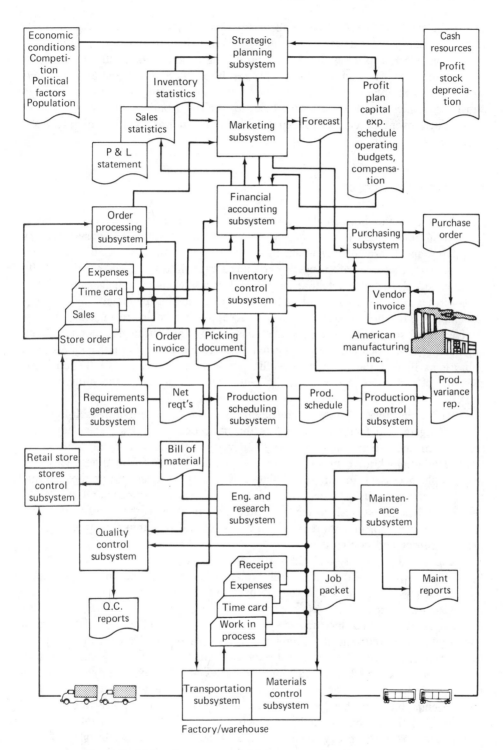

Fig. 3.9 Information system model for a manufacturing company

job packets to the factory (telling them what jobs to work on, the sequence and scheduled completion dates), accepting feedback (including labor, material, expense, and work-in-process data), and producing a variety of quality control and maintenance reports and analyses. The result of these six manufacturing subsystems is to maintain an availability of finished-goods items in the warehouse to satisfy customer demand and interface to the distribution subsystems (order processing, inventory control, accounting, and transportation), which have been described previously.

SUBSYSTEM CLASSIFICATION

Now that the horizontal subsystems have been described and their interconnection illustrated, it is useful to categorize or classify the subsystems. By classifying and characterizing them, the MIS designer can better determine where to start, what resources are necessary, required capabilities, the degree of difficulty to be expected, and the potential benefit to various levels of management. Figure 3.10 further classifies the 15 subsystems illustrated in the manufacturing information model. The three major categories are supportive, mainstream, and administrative. The supportive category includes marketing, strategic planning, and engineering and research. The supportive subsystems differ from the mainstream subsystems in that the latter control the physical line operation of the business, the flow of raw materials through the plant into the hands of the ultimate consumer.

The supportive subsystems are obviously most significant in establishing the plans, budgets, and facilities, as well as the basic decision rules embedded in the mainstream subsystems; however, they differ from the line or mainstream functions. The administrative subsystems involve the accounting for facilities, activities, and people necessary to run the business. These subsystems satisfy the external requirements of a business placed upon it by various government and regulatory agencies. Thus taxes must be paid, profitability reported to the Security and Exchange Commission, and the business must be operated within the framework of proper licenses and contracts.

Figures 3.11, 3.12, and 3.13 further characterize the subsystems on the basis of 12 criteria. An example will explain how to read the charts. The sales analysis subsystem is marketing supportive and aimed at operating and middle management. Sales analysis reports are usually produced on a weekly basis; the decision rules required by the subsystem are well understood, straightforward, and highly structured; and the complexity level of mathematics or computer processing required is low. The principal data base element from which the necessary information is extracted is the customer and sales file. The type of data is internal to the company's operation (sales history) as contrasted to external data (economic trends, buyer profiles) and the time demand is medium; that is, the information must be timely, but normally it can be produced on a scheduled basis. The transaction volume is heavy because the analysis is built from customer orders. Because the sales analysis can be scheduled and because it requires a compilation of data, the typical mode of operation is batch. The historical frequency of imple-

SUPPORTIVE

Marketing
Sales analysis
Sales forecasting
Advertising
Sales administration

Strategic Planning
Econometric models
Market models
Simulation
Decision theory
Investment analysis
Facilities planning

Engineering and Research
Design automation
Project control
Numerical control
Configuration management
Industrial engineering
Bill of material generation

MAINSTREAM

Sales Order Processing
Customer billing
Order filling
Transportation

Inventory Reporting and Control
Stock status reporting
Statistical replenishment.

Requirements Generation
Gross requirements generation
Net requirements generation

Production Scheduling
Fabrication and assembly scheduling
Shop loading
Issuance of job packets

Production Control
Performance vs plan analysis
Variance reporting

Purchasing
Receiving
Quality Control
Maintenance

ADMINISTRATIVE

Financial
Accounts receivable
Accounts payable
General ledger
Cost accounting
Fixed asset accounting
Budgeting
Financial models
Key rated analysis
Profit and loss statements

Personnel
Payroll
Payroll reports
Wage and compensation analysis
Performance appraisals

Legal

Fig. 3.10 Information subsystem classification

67

Subsystem	Type of function	Major management focus	Cycle	Form of processing	Processing complexity	Data base	Type of data	Time demand	Transaction volume	Typical mode of operation	Frequency of implementation	Difficulty of implementation
Sales analysis	Mktg. supp.	Opert'g & middle	Weekly	Structured	Low	Customer & sales files	Internal	Medium	Heavy	Batch	High	Low
Sales forecasting	Mktg. supp.	Middle	Monthly	Structured	High	Sales history	Internal	Low	Heavy	Batch	Med.	Med.
Advertising	Mktg. supp.	Middle	Monthly	Unstructured	High	Sales history	Internal external	Low	Light	Batch	Low	High
Sales administration	Mktg. supp.	Opert'g & middle	Daily	Highly struc.	Med.	Customer & inventory	Internal	Med. to high	Heavy	Direct & Batch	High	Low
Econometric models	Plan'g supp.	Middle & top	Monthly	Structured	High	Gen. Ledger accounting	Internal	Low	Light	Batch	Low	Med.
Market models	Plan'g supp.	Middle & top	Monthly	Unstructured	High	Sales history	Internal external	Low	Med.	Batch	Low	High
Decision theory	Plan'g supp.	Middle & top	Weekly	Unstructured	High	— —	Internal external	Med.	Low	Batch	Med.	High
Investment analysis	Plan'g supp.	Middle & top	Monthly	Sturctured	Med.	Gen. Ledger accounting	Internal	Low	Low	Batch	Low	Med.
Facilities planning	Plan'g supp.	Middle & top	Monthly	Structured	Low	Gen. Ledger accounting	Internal	Low	Low	Batch	Low	Med.
Design automation	Engr'g supp.	Opert'g & middle	Daily	Structured	High	Product file	Internal	Low	Med.	Batch	Low	High
Project control	Engr'g supp.	All levels	Weekly	Structured	Low	— —	Internal	Low	Med.	Batch	Med.	Med.
Numerical control	Engr'g supp.	Operating	Weekly	Structured	High	Product file	Internal	Low	Med.	Batch	Low	High
Configuration management	Engr'g supp.	Opert'g & middle	Weekly	Structured	Low	Product file	Internal	Low	Med.	Batch	Low	Med.
Industrial Engineering	Engr'g supp.	Opert'g & middle	Daily	Structured	Med.	Personnel file	Internal	Med.	Med.	Batch	Low	Med.
Bill of Mat'l generation	Engr'g supp.	Operating	Daily	Highly struc.	Med.	Product file	Internal	Med.	Heavy	Direct & batch	Med.	Med.

Fig. 3.11 Supportive subsystem characteristics

Subsystem	Type of function	Major management focus	Cycle	Form of processing	Processing complexity	Data base	Type of data	Time demand	Transaction volume	Typical mode of operation	Frequency of implementation	Difficulty of implementation
Customer billing	Main-stream	Operat-ing	Daily	Highly struc.	Low	Customer file	Internal	Med.	Heavy	Batch of dir.	High	Low
Order filling	Main-stream	Operat-ing	Daily	Highly struc.	Low	Customer file	Internal	Med. to high	Heavy	Batch or dir.	High	Low
Transporta-tion	Main-stream	Operat-ing	Daily	Highly struc.	Med.	Cust.& vehicle	Internal	Med.	Heavy	Batch or dir.	Med.	Low
Stock status reporting	Main-stream	Opert'g & middle	Daily	Highly struc.	Low	Inventory file	Internal	Med.	Heavy	Batch	High	Low
Statistical replenishment	Main-stream	Operat-ing	Daily	Struc-tured	High	Inventory file	Internal	Med.	Heavy	Batch	Med.	Med.
Gross Require-ments gen.	Main-stream	Opera-ing	Daily	Highly struc.	Med.	Inv. & pro-duct file	Internal	Med.	Med.	Batch	Med.	Med.
Net requirements generation	Main-stream	Opera-ing	Daily	Highly struc.	Med.	Inv. & Prod file	Internal	Med.	Med.	Batch	Med.	Med.
Fabrication & Ass'y scheduling	Main-stream	Operat-ing	Daily	Struc-tured	High	Inv.Prod.& facil.file	Internal	Med.	Med.	Batch	Low	High
Shop loading	Main-stream	Operat-ing	Daily	Struc-tured	High	Inv.prod.& facil.file	Internal	Med.	Med.	Batch	Low	High
Issuance of job packets	Main-stream	Operat-ing	Daily	Struc-tured	Med.	Inv.prod.& facil.file	Internal	Med.	Med.	Batch	Med.	Med.
Performance vs plan analysis	Main-stream	Opert'g & middle	Weekly	Struc-tured	Med.	Inv.work in process	Internal	Med.	Low	Batch	Med.	Med.
Variance reporting	Main-stream	Opert'g & middle	Weekly	Struc-tured	Med.	Inv.work in process	Internal	Med.	Low	Batch	Med.	Med.
Purchasing	Main-stream	Operat-ing	Daily	Highly struc.	Med.	Vendor file	Internal	Med.	Med.	Batch	Med.	Med.
Receiving	Main-stream	Operati-ing	Daily	Highly struc.	Low	Inventory file	Internal	Med.	Med.	Batch	Med.	Low
Quality control	Main-stream	Opert'g & middle	Weekly	Struc-tured	Med.	Product & facilities	Internal	Med.	Med.	Batch	Low	Med.
Maintenance	Main-stream	Opera't'g & middle	Weekly	Struc-tured	Med.	Prod. & facil.file	Internal	Med.	Med.	Batch	Low	Med.

Fig. 3.12 Mainstream subsystem characteristics

Subsystem	Type of function	Major management focus	Cycle	Form of processing	Processing complexity	Data base	Type of data	Time demand	Transaction volume	Typical mode of operation	Frequency of implementation	Difficulty of implementation
Accounts receivable	Admin. finan.	Operating	Daily	Highly struc.	Low	Customer	Internal	Med.	Heavy	Batch	High	Low
Accounts payable	Admin. finan.	Operating	Daily	Highly struc.	Low	Vendor	Internal	Med.	Med.	Batch	High	Low
General ledger	Admin. finan.	Operating	Weekly	Highly struc.	Low	Acct'g	Internal	Low	Low	Batch	Low	Low
Cost accounting	Admin. finan.	Opert'g & middle	Weekly	Structured	Med.	Inv. & gen.ledger	Internal	Med.	Low	Batch	Med.	Med.
Fixed asset accounting	Admin. finan.	Opert'g & middle	Weekly	Highly struc.	Low	General ledger	Internal	Med.	Low	Batch	High	Low
Budgeting	Admin. finan.	All levels	Monthly	Structured	Med.	General ledger	Internal external	Med.	Low	Batch	Med.	Med.
Financial models	Admin. finan.	Middle & top	Monthly	Structured	High	General ledger	Internal external	Low	Low	Batch	Low	High
Key ratio analysis	Admin. finan.	Middle & top	Monthly	Structured	Med.	General ledger	Internal	Low	Low	Batch	Low	High
Profit and loss statements	Admin finan.	Middle & top	Monthly	Structured	Low	General ledger	Internal	Low	Low	Batch	Med.	Med.
Payroll	Admin. pers'1	Operating	Weekly	Highly struc.	Low	Personnel file	Internal	Med.	Med.	Batch & dir.	High	Low
Payroll reports	Admin. per's1	Operating	Weekly	Highly struc.	Low	Personnel file	Internal	Med.	Med.	Batch	High	Low
Skills inventory	Admin. pers'1	Opert'g & middle	Weekly	Structured	Low	Personnel file	Internal	Low	Med.	Batch	Low	Med.
Wage and compensation analysis	Admin. pers'1	Opert'g & middle	Weekly	Structured	Low	Personnel file	Internal	Low	Med.	Batch	Low	Med.
Performance appraisals	Admin. pers'1	Opert'g & middle	Weekly	Structured	Low	Personnel file	Internal	Low	Med.	Batch	Low	Med.
Legal	Admin. legal	Middle & top	Weekly	Structured	Low	Specially prepared	Internal external	Low	Med.	Batch	Low	Med.

Fig. 3.13 Administrative subsystem characteristics

menting this subsystem is high, and because of the composite of characteristics, the degree of difficulty in implementing is low.

Additional study of the characteristics chart can help establish a priority analysis of subsystems based on the relative weights placed on the various criteria. Thus it may be wise to start with subsystems that are easy to implement; conversely, if the systems capability is present, the company may choose to tackle subsystems that are aimed at higher levels of management, thereby going after the bigger payoff and benefit. These trade-offs will be discussed in more detail in the subsequent chapter.

SUMMARY

This chapter has developed an information subsystem model based on a hypothetical company in the distribution business. The system road map was used to further analyze the horizontal subsystems (first described in Chapter 1), which constitute a management information system. The model facilitated a focus on specific characteristics of management information systems and elements, including the need for integration in MIS, the priority of subsystem selection, system trade-offs, time frame and phasing plan, implementation considerations, and the concept of the central data base. The system model of the distribution company was extended to include the subsystems pertinent to a manufacturing company. Then a method for classifying subsystems was presented, and each subsystem was viewed in accordance with a set of descriptive criteria.

Emphasis has been on the management and business elements in MIS. Up to this point there has been scant mention of computers. This omission is deliberate, for a major premise of the book is that marrying a computer to a business operation begins with management and a thorough study of business operations, not with the computer.

STUDY CASETTES

MIDEASTERN ELECTRIC

A large utility with over two million customers, Mideastern has been using computers for over 15 years. A conservative approach to computers and organization has resulted in the situation where the president has become upset with the lack of progress in EDP. Upon his return from an advanced computer seminar, he asked his staff assistant to make a quick assessment of their use of computers in relation to other utilities doing about the same volume of business.

The report, which the assistant indicated was only a cursory treatment in view of the six-week deadline the president had placed on its completion, centered on the lack of imagination and rather prosaic approach that the current EDP staff had taken. It was true that customer billing was running smoothly, but the computer offered management minimal help in areas such as power loading or in improving cost effectiveness; in other words, the company was paying over a million dollars per year in computer hardware costs alone, but was reaping very few benefits in the management area. The report was most direct, hard-hitting, and very critical of most of the computer operations. While it didn't single out current EDP management, the conclusions were tantamount to a severe indictment.

The EDP Director was a long-term Mideastern employee, having been with the company for 22 years. He ran the punched card equipment when Mideastern started with mechanical data processing and slowly evolved into his current position over the period of time that the company was going through three generations of computer hardware.

On the basis of the report and his own intuitive feeling, the president had decided on a change in EDP management. He wanted the current Staff Assistant to the Vice-President of Engineering, Bill Vosbury, to take over the job. The staff assistant had been with Mideastern 15 years, was involved in a variety of management jobs, most of them important line functions, and always performed these functions most effectively. He had a record of achievement and was also a technically competent individual, not afraid to tackle new jobs which weren't exactly in his area of expertise. He knew very little about computers, particularly about running a large scale EDP department. He had a bachelor's and master's degree in Electrical Engineering so that he knew the basic principles of computers and the electronics that powered them.

Vosbury had given a great deal of thought to the president's insistence that he take the job; however, because of the importance of the job and the fact that it was different from any other job Vosbury had held, the president left the final decision to Vosbury. Vosbury had two days before his meeting with the president. The president would expect his decision on taking the job as well as his initial feelings on the approach to be taken to improve Mideastern's data processing function. Vosbury was spending considerable time mulling over what he would say to the president; he knew it was an important crossroad in his career.

Study Questions

1. Is Vosbury qualified for the job?
2. Did the president act with intelligence on the basis of the report by his assistant?
3. What should Vosbury do if he accepts the job?
4. What should be the role of the old EDP director in the new organization?
5. How long do you think it will be before Vosbury gets results?
6. Does Mideastern have management involvement?

THE BROWN COMPANY

TO   Harvey Williamson, Manager of
              Data Processing
FROM   John J. Warren, Director of Marketing
SUBJECT   Viewpoint on Data Processing
DATE   February 12, 1972

At our last executive committee meeting, the subject of data processing at the Brown Company was one of the agenda items. President L. J. Parsons suggested that it might prove helpful if the department heads each write you a letter indicating their feelings and opinions about the progress we have made with EDP over the past several years. I do not know how typical my response will be because I have not discussed the subject with the other department directors; however, I have decided to be extremely frank and candid in giving you my personal reactions. In so doing, I may appear to be over-critical, but I hope you will take my remarks in the constructive way they are intended. I realize the situation is a two-sided one and that I have not done everything I could personally do to take advantage of EDP. Hopefully, this letter and the others you receive can lead to the establishment of meaningful dialogue that can help resolve some of our existing problems and help us move ahead to improve the situation.

I do not think EDP meant too much to me until three years ago when we installed the third generation computer that is currently in operation. Let us discuss the routine computer applications that were tackled first, things like processing orders and analyzing sales history. It appears to me that we have made some progress; however, I must state frankly that it has been somewhat slow and painful. In looking back at the cutover to our new order processing system, which occurred two years ago, I know I was quite upset at the time and lost a great deal of faith in computer processing. I know we antagonized several of our key customers by sending them erroneous invoices and also by indicating we had certain items in stock when, in reality, we did not. I remember the embarrassment, for example, when the system treated a request to expedite an order as an order itself. As a result, the J. L. Craemer Company received two carloads of its order.

You and your staff had done quite a job in convincing us that this new system would be a great success. We believed you because we really wanted to, and we looked forward to the new approach with a great deal of enthusiasm. In retrospect, I think we were oversold. You should have felt free to tell us potential problem areas and pitfalls. Presenting us a more balanced picture would have prepared us to face the cutover period with far better perspective. We could have been in a position to support the system rather than castigating it. I'm told I still have an order clerk who uses your inventory report for posting her manual cardex files. I don't think that's exactly what you meant when you said we were going to have a common data base system. We survived that period and finally did see the improvements that you promised us, even though they were from six to 12 months late in occurring.

Another element that was overlooked (and this probably is our fault as much as yours) was that we had very little to do with the design and development of the system. True, our people attended a course on EDP, but I thought the instructors spoke over our heads and in terminology that was at best very difficult to understand. I still can't see what bearing an "octal patch" has to my operation. This one-shot instruction was not enough to cover all the things we should have known about the implementation of a new system. I probably should have assigned one of my sales analysts to represent our interest as the system was developing. Not having participated in the development, I naturally tend to resist changes that are forthcoming. One of the areas in which I think we should have pressed harder is that of constructing the system in a manner that would allow for later additions and changes. It is true that one of your system analysts discussed with me at the very beginning what type of sales analysis reports we needed. However, I never saw him again. The marketing situation is a most dynamic one as you know, and our needs today certainly differ from our needs two years ago. I hate to think that we are locked out now because we didn't request something two years ago.

Now, I'd like to turn to the more sophisticated application areas. I remember a presentation you made when we started the conversion to the new system. You spoke about an integrated data processing system built around a common data base. You indicated, at the time, that a complete sales history file would be maintained and indexed in such a way that we could obtain almost any type of analysis required and in a short response time. Though this can be done to a limited extent, it hardly satisfies all our current needs. It seems to me that we spent a good deal of time working along with your people in capturing information that was to become part of this data base. Other departments also were to compile information for the data base. For example, we were told we could get an up-to-date status of in-process orders from the factory. In order to do this, we had to change a number of our existing procedures and expend a considerable amount of clerical effort. Very frankly, I have seen little results from all the work that we put in.

I think the idea of on-line order entry directly to the computer that you spoke about several years ago still presents a great opportunity for us to materially reduce our order cycle time. This would improve customer service in an area that I am sure costs us dearly. Another area I am vitally interested in is an improved sales forecasting system. With our other data processing problems, I wonder if we will ever get to these things before you are ready to change computers again and go through a lengthy conversion process.

In summary, I hope I have not been too critical and I want to state again that I realize I share a good deal of the responsibility for your problems. Maybe the following set of ground rules will help us both:

1. Be frank with the operating departments. We want to work with you, but we need to have a balanced picture.

2. Let's cooperate in determining system specifications. I realize that I need more computer education and I am most certainly willing to get it if I can participate more effectively in EDP operations. This is true of all the people in my department.

3. Let's work together to map out a plan for getting to the real payoff areas that I have mentioned. I realize it will take time, but I will be satisfied if we have long range goals and are headed toward those goals.

Sincerely,

John J. Warren

JJW/rc

Study Questions

1. What do you think of Warren's treatment and opinion of EDP?

2. How would you take it if you were Williamson?

3. How typical do you think this situation is?

4. What should be Williamson's next actions?

BIBLIOGRAPHY

CHURCHILL, et al., *Computer Based Information Systems for Management—A Survey.* National Association for Accountants, New York, 1968.

EMERY, JAMES C., *Organizational Planning and Control Systems.* The Macmillan Company, London, 1969, 166 pp.

HOUSE, WILLIAM, *The Impact of Information Technology on Management Operation.* Auerbach Publishers, 1971, 436 pp.

KELLY, J. F., *Computerized Management Information Systems.* The Macmillan Company, New York, 1970, 533 pp.

MARTINO, R., *Information Management: The Dynamics of MIS.* Management Development Institute, Wayne, Pa., 1969, 163 pp.

McCARTHY, E. J., J. A. McCARTHY, and D. HUMES. *Integrated Data Processing Systems.* John Wiley & Sons, New York, 1966, 565 pp.

McKEEVER, J. M., and B. KRUSE. *Management Reporting Systems.* John Wiley & Sons, New York, 1971, 94 pp.

PRINCE, T. R., *Information Systems for Management Planning and Control.* Richard D. Irwin, Homewood, Illinois, 1970, 523 pp.

ROSS, J., *Management by Information System.* Prentice-Hall, Inc., Englewood Cliffs, New Jersey, 1970, 322 pp.

SCHWARTZ, N. H., MIS Planning. *Datamation,* September 1, 1970, pp. 28–31.

Chapter 4

DEVELOPMENT AND IMPLEMENTATION

OF SUBSYSTEMS—

THE VERTICAL DIMENSION

Chapter 1 briefly described the steps that an application must go through to become operable on a computer. Once the total information model is developed as in the previous chapter, the subsystems identified, and the implementation priority determined, each application must be thoroughly planned, documented, programmed, tested, and, finally, put into productive computer operation. This activity is called the vertical dimension of MIS and is the subject of this chapter.

Figure 4.1 illustrates the application development and implementation cycle. The core of the wheel indicates that there are three general phases in this process. They are (a) analysis, (b) synthesis, and (c) implementation. Analysis is defined as the separation of anything into its constituent parts or elements. This phase of the computer acquisition cycle is concerned with this initial step. Applied to computer acquisition, analysis involves the review and analysis of company operation and the division of the total operation into logical and workable units for measurement and evaluation to see if there are better ways of accomplishing the objectives of the business.

Synthesis, the opposite of analysis, begins to combine and build the parts or elements into a whole. The analysis stage dissects business operations to show up weaknesses and areas in need of improvement, particularly the area of information analysis and its effect on the control of operations. The synthesis phase combines these elements in such a way as to improve the original operation.

The implementation phase is the proof of the pudding. Here the synthesis (or improved solution) is actually designed, programmed, and put into operation. The conclusion of this phase is the maintenance and modification of operational applications to ensure that they remain free of errors and discrepancies.

A further breakdown of the computer selection cycle indicates that the

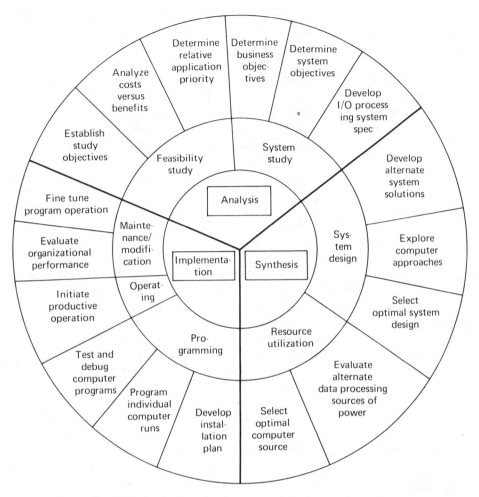

Fig. 4.1 Application development and implementation cycle

analysis phase consists of the feasibility study and system study subphases. The feasibility study begins with the establishment of objectives, including the time and cost of the study, selection of the people who will conduct the study, and the general manner in which the study will be conducted. The feasibility study is directed to the question: Does a computer offer sufficient benefits to a company to warrant further investigation? An effective system study requires a considerable investment in time and money and should be undertaken only if a preliminary study indicates that a computer presents a feasible solution to problems. It is possible that further system study will indicate that a computer is not justified, but a company should be reasonably sure that it is before embarking on a comprehensive system study.

The system study begins with an analysis of overall business objectives and focuses on the information and control system, which enables a company to plan and schedule operations better in order to produce the product at the lowest possible cost and still satisfy customer demand. The total information system will be broken down into progressively smaller and smaller units of study until the focus is on meaningful and manageable subsystems. The input, output, and processing steps of these subsystems will be carefully analyzed to form the foundation for the synthesis phase of the computer selection cycle.

The synthesis phase consists of the system design and resource utilization subphases. The system study answers the question of what is being done and compares it to what should be done. System design is concerned with how it is being done and compares that with how it should be done. In system design, the detail produced during the system study is used to develop alternate solutions that will better achieve the defined business and system objectives.

The resource utilization subphase explores various alternatives for providing the EDP resources necessary to accomplish the job. These alternatives range from using a company's own system and programming personnel, and its current computer if there is available capacity, to employing outside assistance in the form of system help, software help, computer time, or time-sharing service.

The implementation phase includes developing the installation plan, which outlines the resources necessary to prepare for the computer installation. The installation plan and schedule determine the delivery date of the necessary equipment. The implementation phase includes the programming, operating, and maintenance-modification subphases. The implementation staff, after selection and training, transforms the system design specification into progressively greater and greater detail, thus preparing the system for computer processing.

The resultant programs are tested and finally put into productive operation. The productive programs are then reviewed to determine if they meet the system objectives and, therefore, the business objectives. The resultant improvements and benefits are measured against those that were projected.

The implementation phase does not end at this point but includes the important maintenance-modification subphase. The overall operational performance must be evaluated as a preliminary step to fine-tuning the running applications. It is inevitable that operational errors and program discrepancies will occur with time; a plan must be instituted for their resolution and correction. With the fine tuning accomplished, both short- and long-range plans for future growth are refined.

In reality, the phases of analysis, synthesis, and implementation are never-ending cycles. As soon as initial computer applications are put into productive operation, additional ones are tackled. The operational applications must be periodically reviewed and updated to run more efficiently and to adapt to changing business conditions and needs. As more applications are put on the computer, it is not too long before the company reaches the capacity of its current computer and the entire computer selection cycle must be reinstituted. This continued and seemingly never-ending cycle may appear a bit frustrating, but it can be one of the most rewarding activities in which a company is involved.

This chapter is not intended as an all inclusive chapter on systems development. I will attempt to emphasize those aspects that are most pertinent to MIS development as opposed to generalized system development. Obviously, after the information model and MIS road map are completed, application development is a fairly generalized function whether one is designing a system aimed at management or a system primarily aimed at reducing cost at the clerical level. Therefore more attention will be given the feasibility and system study phase. As the cycle begins to fan out into progressively more and more detail, the steps are similar for all types of systems. For example, the process of writing computer instructions is roughly the same type of activity whether the application be a payroll or a financial model.

FEASIBILITY

Feasibility is a significant phase of the system development cycle. Many companies have launched major computer programs and were well along in a dedicated productive effort when someone raised the question: We're making good progress, but are we working on the right problem? This is the purpose of the feasibility phase—to develop a set of selection criteria, a selection procedure, and an effective decision-making organization such that a company can be certain that it is working on the right problem and in the right sequence. The feasibility phase is a vital underpinning of MIS. Too often the selection of applications has been left to EDP people or has been rubber-stamped by management without real study or analysis.

FEASIBILITY CRITERIA

Figure 4.2 indicates that there are three general feasibility considerations: (a) technical, (b) economic, and (c) operational. It is important that all three be carefully considered by management, in addition to establishing their relative weight and significance. The technical considerations are directed at the question of whether the necessary hardware, software, and application tools are available or will be available when required by the particular applications under study. Often there is a risk or probability factor because one or several of the technical elements may be future items promised by a certain date but not yet available. In this event, management must consider the reliability of vendor claims, whether the particular item is on the critical path and what insurance if any can be established in case of late delivery. Of course, the risks increase greatly when several key items are in the future category. The technical considerations in MIS will be discussed fully in the succeeding chapter. Certain hardware items are required, such as input-output devices, communication capabilities, and bulk magnetic storage devices. Software items, such as data base management, operating systems, and special languages, as well as application packages and management science techniques, may be MIS requirements. Each of the required items must be carefully evaluated to ascertain its relevance to MIS development. The higher the dependence on sophisticated and/or technical items yet to be field-tested, the higher the risk factor in selecting a particular application for development. It may be wiser to proceed along the safer route, particularly if this represents a first venture into MIS. A look at the economic and operational feasibility will further qualify application feasibility.

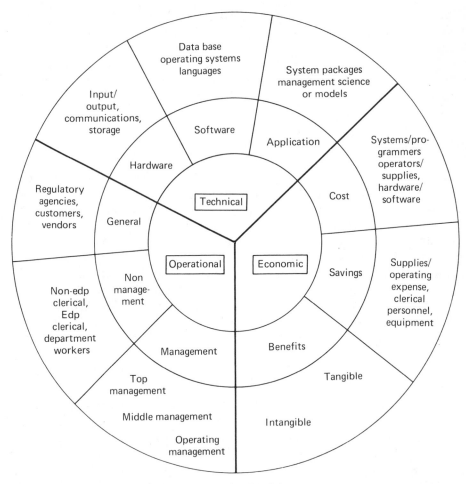

Fig. 4.2   Application feasibility criteria

Economic considerations represent the single most important feasibility criteria. If a company cannot improve its profit picture or return on investment in the short or long run, then it should not be considering MIS. In looking at the economics of MIS, one must consider the cost of MIS compared to the savings that MIS can accrue and/or the added benefits derived from the system. The costs can be divided into three major categories: (a) hardware/software, (b) system/programmers, and (c) operators/supplies. Analysis of EDP costs has concluded that the percentage breakdown of these costs is roughly 35/40/25; that is, of every dollar spent by a company on EDP, 35 percent represents the cost of computer and software rental, 40 percent represents system and programming salaries, and 25 percent represents operator salaries and operating costs (cards, paper forms, and the like). If a company already has an underutilized computer, only the incremental costs—the last two elements—should be considered. System designers are prone to underestimate the system and programming costs and time that are necessary to develop and implement an application fully. An application is not completed until it is completely tested, documented, and in full productive operation. The testing includes computer time, which must be reflected in the cost. As in a cost accounting system, a distinction must be made between fixed and variable costs and also between one time and recurring costs. A fixed cost, for example, may be computer time if the computer is underutilized or is purchased. A one-time cost is the initial development effort to design and implement an application as opposed to the variable cost of regular program maintenance and daily operational running.

A saving is a definite data processing cost reduction caused by the introduction of a computer application. The saving could consist of equipment reduction if a computer replaces bookkeeping machines or punched-card equipment. It could be the reduction of supplies and operating costs or the reduction of clerical personnel as the computer system absorbs the routine administrative functions. More often than not, the introduction of MIS, although not without some clerical cost savings, will result in an overall cost increase because of the introduction of more powerful computing equipment. Even in smaller installations, companies have found that the payoff of computerization is not in reduced costs but in providing benefits in the form of more meaningful and more timely information.

Turning now to the type of benefits that can be expected from a computer program, we can distinguish two general categories—tangible and intangible. A tangible benefit is one that can be accurately measured and that can be directly related to the introduction of a computer system. An example is a cost reduction where work formerly accomplished on overtime has been eliminated because of an improved production scheduling system. An example of an intangible benefit is an improvement in customer service brought on by a more responsive order processing system. Although it is often clear that the improvement is a result of the computer, it is difficult to place a monetary value on the effect this has on overall company profitability. There are degrees of tangibility in computer benefits. Certainly the benefit of improved company image as a result of the computer installation is less tangible a factor than the benefit of improved customer service, although both benefits fall into the intangible category.

It is interesting to note the major benefit areas experienced by companies that have installed computers. In order of significance, they are as follows:

1. Ability to obtain reports and information heretofore unavailable.

2. Availability of reports and information on a more timely basis.

3. Improvement in a basic operating area of a business.

4. Increased ability to perform computations that were not practical before.

5. Reduction in clerical cost.

6. Maintenance of competitive position.

7. Aid in management decision making.

8. Intangibles, such as customer image, leadership in the industry and community, increased customer morale, and management confidence.

Significantly, clerical cost reduction falls well down the list as a principal benefit. Most companies first entering data processing have a tendency to overemphasize this element; later they discover that benefits have come in those areas listed in the first four categories.

In assembling the final feasibility study, the time dimension of when the benefits will occur is important. If the study encompasses the entire information system of a company, it is clear that such a development will take a rather lengthy period of time to implement. Some type of phase-in plan must be instituted, which means that the benefits will come gradually and not all will be apparent during the first year of installation. The feasibility study return on investment analysis should reflect this fact.

Placing a dollar value on anticipated computer benefits is a difficult task. An example in a specific area may serve to illustrate the type of analysis that can be used for this purpose. Many companies have inventory problems that result in a major overstocking of certain items and understocking of others. The key consideration in inventory control is maintaining a balanced inventory that provides the required level of customer service. If asked how much reduction can be accomplished by automating the inventory control operation, most business managers would say "Plenty." However, this is hardly a quantified statement of fact. One might look at other companies with similar operations that have computer-based inventory control systems to determine what reductions they have obtained. Another way is to use a computer to analyze past history of demand and prior levels of inventory. This process, necessarily, will have to be on a service bureau machine or at some other facility if the company is conducting its initial feasibility study. Through a process called simulation (which uses mathematical inventory decision rules), the computer can indicate what levels of inventory would have been required in order to meet the desired level of customer service. Comparing these simulated levels with actual levels gives a company a good idea of potential inventory reduction.

Although the simulation procedure described gives a solid indication of what is possible, it still may not be completely convincing. Another approach is to work backward, utilizing a breakeven analysis. After accumulating the projected computer costs, a calculation of the amount of inventory reduction necessary to cover these costs can be ascertained. Maintaining inventory results in carrying such costs as taxes, insurance, investment on the capital, spoilage, obsolescence, and space. These costs usually amount to between 15 and 20 percent of the inventory value. If the total computer costs (rental, operating, and system costs) are $60,000 per year, it can be calculated that an inventory reduction of $400,000 is necessary to offset these costs ($15\% \times \$400,000 = \$60,000$). Management now can focus on the question of how likely it is that an automatic inventory control system can reduce inventory to that extent. This type of breakeven approach can be used in assessing computer benefits in other operating areas as well.

An often-overlooked element of feasibility is the one called operational feasibility. It has been found that a particular application may be technically and economically feasible but fails to produce the forecasted benefits because a company is not able to get it to work. This is often perplexing to EDP management who cannot understand why a well-conceived and designed system cannot be successfully utilized by the operating departments. There are several reasons for this situation. Some of the problems are motivational and psychological in nature and can be resolved by proper training and indoctrination. However, some of them are serious enough at the outset to warrant placing a lower priority on a particular application area until the problem is resolved. An example is the development of a sales report that shows profitability of sales by item and product line. If a salesman is compensated the same whether he sells item A or item B, the report will be meaningless to him and of little value. In another case, a decentralized sales administration function is computerized as part of a MIS concept. Where local sales branches processed orders and billed customers directly, these activities are now accomplished centrally. The new system is designed and installed with minimal local participation or involvement. As a result, the branches utilize tactics that serve to circumvent the system. The new system develops a billing backlog, customers become irate, management becomes disillusioned, and the system eventually fails. In these two cases, it may be wise to assign a lower system priority until specific policies are changed and tested. If this is not done, the computer and MIS will bear the blame for the failure whether it is the real reason or not.

It is necessary to assess management, nonmanagement, and general operational considerations as indicated in Figure 4.2. The major focus of the application must be ascertained, with the resulting impact on top, middle, and operating management carefully analyzed. For example, a system may be built on a rather revolutionary approach to production scheduling. This factor obviously has a direct impact on the production scheduling supervisor and the production manager. If the production manager is a former production worker who has worked his way to his current position, is very conservative, and has shown an antagonistic point of view toward computerized production scheduling systems in the past, this situation obviously represents a negative operational feasibility consideration. It must either be dealt with and resolved or should be a strong factor in establishing a lower priority for the production scheduling subsystem. This is true for nonmanagement personnel as well, although not as much as for management personnel. A positive attitude and an acceptance of the system on the part of management can be reflected downward to the people who must implement the system. Frequently, the development of MIS can require greater demands on clerical personnel, in the form of learning new ways of doing business, in the addition of duties that add to their total work load, or, in some cases, a combination of both. These demands are important considerations in operational feasibility.

The "general" category under operational feasibility is a most significant one and must not be overlooked. The stories of customer reaction and the rigors of converting to a new billing system are legion. Most of us have received notices apologizing for dunning us for bills we have long paid, or for the myriad of other problems encountered because the company was converting to a new computer system. This situation is obviously a consideration in operational feasibility. An example of a vendor consideration is in the development of an inventory control system. If an automatic reordering system requires the delivery of a greater number of smaller orders with less lead time, the vendor must be conditioned to respond to this new policy, particularly if the items in question are in short supply. Similarly, the potential impact of MIS on regulatory external agencies must be considered. For example, if the system is designed to provide magnetic-tape audit trails, this procedure should be reviewed with the company's auditors and the Internal Revenue authorities. Thus it is important to consider carefully the three elements of feasibility described in Figure 4.2. A proper blending, analysis, and weighing of the technical, economic, and operational elements will ensure that the correct priority is placed on application subsystems within a MIS and that a company is indeed working on the right problem.

RETURN ON INVESTMENT ANALYSIS

Another way to view MIS feasibility is to measure the overall impact on return on investment. The assumption is that if a computer is a beneficial tool, it will increase the profits of a company and/or reduce investment and thereby have an effect on improving return on investment. Although a simple return on investment analysis may seem so basic as to be naive to the businessman, it is not that common to the EDP side of the house. The ROI concept (return on investment) is briefly mentioned here to reinforce its significance to EDP projects, many of which have been immune even to the most basic of business measurement tools. Profitability and return on investment are the two key yardsticks of measuring business performance. Figure 4.3 illustrates a simplified schematic of a return-on-investment analysis. The top portion is a profit-and-loss statement for the company, starting with sales on the first line, subtracting cost of sales to arrive at net earnings before taxes, and then subtracting taxes (a 48 percent rate is assumed) to arrive at net earnings after taxes. Cost of sales consists of variable costs (labor, material, etc.), fixed costs (depreciation, rent, equipment cost, etc.), and administrative costs (legal, personnel, accounting, etc.). Thus the $1,499,000 is the company profit for the year and forms the numerator of the return on investment equation.

The investment or denominator of the equation consists of fixed investment (money tied up in machinery and buildings) and net working capital, made up of current inventory, accounts receivable, and other current assets. The ratio of net earnings to total investment is equal to the company's rate of return on investment. ROI is really what a company is trying to improve, as it is the true measure of how well it is using the stockholders' money. If a computer can have an appreciable effect on improving this rate of return, then it is most certainly a desirable investment. For illustrative purposes, assume that Figure 4.3 represents the company's ROI at the point in time it is evaluating the possibility of a computer. The figures exclude the last three zeros, so that the company in question is netting approximately $1.5 million on $29 million sales and has an ROI of 5.4 percent.

The ROI analysis can further determine whether you are working on the right problem or not. For example, a 1 percent improvement in material cost can add $102,000 to profit, whereas a 1 percent improvement in labor cost adds only $41,000. The reason is obvious, for material constitutes a greater portion of the total variable product cost. Consequently, everything being equal, it would seem wiser from an economical point of view to focus a MIS on improving material costs (i.e., a purchasing system that could take advantage of quantity discounts or a production control system that could reduce material variances and scrap loss).

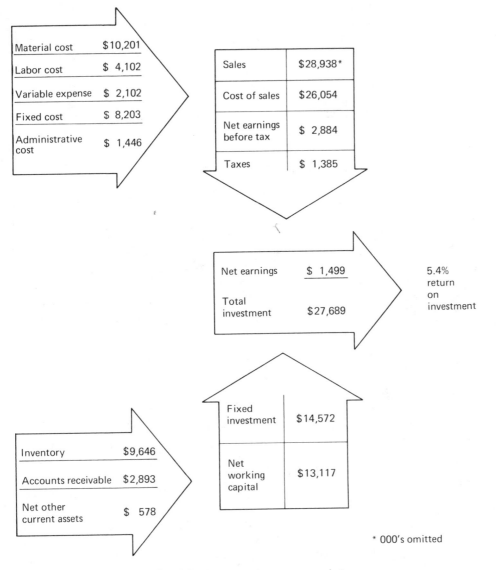

Material cost	$10,201
Labor cost	$ 4,102
Variable expense	$ 2,102
Fixed cost	$ 8,203
Administrative cost	$ 1,446

Sales	$28,938*
Cost of sales	$26,054
Net earnings before tax	$ 2,884
Taxes	$ 1,385

Net earnings	$ 1,499
Total investment	$27,689

5.4% return on investment

Fixed investment	$14,572
Net working capital	$13,117

Inventory	$9,646
Accounts receivable	$2,893
Net other current assets	$ 578

* 000's omitted

Fig. 4.3 Return on investment analysis

A simple calculation shows that a decrease of material costs of 3 percent through improved purchasing or production control can improve the company's ROI from 5.4 to 6 percent.

Another area of real payoff on the investment side is that of inventory. Almost 75 percent of the net working capital consists of inventory. A computerized inventory control system that could better control and balance inventories would have a significant impact on ROI. A projected 20 percent inventory reduction would amount to $1.9 million. In addition, the reduction in inventory reduces the inventory carrying costs (storage, movement, taxes, insurance, and so on, historically calculated at about 15 percent of the inventory value). This reduction in carrying costs reduces variable costs by $285,000 and adds to the yearly profit. The effect of these changes is to increase ROI from 5.4 to 6.4 percent.

These are merely examples of what an ROI analysis can indicate. It is not important to argue whether a computerized MIS can reduce material costs 1, 3, or 5 percent or to discuss the specific impact it can have on inventory investment; it obviously depends on the particular situation. The point being stressed here is the desirability of looking at MIS as an integral part of the business operation, as an element in increasing profit, reducing investment, and improving ROI.

MARGINAL VALUE OF INFORMATION

Marginal value or marginal utility is a common economical term. The definition of marginal value is that it represents the value (utility) to a buyer of each additional (marginal) unit of a product. It defines the price the end user or consumer is willing to pay for each additional unit of a product. The greater the quantity the user already has, the less, supposedly, he is willing to pay for an additional unit. The law of supply and demand takes effect, and when the supply reaches a certain point (the saturation point), then demand, theoretically, becomes zero. The supplier must then wait to replace the item as it depreciates or becomes obsolete, or he must develop an innovative or attractively priced new item that eventually induces the buyer to buy it. An example is a suit of clothes. The typical male businessman wears a suit to work 5 days a week. He may possess three or four suits, but as he buys his fourth or fifth, the marginal value is reduced significantly. He can only wear one per day, and, assuming that he is content with his first five, the sixth offers him little satisfaction. There are obvious psychological factors that affect this situation (i.e., there are many men who for one reason or another own 20 or 30 suits or more), but, for the most part, the preceding analysis is true for the average businessman and explains the marginal value concept.

Let us see if this concept can be applied to information produced by a management information system. Is there a marginal value? What is the point at which the value becomes zero? Some would say that, in the case of information, not only is there a marginal value, there is also a negative value. A condition exists in some companies that might be called "information glut." This is a condition where the organization seems to be choking with information. Report and analyses have proliferated, partly because of the ease and speed of today's high-speed print-out systems. The company may not have made a report utilization survey or study for years. Reports are added on top of reports and no effort is made to streamline, combine, or eliminate. While formal reevaluation and reassessment may be common practices for the external products the company produces, they are not practiced in the case of computer products (printed reports). The development of MIS should serve as a catalyst to trigger the much-needed appraisal of current information outputs. The system should encourage the management by exception concept as opposed to management by the ton (referring to mounds of paper spewed out by computer systems). If not controlled, the "information glut" can reach the proportions facetiously characterized by columnist Art Buchwald in an article called "The Great Data Famine."

One of the major problems we face in the 1970s is that so many computers will be built in the next decade that there will be a shortage of data to feed them.

Prof. Heinrich Applebaum, director of the Computer Profileration Center at Grogbottom, has voiced concern about the crisis and has urged a crash program to produce enough data to get our computers through the seventies.

"We didn't realize," the professor told me, "that computers would absorb so much information in such a fast period of time. But if our figures are correct, every last bit of data in the world will have been fed into a machine by Jan. 12, 1976, and an information famine will follow, which could spread across the world."

"It sounds serious," I said.

"It is serious," he replied. "Man has created his own monster. He never realized when he invented the computer that there would not be enough statistics to feed it. Even now, there are some computers starving to death because there is no information to put into them. At the same time, the birth rate of computers is increasing by 30% a year. Barring some sort of worldwide holocaust, we may soon have to find data for 30,000,000 computers with new ones being born every day."

"You make it sound so frightening."

"It is frightening," Prof. Applebaum said. "The new generation of computers is more sophisticated than the older generation, and the computers will refuse to remain idle just because there is nothing to compute, analyze, or calculate. Left to their own devices, the Lord only knows what they will do."

"Is there any solution, professor?"

"New sources of data must be found. The government must expand, and involved studies must be thought up to make use of the computers' talents. The scientific community, instead of trying to solve problems with computers, must work on finding problems for the computers to solve."

"Even if the scientists really don't want the answers?"

"Naturally. The scientific community invented the computer. Now it must find ways of feeding it. I do not want to be an alarmist, but I can see the day coming when millions of computers will be fighting, for the same small piece of data, like savages."

"Is there any hope that the government will wake up to the data famine in time?"

"We have a program ready to go as soon as the bureaucrats in Washington give us the word. We are recommending that no computer can be plugged in more than three hours a day.

"We are also asking the government for $50 billion to set up data manufacturing plants all over the country. This data mixed with soy beans could feed hundreds of thousands of computer families for months.

"And finally we are advocating a birth control program for computers. By forcing a computer to swallow a small bit of erroneous information, we could make it sterile forever, and it would be impossible for it to reproduce any more of its kind."

"Would you advocate abortions for computers?" I asked Applebaum.

"Only if the Vatican's computer gives us its blessing." *

Although I do not believe the marginal value of information can be determined as precisely as it can be for other economic goods, the general concept does hold and, at a minimum, should serve as a design guide for a management information system. There are specific examples when the marginal value of information can be fairly accurately determined, whereas it is difficult if not impossible in other situations. The value of information should always be a prime consideration in system design, even in the latter case.

A fairly clear–cut example is the value of calculating automatic reorder points and economic order quantities, as mentioned previously. Simulation (later confirmed by actual operation) can illustrate the specific monetary value expressed in lower inventory levels and improved customer service. If the inventory control system can reduce inventory by $200,000, then the value of the information generated by the system that accomplishes it is worth somewhere around $30,000 (15%, the carrying cost, × $200,000). Let us pursue this subject a step further. A basic ingredient of an effective inventory control system is a sales forecasting subsystem. Suppose that the current inventory control system utilizes forecasting technique A, whereas another method, forecasting technique B, is conceded to be a superior statistical method. It may well be that the forecast error has minimum leverage on the savings that can accrue from an inventory control system. Simulation may indicate that a forecasting system that is 20 percent more accurate has only a 3 percent influence on inventory levels. If there is a sizable system and programming cost in implementing the new forecasting technique, it may more than offset the value of the information. In this case, the marginal value of information is negative; the cost of acquiring the information is greater than the resultant benefit.

Another example is the use of information in a strategic planning subsystem. Here the marginal value is difficult to assess. Often the cost of the information is quite exact, particularly if the information is obtained from an outside agency. A market survey may be directed at answering questions, such as what are the user's criteria for changing vendors, for replacing their current product, or for adding another vendor's product. Assume that such a survey, because of its competitive implications, can only be conducted by an outside agency and that the price of such a survey is $20,000. How can one assess the marginal value of this information? If this information is part of the market analysis preparatory to designing a new product line, it is obvious that the stakes are quite high. But the strategic planning group has already assembled an extensive and comprehensive data base, one reflecting the future marketplace for the company's products. What is the marginal value of additional information? Is it greater than $20,000? This is a most difficult question to answer. One might begin by asking a counter-question: What action might be taken as a result of the information? Assume, for example, there exists a question as to the impact of adding a specific and costly feature to a product, and assume further that the incorporation of the feature would result in a $200,000 development cost. If the survey will indicate without a doubt whether such a development is feasible, one might argue that it is worth $20,000 to save $200,000. However, the survey may not be conclusive and may only improve the probabilities of making the correct decision. Then management must weigh the costs and probabilities of improved product development and resultant profit as an outgrowth of the additional data. It may be that similar surveys have reduced the risks in decision making such that the additional information is indeed marginal in value.

In conclusion, although there is no clear-cut method of assessing the marginal value of information, the need to do so is important. The value of some information can be accurately determined and weighed against the costs necessary to produce it, whereas the marginal value of other information is difficult to assess. This fact should not preclude the analysis of marginal value; it is certainly more desirable than following the supposition that all information has value. The consequences of the latter concept are often "information glut" and the development not of a management information system but of a management proliferation system.

APPLICATION BUSINESS PLAN

A growing number of companies that have a mature and comprehensive planning process are using the concept of a product business plan. For each major product or project undertaken, a planning guide is utilized to ensure that all the elements needed for the success of the program are included and properly reflected. I feel that this concept can and should be carried over to the planning of major application subsystems within MIS and, indeed, to the entire MIS development process. I call this the application business plan. All too often the planning approach to MIS is a fragmented one. Different individuals and different groups get together and frequently accomplish effective work, but their efforts are not coordinated and their overall game plan is not set down and documented in an official document. This is the purpose of an application business plan—to provide a vehicle for stating the pertinent agreements and rationale under which the activity must proceed. The application business plan must be a live document that is continually updated and modified. If a new system analyst or operating manager enters the project, the application business plan is the first document to read in order to gain pertinent background.

Figure 4.4 presents an outline of the contents of an application business plan. The first section covers the rationale of the particular program—the purpose, objectives, goals, and similar factors—and the connection with the other portions of the management information system. The second section covers the definition and characteristics of the application. An individual not familiar with the application can obtain a concise but definitive explanation by reading this section. The next section covers the feasibility of the application. This area is obviously important and reflects an analysis of the feasibility considerations discussed earlier in the chapter. Whatever feasibility criteria a company employs, whether cost versus benefit analysis or return on investment, the criteria and financial data are recorded in this section.

The remaining sections cover more detailed information about the application, the design and specification, the schedule and implementation plan, and, finally, the implementation status and review section. Thus the application business

- . Purpose
- . Application objectives
- . Strategies
- . Fit with information system model

} Rationale

- . English Language Narrative
- . General flow chart
- . Major reports
- . Special features

} Definition and characteristics

- . Projected costs
- . Projected savings
- . Projected benefits
- . Cost vs benefit analysis
- . Breakeven analysis
- . Return on investment

} Economics

- . Detailed flow charts
- . Input/output/processing requirements
- . Data base requirements
- . Program run breakdown
- . Special considerations

} Design and specification

- . Major milestones
- . Programmer assignement
- . Conversion schedule
- . Testing and debugging
- . Parellel operation

} Schedule and implementation plan

- . Milestone analysis
- . Management reports
- . Contingency plan

} Implementation status and review

Fig. 4.4 Application business plan

plan is an on-going document that covers the life cycle of the application from feasibility, justification, and design to implementation, schedule, and, finally, productive operation. A company must insist that no major program be authorized without a business plan.

Of equal importance to the application business plan is the manner in which it is conceived and implemented. The proper MIS organization must be established in order for the business plan concept to be effective. Figure 4.5 illustrates four application business plan decision groups—in effect, three groups reporting to an overall MIS steering group. The top group is responsible for establishing the business plan for the entire management information system. The basis of this application business plan will undoubtedly be the information system model or MIS framework described in the preceding chapter. The group is headed by a prominent member of top management who must be able to devote a good amount of time to the program; in this case, it is the executive vice-president. The heads or key decision makers of the departments to be affected by MIS are also members

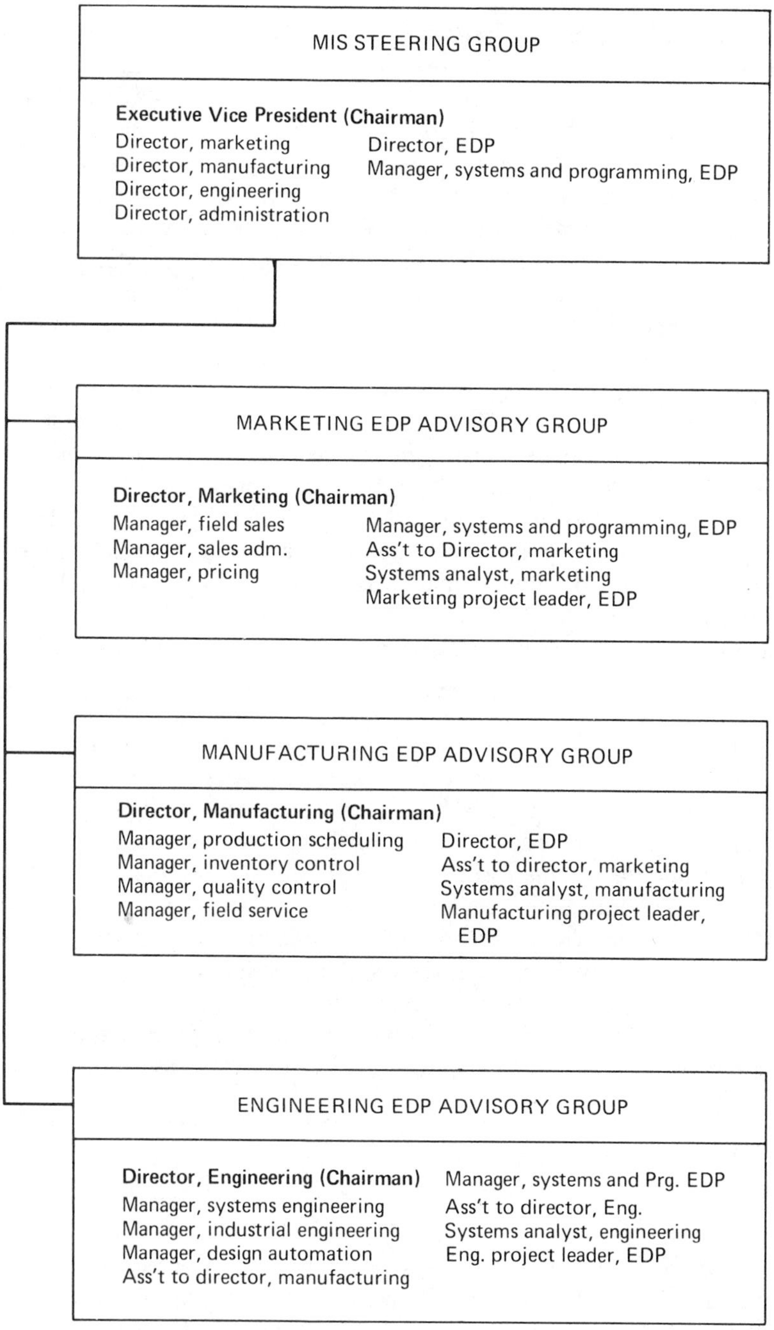

MIS STEERING GROUP

Executive Vice President (Chairman)
Director, marketing   Director, EDP
Director, manufacturing   Manager, systems and programming, EDP
Director, engineering
Director, administration

MARKETING EDP ADVISORY GROUP

Director, Marketing (Chairman)
Manager, field sales   Manager, systems and programming, EDP
Manager, sales adm.   Ass't to Director, marketing
Manager, pricing   Systems analyst, marketing
                               Marketing project leader, EDP

MANUFACTURING EDP ADVISORY GROUP

Director, Manufacturing (Chairman)
Manager, production scheduling   Director, EDP
Manager, inventory control   Ass't to director, marketing
Manager, quality control   Systems analyst, manufacturing
Manager, field service   Manufacturing project leader,
                                   EDP

ENGINEERING EDP ADVISORY GROUP

Director, Engineering (Chairman)   Manager, systems and Prg. EDP
Manager, systems engineering   Ass't to director, Eng.
Manager, industrial engineering   Systems analyst, engineering
Manager, design automation   Eng. project leader, EDP
Ass't to director, manufacturing

Fig. 4.5   Application business plan decision groups

of the steering group. The director of EDP and the manager of systems and programming represent the EDP department. This group meets periodically to update the MIS business plan as well as to review the status of the three advisory groups reporting to them.

An advisory group is formed for each of the major application subsystem areas: in this case marketing, manufacturing, and engineering. The group is chaired by a top executive of the department concerned and includes key people within the department as well as the key EDP personnel involved in system development. Note that in each group there is a system analyst representing the department affected. His inclusion is extremely important and ensures that the department's interests and objectives are represented in the detailed implementation steps as well as in the overall planning. The key system designers within the EDP department, entitled the marketing, manufacturing, and engineering project leaders, are also members of the group. They are the EDP personnel responsible, together with the department's system analyst, for the full–time direction of the particular application area. Note, also, that there is cross–representation on each of the committees. The directors of manufacturing, marketing, and engineering are on the steering group, and they also head one of the advisory groups. The director of EDP and the manager of systems and programming also sit on advisory groups. Thus there are continuity and tie-in.

An additional point is the possibility of dovetailing the application business plan concept with the company's program or project management organization. Many companies have a program management office that assigns program managers to major projects. Although they do not control the departments responsible for implementing the project, they are responsible as catalysts and coordinators to see that the project is completed on schedule and as specified. It is possible that a program manager may be assigned to one of the advisory groups. It then becomes his job to schedule the meetings, see that the written plan is prepared, the schedules monitored, and action taken to remain on schedule. Most firms have not considered major MIS subsystems as candidates for program management. The contention presented here is that perhaps they should. More systems have failed because of lack of management direction and leadership than for any other reason. The application business plan, the formation of application decision groups, and the employment of program management are powerful techniques for ensuring the success of a management information system.

THE SYSTEM STUDY

As indicated in Figure 4.1, the system study focuses on the determination of basic business objectives, the establishment of system objectives based on the business objectives, and the development of an input-output processing system specification for each application being implemented. The system study begins with the development of the information system model of the previous chapter.

Figure 4.6 presents a more detailed schematic of the system study phase. The starting point is the marketplace in which the company competes. Although it is not the responsibility of the system study group to develop the overall business

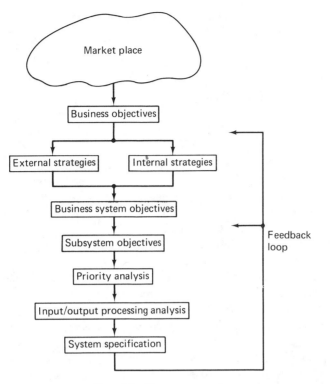

Fig. 4.6 The system study

objectives from the nature of the marketplace, the group must be aware of the developments and the policies at this level. The fact that the system study begins at such a high level may seem presumptuous, but it is essential if the resultant system study is geared to improving company operations.

Definitions of the terms business objectives, external and internal strategies, and business system objectives are in order at this time.

Business Objectives

Business objectives state the reason the company is in business. A direct parallel is the job description of an individual, which explains the purpose and nature of his job and the objectives he is to accomplish. For a business, the broadest category usually is to maximize revenue, keep costs down, improve profit, and increase rate of return on investment. These goals normally are quantified by specific dollar figures.

Business Strategies

Of more significance to the systems study group are the specific external and internal business strategies evolving from the business objectives.

External strategies are related to the marketing function and state the way the company plans to attain the necessary sales revenue from the marketplace in which it competes. The external marketing strategies generally revolve around the answers to three basic questions:

1. With whom do I want to do business?

2. What should I sell them?

3. Why should they buy from me?

The answers to these questions will lead to strategies like extending the geographical boundaries of the marketing area, concentrating a homogeneous product line in a specific marketing area, expanding product offerings to provide a full line, expanding sales 15 percent per year, and so on. These external objectives have considerable influence on the system study group.

Internal strategies concern those functions related to turning out the product or service offered to the market. These strategies are built around the central focus of providing the product and/or service that meets the external marketing strategies and yet utilizes the company's resources in such a way as to minimize the costs, thus attaining the company's profit and return-on-investment goals. These internal strategies affect the basic production, purchasing, inventory, quality control, accounting, personnel, and engineering and research functions of a company. As a rule, specific internal strategies have great bearing on the system study group. A strategy might be to level production because of the scarcity of skilled labor or to achieve a 98 percent quality control standard because of the costly impact of product failure to a customer. Another internal strategy might be to institute a standard cost program to control production costs and establish a better basis for pricing. The system study must be aware of these internal strategies, the probabilities of each occurring, and their expected time frame.

The combination of the external and internal strategies is the necessary "front end" of establishing business system objectives. It is true that system objectives can be established independently of this type of analysis, and many reasons can be presented for so doing. For example, it is apparent that some companies have ill-defined or undefined overall strategies. The decision then becomes one of waiting until the strategies are determind or of assisting in the establishment of the strategies before embarking on the system study. This is a trade-off that a company must face, realizing that a system that is inconsistent with overall company objectives can prove quite detrimental. It is possible to assume on one's own what strategies the company should have and to build a system from there, but doing so can be risky. This is one of the underlying and hidden reasons that a system study takes so long; often it is not the fault of the system study team but the result of management's inability to agree on basic business strategies. System people, in their zeal to begin, may tend to avoid the major overriding issues in an effort to bypass what they consider top management red tape. The system group can take this attitude, but in many cases it is like building a house on quicksand. It is better to face the issues, convince management that it must reach decisions, and begin the system study on solid ground.

Business System Objectives

The next term requiring a definition is business system objectives. A business system is defined as the paperwork complex that parallels the physical operations of a company. As was explained in the previous chapter, a business system is not the physical operation itself, although the two go hand in hand. For example, a manufactured product is produced by fabricating and assembling various raw materials, piece parts, and assemblies at various work centers. The physical process of bringing together the necessary materials and machines to produce a product is an example of a physical operating system. On the other hand, the process that produces a production schedule telling the foreman what materials and what machines are needed to produce a specified number of products by a specified time is defined as a business system. It is the paperwork system that controls the operating system.

Subsystem Objectives

As has been discussed in Chapter 3, in analyzing a company's operations, it will be obvious that the overall business system can be broken down into a hierarchy of subsystems, and the subsystems in turn into other subsystems. The starting point of the system study should be an analysis of the hierarchy that exists within the company being studied. Such an analysis will enable a clearer definition and statement of system and subsystem objectives.

Priority Analysis

After the definition of the system and subsystem objectives, it becomes apparent that the achievement of the entire range of objectives is a Gargantuan task and that some type of phasing or priority analysis must be undertaken. The feasibility study should have established some framework for determining priorities. The system study by now should enable the system group to present various alternatives to management for its evaluation. The establishment of priorities is a management, and not a system, prerogative.

Input-Output Processing Analysis

Once study priorities have been established, detailed data comprising the input, output, and processing requirements of each subsystem are gathered, categorized, and analyzed.

System Specification

The final result or output of the system study is a system specification. System specs should be developed along the same lines as engineering specs for a specific piece of equipment. The clearer and less-ambiguous the spec, the more realistic the proposed computer solution will be. If, for example, the spec omits a requirement to handle a volume up to 20 percent greater by the time the system is installed, the computer configuration will be underbid, thereby posing a serious problem at the time of installation. It is significant at this point to take a look at the ingredients of a system specification.

For illustrative purposes, an order processing system is described. The level of detail is intentionally sparse in order to facilitate understanding. The components of a system spec are as follows:

1. System description

2. System objectives

3. General flow chart

4. Input-output requirements

5. File considerations

6. Volumes and other specific details

7. Complementary subsystems

8. Cost and other ground rules

Addendum 1 presents a synopsis of the type of information found in each of the eight sections of the system specification. The reader may wish to refer to the addendum while reading the following description. The system description (section 1) is a written narrative of either the current system, the new system, or both. It usually is advisable to develop a good degree of detail on the existing system because the phase-in plan is based on where the company stands at the time the new system is implemented. It also is important because the cost considerations may dictate the maintenance of portions of the old system. For example, there may be a cost limitation on input equipment, and if the company has a purchased paper-tape input system, it may be mandatory to keep the old input devices even though new techniques may be more efficient. In this instance, the old system is described in very brief terms.

The system objectives (section 2) are extremely important because they form the raison d'etre for the system study. Objectives can take the form of rather modest streamlining of existing data processing methods, eliminating duplication, cumbersome operations, unnecessary time delays, and so on, or the objectives can envision a 5-year master plan to develop a total management information system.

The general flow chart (section 3) illustrates in symbolic form the written system narrative of section 1. It is easier to follow than the written word and begins to shape the system for eventual computer solution. The flow chart described in the addendum is an extremely simplified one and shows only the most general functions carried out by the system. Subsequent flow charts pinpoint specific areas in progressively greater detail to the point where there is a full understanding of each step in the operation.

Input-output requirements (section 4) move into the more specialized areas of the system study. The output is particularly important because this is how management and operating personnel view the system. Two examples of the reports emanating from the sales-order processing system are presented. These reports are the ones that enable the company to reach the system objectives listed previously.

Once the output requirements are established, the system study works backward to determine the input necessary to produce the output. For example, it is essential to know the item ordered and the quantity before the order can be extended and priced. This data comes from the individual salesman or sales office. The maximum size of the alphanumeric characters in each field is listed.

File considerations (section 5) describe the amount of storage required to maintain the necessary fixed information required by the system. By adding up the number of alphanumeric characters in the customer file and inventory file, and multiplying by the number of customers and number of inventory items, the file storage capacity required of the computer system can be determined. Also, by superimposing the time requirements on the various files, the response capabilities of the file storage media can be ascertained. For example, if a salesman must know immediately if an item is in stock, the inventory file must be located in immediate access storage.

Volumes and other specifics (section 6) are important to determine the input and output speeds required of the system. The basic input and output documents were described in section 4. These now must be viewed in light of the volume considerations listed in this section. For example, the daily average input load to the system can be calculated by multiplying the number of orders per day by the number of alphanumeric characters per order. The system must also be designed to handle peak input loads.

Unless the system is an isolated one, which is rare, it is necessary to know the complementary systems (section 7) that either feed the system or are fed by it. The system may be designed to run by itself, but the necessary flexibility must be established to enable the order processing system to tie into other systems that are added at a later date.

Finally, cost and other ground rules (section 8) must be stated, for they are significant parameters that bound the system. It may be that the company does not wish to state definite cost ground rules lest it unnecessarily limit the scope of the system solution. In this event, this section can be omitted. However, particular cost parameters may be most significant. For example, it may be that the company owns several bookkeeping machines and wants to make use of them until they are fully depreciated. Although the economic validity of the company's depreciation practices may be challenged, if this is a company policy, the system study must be consistent with it.

This, then, represents the contents of a system specification. Figure 4.6 indicates a feedback loop which implies that the system study group should continually reevaluate its work against the original business objectives and business system objectives that were established. The business world is a dynamic one and it is important that the resultant system reflect the current business environment. Constant tuning of the system study with the business and business system objectives is extremely important.

SYSTEM DESIGN

Figure 4.7 indicates that the system design phase is directed at developing alternate system solutions, exploring the various computerized approaches, and then selecting the optimal system design. The goal is to design a system that accomplishes the applications at hand but does so in the fastest, most efficient, and most economical manner. The approach is to develop as many alternate solutions as possible within the time restraints and then to test each against the computer configuration necessary for its solution.

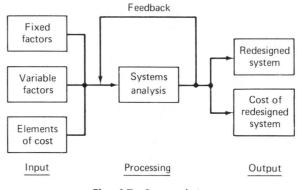

Fig. 4.7 System design

No mention has been made to this point of particular computer or particular hardware characteristics. It would have been premature to do so. The data requirements, the input and output needs, and the flow of information processing steps have been analyzed and categorized thoroughly. Now is the time to impose a hardware or computer solution and to discuss such elements as file storage media, input devices, printing facilities, computer capacity, and processing speeds. These items must be combined in such a way as to provide an optimum solution consistent with the time frame allocated to the job, the personnel resources available to accomplish it, and the particular computer system available. The purpose of the design is to satisfy the system requirements in the most efficient manner and at the lowest possible cost. In order to do so, one must consider what is fixed about a system, what is variable, and how the fixed and variable elements can be combined in such a way as to produce the optimum redesigned system (see Figure 4.7). In practice, various iterations are made as different combinations of fixed and variable elements are evaluated and compared until the best design is developed.

The terms *fixed* and *variable* warrant clearer definitions. The fixed elements are those that cannot be changed and must be adhered to in designing the new system. For example, a company may have an existing computer system that it wants to maintain as the core of any new approach.

A variable factor is one that can be changed to arrive at a new design, such as whether a report is printed and sent to a manager or is available on request by means of a cathode ray tube in the manager's office. Either the printed report or visual display may satisfy the information needs of the manager, but one method may do so more efficiently and effectively. Obviously cost also plays a part in this decision. One may argue that fixed factors are arbitrary in nature, for it is obvious that anything can be changed if there is good reason to do so. However, in a practical sense, these fixed elements exist.

Thus the fixed and variable elements, along with the costs associated with each, are blended into a system design. Figure 4.7 shows a feedback loop, indicating that the process is repeated until the best system is found. It can be stated realistically that the final redesigned system is not necessarily the optimum. It is true that there will always be room for an imaginative mind to improve the final system even further. However, it is unwise to pursue system design to a point of diminishing returns for the efforts expended.

RESOURCE UTILIZATION

Figure 4.1 indicates that the resource utilization phase of the synthesis process is evaluating alternate sources of EDP power and selecting the source(s) that best fulfill the needs. This was not a difficult job five years ago, but with the proliferation of hardware, software, and service companies, it has become a real challenge. If a company has the necessary personnel capability and hardware capacity, then it should probably consider using its own internal resources. However, more often than not, the demands of MIS outdistance the supply of available resources. In this event, the company must look to outside assistance. This subject will be discussed more fully in the next chapter. It is sufficient to say here that there are alternative resources to evaluate. For example, one service that might appear extremely attractive in MIS design is "subscription service." These services offer application packages geared to a specific application or specific industry. Some subscription service companies specialize in the design and implementation of packages ranging from basic payroll and accounting systems to more sophisticated application areas, such as statistical forecasting or simulation. Other subscription service companies concentrate on providing packages aimed at specific industries, like hospital accounting or school administration. If these packages are flexible, modular, and well designed, and if they reflect the practical business environment, then they can indeed prove quite attractive to a company evaluating its own MIS. The rationale for subscription services from the service company's point of view is that it is possible to offer a lower price because of the use of the packages among several customers. If the cost incentive is present, it may be feasible for a company to change its operation to adapt to the specifications of the package. However, this step should be evaluated carefully.

Another outside resource that should be carefully analyzed is time-sharing services. Time-sharing companies have developed hardware and software systems aimed at specific areas of operation that may be extremely critical to MIS. For example, some time-sharing services are focused on scientific or management science applications. It may be possible to satisfy a good portion of the engineering and research department's system needs by utilizing such a service. A terminal can be placed in the engineering department. The central computer has access to a library of scientific subroutines, regression analysis, coordinate geometry, stress analysis, and the like, allowing the engineer to enter variable data pertinent to the products being designed. He then calls forth subroutines from the time-sharing service company's scientific library to solve his particular problems.

Also available are a variety of support arrangements ranging from the use of part-time programmers to the utilization of "facilities management" firms. The latter will undertake to bid on any job or system requirement. This area may involve (a) basic consultation on a specific subsystem or (b) full responsibility for the resources (including the computer itself) necessary to accomplish a major system. For example, a company might subcontract the development and implementation of its entire marketing system to a facilities management firm.

As mentioned earlier, the proliferation of hardware, software, and service companies presents a challenging dilemma for the EDP manager. Available to him are a wide variety of alternatives for obtaining computing power. Although there are opportunities for selecting a source or a combination of sources that can get him where he wants to be in a faster and more economical manner, he must be careful to base his decisions on an analytical evaluation of the alternatives. The result is an added responsibility for many EDP managers. Since relatively few have experience in this area, EDP managers should avail themselves of the legal, procurement, and management talent within their companies to ensure that the best decisions are made. There is significant risk in contracting the wrong job to the wrong service company.

IMPLEMENTATION

Figure 4.1 lists the major functions that are performed during the implementation phase. If the implementation of a management information system involves a new computer or a major addition of hardware, site preparation work is required. Otherwise the implementation phase involves the individual programming, testing, and operational running of programs that constitute the application subsystems that in turn are part of the MIS. The maintenance and modification phase covers the continued modifications, correction, and updating of operational computer programs. It reflects the fact that continued productive running of computer applications, as well as with the inevitable changes in business conditions, will necessitate periodic changes and alterations. This important maintenance and modification activity must be anticipated and planned for in advance.

Figure 4.8 illustrates the general steps that are required during the implementation phase. The steps are superimposed on a time scale. The numbers denote months, and this particular schedule indicates that it will take 7 months from the time the implementation begins to when the system can be turned over to the user. The system freeze or point beyond which changes will affect the schedule is indicated as 4 months prior to user turnover. This timetable obviously is not for the implementation of all subsystems in a MIS. It would take a far greater time period than that indicated. The assumption, also, is that a good deal of feasibility analysis, system study, system design, and resource utilization have proceeded this schedule, although all this activity is indicated only by the one block prior to beginning MIS implementation. The major lines of activity are divided into the respective responsibilities of planning management, operating management (other than EDP), systems, programming, operations, and plant engineering. The major and most time-consuming activity is that of the system, programming, and operation groups. These activities require a dedicated, well-managed staff of individual system analysts and programmers who can transform the objectives and goals of the management information system into working programs and subprograms that together accomplish the end result.

SUMMARY

We have now completed the description of the horizontal dimension as well as the vertical dimension of MIS. It should be obvious at this point why the horizontal analysis must precede the vertical analysis. Figure 4.1 was used to depict the analysis, synthesis, and implementation phases of the application development and implementation cycle. Top and middle management are directly involved (or should be) in the analysis phase. The major contributors to the synthesis and implementation phases are EDP management and system personnel, although there still must be a strong management direction and involvement. Since management is most concerned with the feasibility and system study, a greater proportion of the chapter was devoted to these functions.

System feasibility is a most important starting point of MIS development. The various feasibility criteria were presented in Figure 4.2. Technical and economical feasibility have received greater attention than operational feasibility. The last criterion recognizes that every company has a special character, philosophy, and way of conducting business. A management information system must fit into this environment. If major organizational changes are planned in conjunction with MIS implementation, they must be carefully analyzed and reflected in the overall schedule. Inadequate attention to operational feasibility considerations has been a major cause of MIS failure.

Return-on-investment analysis and a discussion of the marginal value of information added further background to the economic feasibility considerations. Finally, the concept of an application business plan was proposed. It is significant that the term business plan is emphasized. I have always felt that management has been remiss in not applying to EDP the same basic business procedures and measurements found successful in other areas of their operation. The rather mysterious and esoteric aura of EDP, in many cases, has made it immune to business scrutiny. The time has come for applying business perspective to EDP operation, and the application business plan plus project management represent excellent vehicles for accomplishing this end.

The remainder of the chapter touched briefly on the definition and considerations of system design, resource utilization, and the implementation phases of programming, operating, and maintenance/modification. Addendum 1 contains the contents of a system specification, while addendum 2 presents a comprehensive case study illustrating the principles of system design.

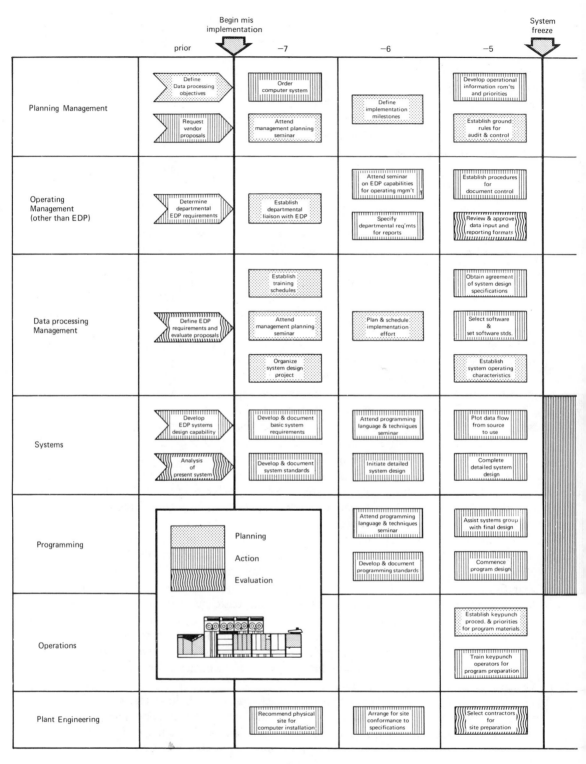

Fig. 4.8 Computer system planning and control

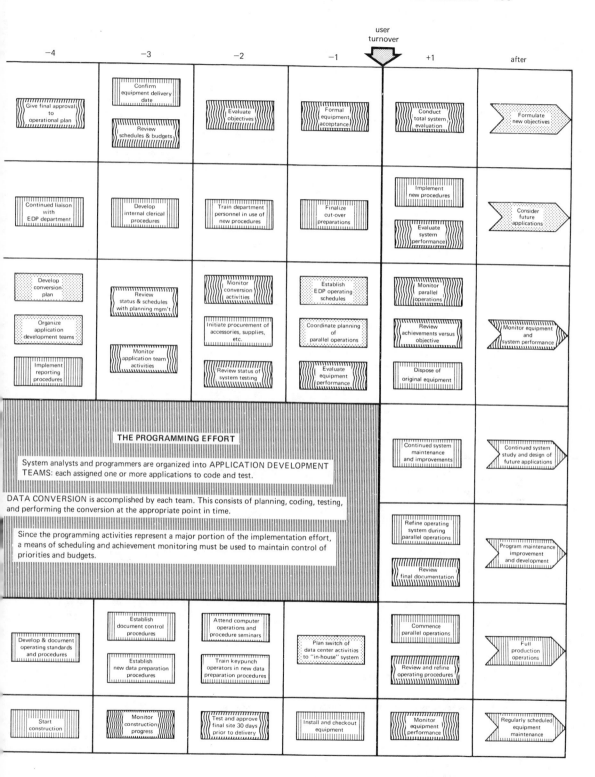

user
turnover

−4	−3	−2	−1	+1	after
Give final approval to operational plan	Confirm equipment delivery date / Review schedules & budgets	Evaluate objectives	Formal equipment acceptance	Conduct total system evaluation	Formulate new objectives
Continued liaison with EDP department	Develop internal clerical procedures	Train department personnel in use of new procedures	Finalize cut-over preparations	Implement new procedures / Evaluate system performance	Consider future applications
Develop conversion plan / Organize application development teams / Implement reporting procedures	Review status & schedules with planning mgm't / Monitor application team activities	Monitor conversion activities / Initiate procurement of accessories, supplies, etc. / Review status of system testing	Establish EDP operating schedules / Coordinate planning of parallel operations / Evaluate equipment performance	Monitor parallel operations / Review achievements versus objective / Dispose of original equipment	Monitor equipment and system performance

THE PROGRAMMING EFFORT

System analysts and programmers are organized into APPLICATION DEVELOPMENT TEAMS: each assigned one or more applications to code and test.

DATA CONVERSION is accomplished by each team. This consists of planning, coding, testing, and performing the conversion at the appropriate point in time.

Since the programming activities represent a major portion of the implementation effort, a means of scheduling and achievement monitoring must be used to maintain control of priorities and budgets.

				Continued system maintenance and improvements	Continued system study and design of future applications
				Refine operating system during parallel operations / Review final documentation	Program maintenance improvement and development
Develop & document operating standards and procedures	Establish document control procedures / Establish new data preparation procedures	Attend computer operations and procedure seminars / Train keypunch operators in new data preparation procedures	Plan switch of data center activities to "in-house" system	Commence parallel operations / Review and refine operating procedures	Full production operations
Start construction	Monitor construction progress	Test and approve final site 30 days prior to delivery	Install and checkout equipment	Monitor equipment performance	Regularly scheduled equipment maintenance

SYSTEM SPECIFICATION

ORDER PROCESSING SUBSYSTEM

1. System Description

The product is handled by 200 salesmen and jobbers throughout the country. The geographical distribution and sales volume are described in section 6. Orders are placed by the salesmen by telephone to the sales administration office in Cleveland. The calls are then backed up by a written order form submitted by the salesman himself or by a sales office, if there are enough salesmen in an area to justify an administrative staff. When the order form is officially received, a credit check is made and a punched card is then produced. This card provides input to the billing system where the individual items are extended, costs and weights calculated, and the various discounts and allowances figured. The card is also used by the inventory system to deplete finished goods if the item is in stock or to trigger "make orders" if the item is not in inventory. When the entire order is assembled, an invoice is issued to the individual customer as a basis of setting up an accounts receivable record.

2. System Objectives

The previous paragraph has described the existing system of order processing. The following list gives the objectives of the new system.

1. Reduce order cycle time from current 30-day average.

2. Reduce out-of-stock condition.

3. Improve accuracy of inventory records.

4. Allow for a 20 percent transaction increase.

5. Facilitate adding new items and removing others.

6. Improve order expediting.

7. Set automatic notation of appropriate substitutions if out of stock.

8. Reduce ratio of cost to order processed.

3. General Flow Chart

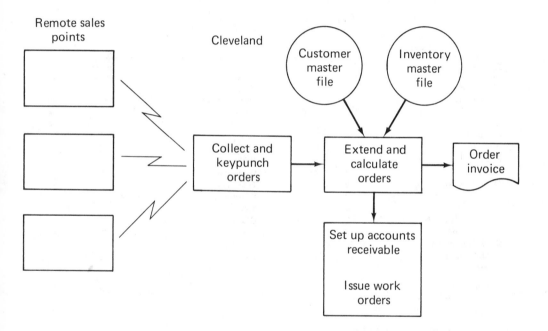

4. Input/Output Requirements

Figure 4.9 describes two basic output forms emanating from the system: the inventory action report and the billing form. These documents describe the required output for the new system. It is believed that these reports will give management the proper control over the order processing cycle. In addition, they present useful statistics not currently available, such as percentage gross margin on each order, reorder points, and economic order quantities. These figures form the basis for periodic inventory and sales analysis reports.

Basic order processing input is submitted by the salesman or sales office and includes the items shown in the table.

Field Name	Numeric	Alpha
Store number	7	–
Item code	5	–
Quantity	6	–
Item description	–	20
Store name	–	20
Store address	–	30
Current month/day/year	6	–
Desired delivery date	6	–
Requested terms	10	–
Shipping instructions	–	20
Insurance instructions	–	25
Total	40	115

5. File Considerations

The two major files required are as follows:

Customer File			Inventory File		
Field name	Numeric	Alpha	Field name	Numeric	Alpha
Store code	7	–	Item code	5	–
Store name	–	20	Item description	–	20
Address	–	30	Size	–	4
Credit terms	10	–	Color	–	4
Discount	6	–	Unit price	6	–
Allowance	6	–	Quantity price	6	–
Region and area code	5	–	Weight	7	–
Open order	8	–	Gross margin	7	–
Open balance	8	–	Economic order quantity	8	–
Maximum credit	8	–	Reorder point	6	–
Order number(s)	50	–	Substitute code	2	–
Customer class	2	–	Cost	7	–
Annual purchases	8	–	Tax	7	–
Date(s) promised	50	–	Insurance	7	–
Overdue status	6	–	Average sales	8	–
Salesman	6	–	Historical sales	12	–
Total	180	50		88	28

6. Volume and Other Specifics

1. Average of 160 orders received per day.

2. Average order six items.

3. 125 company salesmen.

4. 75 jobbers.

5. Two thirds of the orders taken in the spring and in the fall.

6. Eight sales regions; Southwest and West are largest.

7. Teletype network between Cleveland and Los Angeles, and between Cleveland and Atlanta.

8. 200 finished goods items; 150 carried in stock.

9. Average of 20 orders per day expedited.

Inventory Action Report

Item no.	Description	On hand	On order	Total available	Projected demand	Reorder point	Economic order quantity	item no.	On hand	This order	Amount short	% available	Action code	Substitute item no.
Inventory action report								Inventory action report						
					Date							Date		

Billing Form

Store address						Store #	Order #	Date
Store copy								
Item description	Item retail	Unit retail	Item number	Quantity	Discount unit and allowance cost	% gross margin		

Fig. 4.9 Output reports

7. Complementary Subsystems

The sales-order processing system is closely related to the inventory control, accounts receivable, sales analysis, and sales-forecasting subsystems. A prime consideration is to build an open-ended order processing system that can logically lead into subsequent implementation of the other systems. Figure 4.10 illustrates, in flow chart form, the tie-in of the sales-order processing system to these other subsystems (shaded boxes).

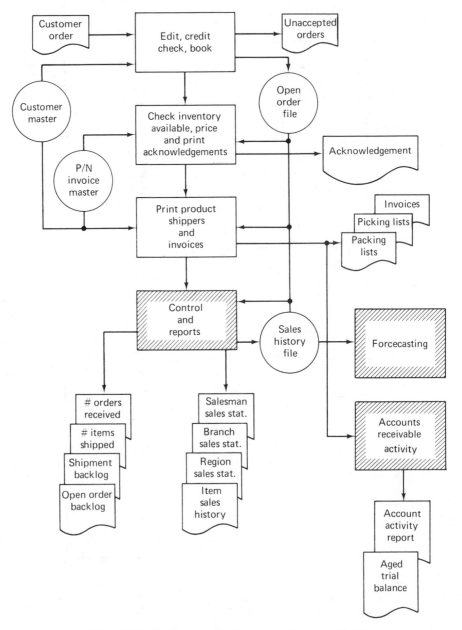

Fig. 4.10 Complementary subsystems of order processing

8. Cost and Other Ground Rules

The system proposed should be able to handle a 20 percent increase comfortably in the current transaction volume over the next two years and a 50 percent increase over the next five years. The hardware cost to accomplish the job (bearing in mind that the sales-order processing and complementary subsystems constitute about 30 percent of the total data processing work load) should not exceed the current hardware cost plus 50 percent. The teletype network should be maintained, for it serves functions other than supplying order processing input. It is desirable that the total data processing job be able to be completed within one machine shift.

SYSTEM CONSIDERATIONS IN MIS

A CASE STUDY

This addendum is an exercise illustrating system principles, design considerations, and trade-offs in the computerization of business applications. It is intended for the reader or student who desires to go a step beyond the discussion of Chapters 3 and 4. Chapter 3 presented a MIS framework for a company in the distribution business. The addendum looks at one of the major subsystems of the company in more depth. The case, although concentrating on order processing, should be viewed in light of its fit within the total MIS framework (see Figure 3.13). Analysis will show the problems in designing a subsystem that is part of an MIS.

The case study is built around Rolco, Inc., a large supermarket chain. The company's organization and operational philosophy are described as a backdrop to the specific business system study. The case illustrates that a computer system cannot be viewed as an isolated entity but is embedded in the business environment and operational framework of the company installing the system. The trade-offs in information system design are not solely within the domain of the electronic data processing department but are system-business trade-offs. The need for inter-action between the system analyst and operating personnel and the management of both is clearly illustrated.

The reader or student is introduced to the principles of flow charting, input-output formats, file design, application timing, and the overall system considerations in computerizing a typical business application. The reader should be in a better position to understand the role of the system analyst, plus the role of the businessman, who is becoming increasingly involved in system design.

The case description is followed by a solution designed by two of my students in the graduate course I teach at Northeastern Business School.

Organization of Rolco, Inc.

Rolco is a large supermarket chain operating in the Midwest and Far West. With sales approaching 2 billion dollars and with 13 retailing divisions and one manufacturing division, it is one of the largest companies in its field. Rolco distributes a wide line of food items through its 13 division warehouses. Each division operates as a relatively autonomous unit with its own general manager, and its own merchandising, buying, personnel, real estate, warehousing, and accounting functions. The manufacturing division supplies about 10 percent of the overall items sold in the stores. The corporate offices of Rolco are located in Los Angeles, as are the manufacturing division and one of the largest retail divisions.

Figure 1 is an organization chart of the company showing three regional vice-presidents and the manufacturing division vice-president reporting to the president. Each of the regional vice-presidents controls the specified number of divisions and has specific sales and profit goals. Rolco operates in a decentralized fashion under the theory that the best performance occurs when a manager has budget and profit goals and is rigorously measured against them. With this in mind, Rolco has established a profit-sharing program that operates at the individual store-manager level. Each retailing division controls from 40 to 90 supermarkets and each store manager receives a bonus at year-end based on his profit performance compared to the previous year and to the established profit plan. The percentage of this bonus as a proportion of the store manager's total salary has been steadily increasing.

The characteristics of the supermarket business are as follows: Supermarket chains operate on a low net profit to sales percentage, usually between 1 to 2 percent. The volume of transactions is extremely high; profitability comes from establishing economically sound store sites, providing products and services to the customer at competitive prices, developing merchandising policies that ensure a complete product line, and from buying, warehousing, and distributing products in the most economical manner. A good proportion of the capital assets are tied up in inventory, for the business centers around procuring, warehousing, distributing, and selling the product. Inventory is maintained at the warehouse and also in lesser amounts at the individual store level. The "backroom" inventory (inventory carried at the store level) varies from store to store, depending on the policies and actions of the store manager. Rolco has 850 stores. The number of items carried in each division warehouse approximates 10,000 and includes grocery products (edible and nonedible), drug items, cosmetics, soft goods, hardware, and miscellaneous. In addition, certain perishables are shipped to the store directly from local bakeries, dairies, produce houses, and meat plants. A store receives perishables daily and orders grocery and other items from the warehouse—three times per week. The trend is to increase the number of orders per week and to improve the ordering cycle so that stock-outs (not having items on the shelf or in inventory) are reduced while "backroom" store inventory is controlled.

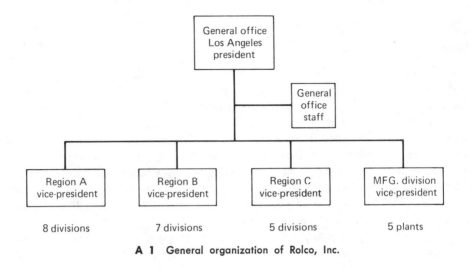

A 1   General organization of Rolco, Inc.

Responsibilities of the Operating Levels

Figure 2 lists the organization at the corporate office level, the division level, and the store manager level. The basic operating unit of Rolco is the division. The regional vice-president has a relatively small staff that coordinates sales, inventory, and accounting statistics; the major control and operating functions are handled at the divisional level.

The corporate office operates as a staff advisory group to the regions and divisions. In general, the control is loose, with major emphasis on coordinating financial reports, distributing general procedures and policies, and assisting the field operators in technical matters. The legal department works closely with the facilities group to select sites for new stores and negotiate store contracts (most stores are under sale and lease-back arrangements). The finance group accumulates and analyzes monthly region and division operating reports and consolidates profit-and-loss and balance-sheet statements. The planning department, in conjunction with top management, establishes 1-year and 3-year sales and profitability goals and is also responsible for evaluation and recommendation of new ventures, mergers, and the like. The merchandising group is mainly a competitive analysis service, continually monitoring and evaluating different products, assessing buying habits and trends, and relating these findings and recommendations to the field operations. They also coordinate nation-wide advertising and promotion programs. There is a certain amount of central buying coordination to ensure that Rolco takes advantage of quantity purchases and has long-term contracts for items in critical supply. The data processing group handles the computer operation for the corporate office and acts in an advisory capacity to the data processing departments of the division. EDP decisions are decentralized, and although there are periodic meetings of the 13 division EDP managers, each manager pretty much runs his own show. The engineering group oversees the physical facilities and is involved in new equipment evaluation. The personnel department establishes general salary

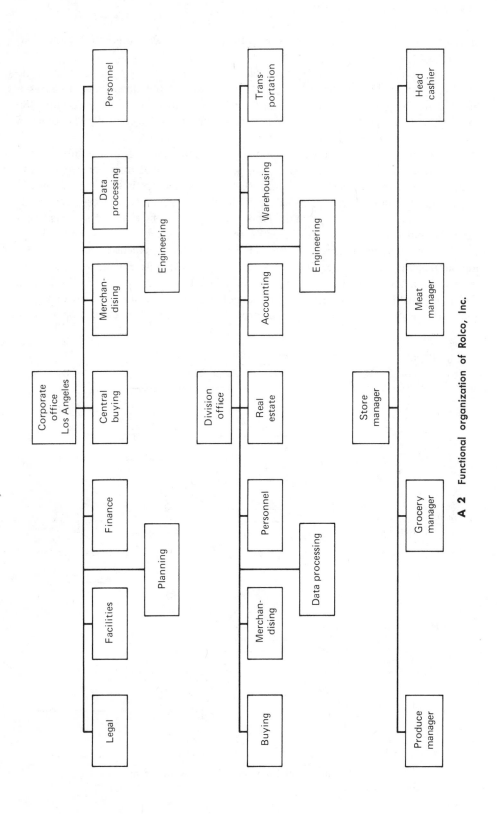

A 2 Functional organization of Rolco, Inc.

and job guidelines and also is heavily involved in nation-wide union and labor contract negotiations.

The division office has an organization similar to the corporate office. The functions are analogous; however, as has been stated, the division operates as a highly autonomous profit center. In order to exploit this concept successfully, top management has given the division a high degree of local control. The division operates with minimum regional or corporate office restraint.

The division office in turn delegates profit authority and responsibility to each store. The store manager has a produce, grocery, and meat manager reporting to him, as well as a head cashier. His profit-and-loss statement is shown in Figure 3. Gross margin (sales, less cost of sales) is developed for meat, grocery, and produce. Controllable expenses include labor, 60 percent of which represents part-time personnel, facility charges, including rent, heat, and light, an inventory charge based on his average backroom stock, and miscellaneous expenses, such as cleaning supplies and paper bags. The total of these controllable expenses is then subtracted from the gross margin to give a net-profit figure for the store. To develop divisional profit figures, noncontrollable expenses (from the store's point of view), such as division-wide advertising, data processing costs, and warehouse operations,

```
Meat sales                    _____
 — Meat cost of sales         _____
     Meat gross margin                      _____


Grocery sales                 _____
 — Grocery cost of sales      _____
     Grocery gross margin                   _____


Produce sales                 _____
 — Produce cost of sales      _____
     Produce gross margin                   _____



Total gross margin                                    _____


Less:  Labor expense          _____
       Facility expense       _____
       Inventory charge       _____
       Miscellaneous expense  _____


Total controllable expense                            _____


Store net profit                                      _____
```

A 3 Individual store profit and loss statement

are reflected against the sum of the individual store's profit. The resulting figure becomes the division's monthly statement, which is submitted to the regional staff and consolidated there for submission to the corporate office.

This, then, is a brief synopsis of the way in which Rolco operates. It is a fairly straightforward operation in that the prime purpose is to get food and related products into the hands of the consumer at a price that permits the company to remain competitive and yet allows for a reasonable profit margin after the costs of getting the product to the consumer are considered. The business is highly inventory oriented—the major capital is tied up in inventory. Effective and efficient movement of that inventory through the division warehouses into the store's backroom and on to the shelves is a highly critical operation. It is here that data processing can make a significant impact in optimizing this flow and supplying valuable by-product information that forms the basis of an effective information system. The basic physical operation and flow of goods is depicted in Figure 4. The Rolco division warehouse is stocked by inventory that is purchased from a variety of vendors and manufacturers of food and related products. These products are then shipped to the various retail stores where they are purchased by consumers who carry them out of the store in shopping carts, into their cars, and finally into their homes. The information system is built around this physical model.

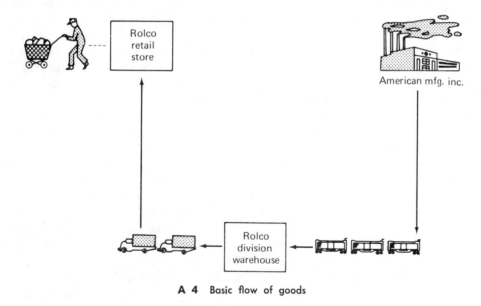

American mfg. inc.

A 4   Basic flow of goods

Trade-Offs in System Development

When an information system for a company like Rolco is reviewed, it becomes obvious that there are a host of trade-off decisions in planning the implementation of the system. An illustration will show the trade-offs in designing a system that blends the following subsystems: order processing, inventory control, and transportation. In developing a set of decision rules for these subsystems, four key management objectives can be ascertained:

1. Increase customer service by reducing stock outs.

2. Keep inventory levels low, thereby conserving working capital.

3. Maintain transportation costs at a reasonable level.

4. Control data processing costs in the order processing cycle.

Analysis shows that these four objectives are conflicting. For example, one way to reduce stock-outs is to maintain higher than normal inventory levels so that there is ample safety stock to handle unforeseen emergencies or changes in buying patterns. Another way to reduce stock-outs is to allow each store to order every day and to ensure one-day delivery service. This process, of course, is desirable from the store point of view and allows the store a great deal of ordering flexibility; however, transportation costs and data processing costs to handle the additional volume of orders will obviously rise.

The solution to these conflicting subsystem objectives is to select the decision rules that optimize the total order processing cycle, based on the relative priority that management places on the four objectives. The point is that in many cases these decisions are made by the EDP manager, often by default. The design of the system makes it mandatory to face these issues. When the subsystems were functioning separately, each department manager (i.e., inventory control manager, transportation manager, sales administration manager, and store manager) designed the system to optimize around his particular requirements. This is not to say that each department ignored the needs of the other. The transportation manager serves the store manager and the order processing department serves both. Since the computer system is often the catalyst that brings the conflicting requirements to light, it was the EDP manager who attempted to bring the various department heads together to agree on a system that came as close as possible to balancing the conflicting needs—to balance the four management objectives.

The way to develop a system that properly balances these and other management needs is to obtain management involvement from the start. The first step is to show management why they should be interested. There are techniques for assessing the trade-offs, for example, of customer service and inventory levels. Based on historical demand patterns of different items and the degree of fluctuation around an expected demand, a level of safety stock is predicated. The amount of safety stock can be based on a stated level of customer service. Thus a 95 percent level of customer service (stock-outs would occur in 5 out of 100 orders) requires more safety stock than a 90 percent level. Also, an item that has a widely fluctuating demand pattern requires a greater amount of safety stock than a stable item with relatively stable demand.

It is also possible to develop the cost trade-offs in ordering more frequently, thus cutting down store backroom stock. For example, daily ordering and 24-hour delivery may completely eliminate backroom stock (items can be loaded directly from the truck onto the shelves at night). The inventory savings must now be viewed in light of the added transportation costs and costs of a night-time store crew. It is here that the data processing department and the computer system can play a role and add a dimension to the trade-off decision. It may be possible to reduce the order processing time by as much as 24 hours by putting communication terminals in the store. Thus, instead of hand carrying the orders at the end of the day to the division office, the orders would be fed directly into the computer each morning. The inventory records could be screened, the order processed, and the picking slip sent to the warehouse within an hour of receipt. The goods could be at the store that evening instead of the following evening. With this ordering flexibility, the store manager might still be able to eliminate backroom stock without increasing his number of orders per week. The communication equipment in each store will obviously add to the data processing costs, but it might be well worth the expenditure.

The foregoing is a classic example of the system trade-off decisions that must be resolved to optimize information systems. These are management decisions. The EDP manager can help resolve the issues by showing the pros and cons of one policy versus another and the relative risks inherent in following various policies. However, middle management must make the final decision, and often the issues are so basic and important to company operations that top management must also become involved.

This discussion illustrates the importance of management involvement in system design, frequently at the executive level. This is so because the system design and resultant system trade-offs often impact and raise questions of top-management strategies and objectives. Thus, while a system trade-off might optimize a conflicting set of costs, the decision reached might run counter to an important company policy, possibly not a short-term but a longer-range one of which the people working on the system are unaware.

The Order Processing Cycle

The current method of ordering involves a store catalog that lists the 10,000 inventoried items at the division warehouse. The order catalog is illustrated in Figure 5. The punched cards correspond to the items ordered and a special pencil is used to mark the quantity desired. The cards are prepunched with the store number and catalog page number. The combination of the page number and the mark sense quantity in one of 50 card columns designates a specific item number. The computer is programmed to convert the page and line number into an item number so that the system can look up the inventory record, multiply the quantity ordered by weight, price, and cost, and print the extended store order. It does not take a system designer long to see that although this system is effective, it can be improved. The store manager or his delegate must make the rounds through the store, look at the shelves, and order what he needs for the next few days. In actual practice, because doing so takes considerable time, the store manager will order half the items in his store for one order and the other half the next order. Since most of the items ordered are fairly stable in demand and the computer extends each order, why cannot the computer automatically produce the order and eliminate

Only one mark per item in this area

Match item number with card item number

SHIP WT.	PRT. LIST	DESCRIPTION	ZONE 1 RETAIL	ZONE 2 RETAIL	ZONE 3 RETAIL	PRICE CHANGE	LINE NO.	ITEM
	12 2LB	STRAWBRY PRSV	65	65	65	65	7550	1
	12 2LB	BLKBRY PRESV	59	59	59	59	7551	2
	24 10 OZ	STRW PRS TMB	29	29	29	29	7566	3
	24 1LB 4OZ	PEACH PRES	39	39	39	39	7567	4
	24 1LB 4OZ	STRAW PRSV	49	49	49	49	7568	5
	24 1LB 4OZ	PLUM PRES	35	35	35	35	7569	6
	24 1LB 4OZ	GRAPE PRES	35	35	35	35	7570	7
	12 1LB4OZ	BLKBERYPRS	45	45	45	45	7581	8
	12 1LB 4OZ	APRICOT PR	45	45	45	45	7580	9
	12 1LB 4OZ	CHERRY PRS	49	49	49	49	7582	10
	12 1LB 4OZ	PINAPL PRS	45	45	45	45	7583	11
	12 100Z K	CHERRY JELLY	25	25	25	25	7765	12
								13
								14
	12 100Z	ELDBERY JELLY	25	25	25	25	7766	15
	12 100Z	APPLE JELLY	25	25	25	25	7767	16
	12 100Z	BLKBRY JELLY	29	29	29	29	7768	17
	12 100Z	BL RASP JELLY	35	35	35	35	7769	18
	12 100Z	STRWBRY JELLY	29	29	29	29	7770	19
	24 200Z	AP BKRSP JEL	35	35	35	35	7771	20
	24 200Z	AP BKBY JELY	35	35	35	35	7772	21
	24 200Z	AP STRW JELY	35	35	35	35	7773	22
	24 200Z	AP ELDR JELY	35	35	35	35	7774	23
	24 200Z	APL GRP JELY	35	35	35	35	7775	24
	24/1LB ORANGE SLICES		25	25	25	25	6302	25

Order guide and price book

A 5

a good deal of effort? There are some problems to be worked out, such as how the computer can spot trends in item movement. However, the store manager could still have the option of overriding the system to handle changes in the automatic order quantity due to changes in buyer demand, special promotions, and seasonal influences. The computer system with the required decision logic could also be programmed to accomplish this step.

The more important question in the preceding system trade-off is what effect it will have on the company policy of autonomous operation with profit center responsibility at the store level. The system, theoretically at least, would save the company a considerable amount of money but might have an unfavorable impact on the store manager. This is a decision that must be made by top management. Rolco management firmly believes in the profit center concept and that performance is optimized when the store manager acts as an entrepreneur who owns his own store. The dollar savings of the system must be carefully weighed against the potential impact it will have on the store manager, who may feel that he has lost control of the ordering function—something he has always controlled and used as a tool to serve his customers better. This feeling may be the governing factor even if the automatic ordering system can be proven more effective in a majority of cases. The answer to this dilemma, perhaps, is to pilot test the system in several stores. Then the store managers can help sell the others on the merits of the system if the system works out in practice.

The store bill, which is the output of the system, shows the store header information at the top. Each line of the bill lists the item description information and shows the extension of the quality ordered times the unit price. A copy of the store bill is used as a warehouse picking document that tells the order pickers what items to pull and assemble for shipment.

Rolco currently utilizes magnetic tape for its storage medium. Each inventory item is carried on magnetic tape in item number sequence and includes the information shown in tabular form.

MASTER FILE (10,000 ITEMS)

Data for Each Inventory Item	Length of Field
Item number	5 Numeric
Item description	32 Alpha
Warehouse slot number	3 Numeric
Zone 1 retail price	6 Numeric
Zone 2 retail price	6 Numeric
Zone 3 retail price	6 Numeric
Zone 4 retail price	6 Numeric
Beginning balance (cases)	6 Numeric
Beginning balance (dollars)	8 Numeric
Receipts (cases)	6 Numeric
Receipts (dollars)	8 Numeric
Shipping weight (gross)	6 Numeric
Shipping weight (net)	6 Numeric
Shipments (cases)	6 Numeric
Shipments (dollars)	8 Numeric
Miscellaneous data	24 Numeric

A punched-card file is used to carry the store header information and consists of the following items.

STORE HEADER CARDS

Data for Each Store	Length of Fields
Store number	4 Numeric
Store address	32 Alpha
Pricing zone	2 Numeric

The batch-order processing cycle is as follows:

1. The store orders are converted from cards to magnetic tape and in the process the page and line number for each item is translated (by a formula) to the item number as carried on the inventory master file. Each store orders three times a week, an average of 1000 items each time. Therefore the total order deck consists of 200 cards, although some cards will have no quantities ordered on them.

2. The ordered items are sorted into the sequence of the inventory master file.

3. The sorted orders are screened against the master file to see if there is inventory on hand, extended (quantity extended by price) and transcribed to magnetic tape as invoice lines.

4. The resultant tape of extended invoice lines is sorted by store number (major index) and by warehouse slot number (minor index). The warehouse slot number is the sequence in which the order is picked.

5. The sorted invoice lines are then printed and sent (a) to the store ordering the items and (b) to the warehouse to pick the order for delivery to the store. The store can then match the physical receipt of the order with the paper invoice.

The reader should be able to describe the receiving process, which in many ways is the reverse of the billing process. Receipts are entered daily. A card is punched up for each item received, with the item number, quantity received, and vendor identification. Receipts average 1000 per day.

Rolco's current method centers around sequential storage on magnetic tape, but the system, as an alternative, could utilize random access storage devices and thus have the ability to process one order at a time. The system would look up the item ordered from a disk storage file, check its availability, update the inventory balance, extend the order, and print the individual invoice. Out-of-stock items and order totals would be punched out on cards as a by-product of the single program run. The receiving process would also be a one-pass operation.

STUDY GUIDE

The study guide lists questions under five headings, ranging from the overall organization philosophy of Rolco through the development of system specifications to future system considerations. These questions can be used either as a checklist for the reader or as a guide for general discussion and work assignments by an instructor. Although the questions center on developing the system much as Rolco now operates, the reader or student should be able to see where he could improve the system and expand the application to accomplish more for Rolco. Doing so, of course, could be an additional assignment.

I have used this case and study guide in the graduate course I teach at Northeastern Business School. Included is a system description and specification developed by two of my students, Edward B. Hyland and John F. Doucette. I think it shows the type of innovative thinking that can result from utilizing the Rolco case for instructive purposes.

A. Rolco Organization and Operation

1. Describe the organizational philosophy and type of business engaged in by Rolco.

2. Do you think this organizational philsophy is sound, considering the type of business?

3. What potential EDP problems are raised by this type of organization?

4. As a store manager, what would be your major concern under this type of operation?

5. What are the key controllable elements in profitable store operation?

6. As a newly appointed vice-president of a region, what are your main concerns?

7. Discuss the pros and cons of centralization and/or decentralization on a function by function basis (i.e., buying, merchandizing, EDP).

B. Trade-Offs in System Development

1. What are the considerations that would cause management to place heavier priority on one or more of the four management objectives listed?

2. What are the relative pros and cons in computerizing the three mentioned subsystems as a single entity? What are the system analyst-operating personnel interaction considerations?

3. Do you think the EDP manager might have a built-in predisposition to installing communication terminals in each store?

4. Who specifically (i.e., what departments and what level of management) would be concerned with computerizing the subsystems mentioned?

5. Can you visualize what the ordering procedures of the grocery store of the future might be? What impact would future considerations have on design of the current information system? How much built-in system flexibility should there be?

6. What advantages does Rolco have because it is a chain operation and owns the individual stores?

C. Initial System Assignment

Initial System Assignment (Assume that the system is for a single division.)

1. Write a simple English narrative of the order processing system, including the objectives and purpose.

2. Assuming that (1) the basic input medium is cards, (2) the file storage medium is magnetic tape, and (3) the output medium is printed copy, flow chart (a) the billing subsystem and (b) the receiving subsystem.

3. Block out the item records on tape and cards.

4. Lay out the store-invoice printer form.

D. Secondary System Assignment

1. Assuming that the basic file storage medium is magnetic disk, flow chart (a) the billing system and (b) the receiving system.

2. Block out the item records on cards and disk.

E. Further Study Questions

1. What are the pros and cons of the tape-batch approach versus the disk-direct access approach?

2. What factors would determine whether you proposed a computer configuration that had higher-speed tapes, disks, and central processor and/or greater capacities?

3. Speculate on what extensions could be put into the system to handle (a) inventory control and (b) truck dispatching. Lay out a sample inventory control report that might emanate from the system.

4. Discuss the desirability of installing communication terminals in the individual stores.

5. How would the system handle items that although listed in inventory are unavailable in the warehouse?

6. What type of internal training would be necessary before installing the system?

7. What impact would the future plans of Rolco have on the initial system design?

8. How long do you estimate it would take to install such a system?

ROLCO ORDER PROCESSING SYSTEM

submitted by
J. Doucette and E. Hyland
for course

THE COMPUTER AND ITS APPLICATIONS II
Northeastern University Graduate School

1. Introduction

2. Narrative of System Differences

3. Order Processing System Flow Chart

4. Receipts System Flow Chart

5. Store Order Card

6. Invoice

7. Inventory File Layout

INTRODUCTION

In designing the order processing system for one of the divisions of Rolco, Inc., we attempted to improve the current system rather than merely duplicate it. In the case study, we are told that most of the items ordered are fairly stable in demand. With this point in mind, and with our belief that the store manager should retain ultimate control over whatever system we may establish, we proceeded to design an order processing system that would permit the automatic reordering of stable items, with the reorder cycle and quantity determined by the store manager and with a built-in capability for altering the cycle and quantity. These conditions would reduce the amount of time the store manager would have to spend in ordering and would allow him, at the same time, to maintain control over the orders received and his backroom inventory.

NARRATIVE OF SYSTEM DIFFERENCES

We first redesigned the store order card. As shown in our card layout, we are allowing only eight items per card, four on each side. At first glance the new design looks much less efficient than the current card, which allows for 50 items per card. However, the big difference is that the store manager submits cards for only the items he orders. At 1000 orders each time, this comes to 125 cards, which is less than the 200 standard card deck now submitted.

How does the store manager find the page and numbers to put on the card? At the time of conversion to our system, a set of labels would be generated for each store, one label for each of the 10,000 items. The label would contain page and item number, and the standard ordering unit, whether it be "case—24 cans," or "case—12 jars," or whatever. At the start, the order code would be zero. We would also print the item description. These labels would be stuck to plastic inserts, which would be placed alongside the price under each item. This might sound like quite a task, but it would be done only once. When the store manager now wishes to place an order, he merely looks at the shelf for the items that need reordering and marksenses (marks with a special pencil that creates machine readable media) the information onto our store order cards from the label below the item. This step eliminates the time-consuming job of matching the card deck with the catalog. Neither item is required now, although the catalog would be needed for items not now in stock. Where does our automatic reordering come in?

The *order code* is the key. If the store manager has an item that he wants ordered regularly, he enters an order code. A 1 will indicate that he wants the item every delivery. A 2 will indicate that he wants it once a week, a 3 indicates twice a week. Additional codes could be established for other possibilities, such as every other week. Whatever the case may be, once the store manager has entered an order code other than 0, he need not order that item again. It will be sent regularly. This process is accomplished through the establishment of what we call a "reorder file." If the store manager wishes to take an item off automatic reordering, he merely enters the page and item number, with an order code of 0. It is clear that we have installed a method for automatic reordering that leaves complete control with the entrepreneur, the store manager.

There is one other major item in our system. This is a method for keeping our labels up to date. We have designed an invoice that has labels on the right-hand side. This label would be similar to the labels used by Internal Revenue on the income tax booklets. The labels must be able to be peeled off twice. When the delivery arrives, the checker would simply peel each label off as he goes down the invoice and would then stick it to the item box. The stock boy would place the new label over the old label when he stocks the item. In this way, our labels would be constantly up to date.

As the store manager goes down the aisle making up an order, he will know which items are on an automatic reorder cycle because the order code is on the label. We also think it would be useful to print the date of order on the label. This step would give the manager immediate information as to how long the item has been in stock, thus indicating the slow movers, which might be dropped.

During the actual processing, inventory would be reduced in exactly the same way as it is now. A unique feature is our back order card, which would be input to the next cycle and which would be continuously generated and sent through until the item became available. In this way, it is not merely a reminder, but it actually saves the store manager from reordering back orders. However, we would still note out-of-stock items on the store invoice.

We have attempted to narrate the differences between our system and the current system. As our flow chart indicates, the major addition to the job flow is the repeat order file. This file, in addition to the order cards, results in a transaction file, which is then processed against the master item file. The results are an updated master file, an invoice file, and the back-order turnaround card.

Our receipts system is pretty much standard except that we generate an accounts payable file, which is expanded with each receipt and which then serves as input to an accounts-payable, check-printing program. We also generate an out-of-stock report, which serves as a reminder to the purchasing department.

In summary, we feel that we have designed a system that might be slightly more complex from a programming standpoint but that releases the store manager from a good part of the tedious job of ordering, thereby leaving him free to concentrate on other areas. And it in no way jeopardizes his control over the ordering process.

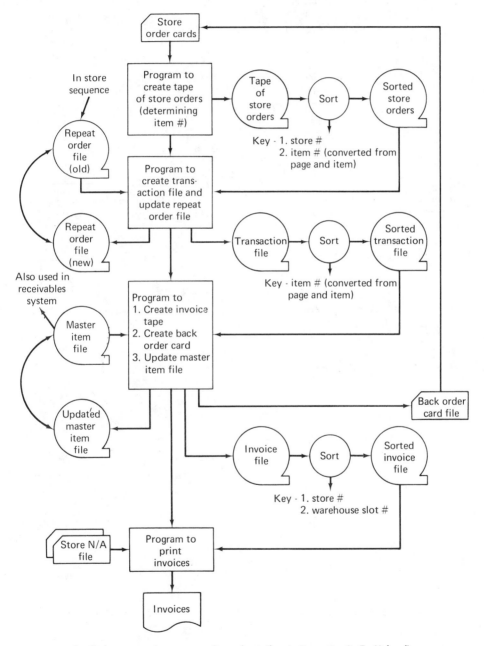

I   Order processing system flow chart (by J. Doucette & E. Hyland)

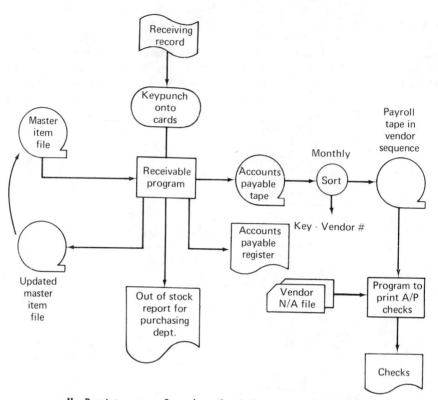

II   Receipts system flow chart (by J. Doucette & E. Hyland)

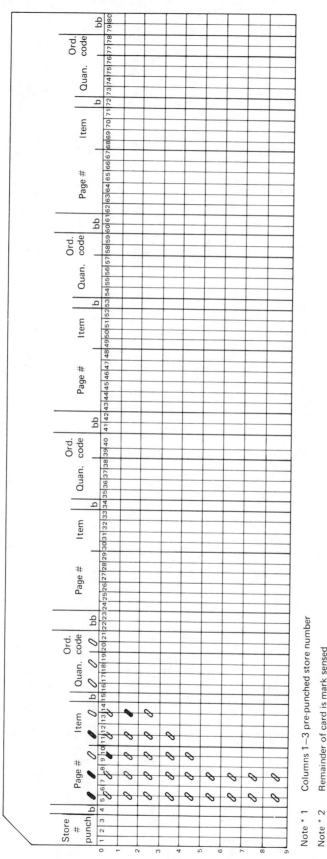

Rolco, Incorporated
Division 1

Store name
Store address

Date xx/xx/xx
Store number – xxx
Warehouse number – x
Pricing zone – xx

Invoice number
xxxxxxx
Page xx

Item count	Item number		Order code	Item description	Slot	Size	Order unit	Qty	Unit price	Cost	
	Page	Item									
xxxx	xxx	xx	x	xxxxxxxxxxxxxxxxxxxxxxxx xxxxxxxxxxx	xxxx	xx	xxxx	xx	x.xx	x,xxx.xx	Label
xxxx	xxx	xx	x	xxxxxxxxxxxxxxxxxxxxxxxx xxxxxxxxxx	xxxx	xx	xxxx	xx	x.xx	x,xxx.xx	Label
											Label
											Label
											Label
											Label
											Label
											Label
											Label
											Label
											Label

Perforation

IV Invoice form

Title   Inventory file

Item number (allow 1 character for expansion.)	Item description	Slot no.	Zone 1 retail price	Zone 2 retail price	Zone 3 retail price	Zone 4 retail price	Allow for expansion	Begin balance cases	Begin balance dollars	Receipt cases	Receipt dollars
5	10 15 20 25 30 35	40	45	50	55	60	65 70	75	80 85	90	95

Title

Shipping weight gross	Shipping weight net	Shipments cases	Shipments dollars	Miscellaneous data
5	10	15	20 25	30 35 40 45 50

Title

5	10	15	20	25	30	35	40	45	50	55	60	65	70	75	80	85	90	95

Title

5	10	15	20	25	30	35	40	45	50	55	60	65	70	75	80	85	90	95

V Record format

STUDY CASETTES

LARABEE STORES, INC.

Sam Greeley was halfway through the fourth day of a planned one-week study of Larabee Stores, Inc., one of the country's big discount department store chains. He had spent most of his time getting data for an inventory-control, order-processing, stock-reorder, sales-analysis application to be presented to Larabee's top management. It was 1:30, and Sam had been with Hugh Lincoln, one of Larabee's four commodity group inventory managers, since lunch.

Hugh: Well, that's about all I can give you. As I said, styles change so fast that half of the items aren't in inventory long enough to control by a system. We buy a lot of something and we sell it and that's that. Out of the 11,000 items I'm responsible for, there's probably less than 1000 that we could put on a reorder basis.

Sam: Maybe so. But I'd like to get into it a little further and see just what we could do.

Hugh: If you like. I'll put you with one of my people. Mike Concannon has been with us a long time and knows everything there is to know.

Sam: Great!

****

Hugh: Mike, I want to present Sam Greeley from the computer section. Sam wants to put our stock control on a computer. Fill him in on some of the details, will you?

Mike: Sure thing, boss. See you later. (turning to Sam) This is some weather we've been having, eh?

Sam: I'll say! Do you have any statistics on how often you order different items, how long they stay in inventory, stock turns, out-of-stock conditions, and so on?

Mike: That's not my line, but I doubt if you'll find anything like that. My group keeps paper balances on about 9,000 items, based on order and receipt slips we receive.

Sam: What do you do when a balance gets low?

Mike: Usually we have a pretty good idea of whether to order more. Depends on the time of year sometimes, or on what seems to be moving well, or on whether the item was a special purchase.

Sam: Special purchase?

Mike: You know, bought somebody's stock going out of business. Something like that. A lot of times we don't order something unless we're specifically told to do so by the marketing staff. Everything is so special that you have to use judgment.

Sam: Then your group is actually responsible for ordering?

Mike: Not exactly. That's purchasing's job. We pretty much control it, though, by the stock level reports we make. We know what's moving better than they do, and when a fast-moving item gets low, we report it to them. This is the case on maybe 5% of the items. The rest of the stock you have to treat as individual cases.

Sam: Could I have a look at some of the forms you use?

Mike: Sure. Here's the main one. You can see how we keep a running balance with each transaction. Look at the whole sheet and you can see how the item is moving. Come on around the department and we'll pick up the other forms and talk to the people who fill them out.

Sam: Great. This should be very interesting.

Study Questions

1. Analyze and comment on Sam Greeley's experience and progress at Larabee Stores.

2. Do you think he is going about the problem in the right way?

3. Do you draw any conclusions about the current order processing, inventory and purchasing system currently in operation at Larabee?

4. What should Sam's next step be after leaving Hugh and Mike?

INGERSOLL MANUFACTURING, INC.

Ingersoll has completed its system study and Dexter Johnson believes he has a good grasp on the information processing requirements of the company. His job now is to design a system solution that meets the system specifications developed during the system study phase. Realizing that management is becoming slightly impatient at the continued delays and departures from the original schedule, Johnson wants to move quickly through the design job.

Johnson has what he considers good specs on the overall total system approach desired by Ingersoll in the long run as well as individual and detailed specs on order processing, inventory control, and those applications currently being performed on punched card equipment. With this in hand, Johnson submits the specs to three computer vendors. He limits the selection to the three vendors who have been calling upon him (his current supplier of punched card equipment plus two others). He issues a covering letter to each as follows:

TO   Computer Vendors
FROM   D. T. Johnson
SUBJECT   Request for Computer Proposal

Attached are system specifications for the major applications of the Ingersoll company. You have been selected as a computer vendor to bid on these specifications. In order to be considered for the eventual contract, you must submit your proposal in writing no later than four weeks from the date of this letter.

Ingersoll desires a computer system to handle the specified applications within one shift of computer operation, leaving the second shift for growth. As mentioned in the overall specification, an open-ended and flexible approach is desired—an approach that will allow Ingersoll to move toward an integrated data processing system in three to five years. A suggested phasing plan with required hardware, software, and personnel resources at each phase is considered optional in your response.

A cost goal is to spend no more than 30% above what is currently being expended. It is assumed that the major portion of our existing hardware will be replaced. The replacement plan, including a timetable, should be defined clearly.

Alternate hardware configurations may be submitted but your reply should state which alternative in your judgment is best suited to handle Ingersoll's requirements. Price and delivery times should be indicated, as well as a complete statement of generalized and specialized system support offered by your company. At the vendor's option, an overall implementation schedule with necessary manpower can be presented.

It should be kept in mind that Ingersoll desires a system that can satisfy current demands while leaving ample growth potential. We do not want to pay any more than we have to; however, we desire a reaistic appraisal of hardware needs. The system must have the power and capacity to do the job. It should be obvious that we will not be content with doing the traditional data processing tasks but must be able to tackle the key money-making applications described in the specifications.

My staff and I will be available to answer questions or elaborate on any area that requires it. Feel free to call upon us, as we realize the importance of your having the necessary data upon which to base your proposal. In addition to your written proposal, you are invited to present the salient features of your recommendations to Ingersoll's management in a two-hour session which will be scheduled after submission of the proposals.

We would appreciate an immediate reply as to your intention to bid on our specifications.

Sincerely yours,
(signed)
_____

Dexter T. Johnson
Director, Data Processing

DTJ/rc

While the vendor's proposals were being prepared, Johnson and his team decided to tackle the system design job themselves so as to be ready to evaluate the responses. The use of consultants was discussed but ruled out at this time. Rather than have a consultant develop an independent system design, it was decided that consultants might well be brought in to evaluate the various vendor proposals after they had been submitted.

Study Questions

1. Is this a good way to evaluate alternate vendors of computing equipment?

2. What additional methods of selection might be utilized in this instance?

3. Do you think Johnson should use consultants or other outside agencies?

4. What should be done after the proposals are received?

5. If a key vendor desires added response time, would you approve of it?

IMPLEMENTATION CONSIDERATIONS

It is surprising that there still are EDP shops that do not utilize any formal method of establishing an implementation schedule. This is true despite the fact that many companies and many EDP directors have passed through three generations of computer hardware. The following recorded dialogue may serve to set the stage for a discussion of implementation considerations.

Interviewer: You've been head of the data processing department for three years now. You were in charge of the feasibility study, recommended your existing computer, and managed the entire program since installation a little over a year ago. As you look back, what do you think your major problems have been?

EDP Director: My major problem has been the lack of communications with management. Somehow, despite everything, they don't seem to understand how to make the most effective use of EDP. We should have meetings where the basic problems are recognized, explored, and resolved, but for some reason we don't. I have a difficult time selling them my program.

Interviewer: What would you say are your secondary problems?

EDP Director: Next in importance is the problem of hiring and keeping good system and programming people. Somewhat related is the problem of getting applications on the computer in a reasonable time frame. I have an existing application backlog that is about 20% of my current work load.

Interviewer: Do you use any type of project control techniques to schedule the implementation of applications?

EDP Director: We don't have a formal method. I can pretty well estimate how long it's going to take from previous experience. I can tell you at any one time how far along each application is and the estimated operational date. However, because business keeps changing and the information system changes along with it, the completion date is always highly problematical.

Interviewer: Do you have historic records of the time and cost of computerizing the applications that are currently operational?

EDP Director: No, but I can tell you within reasonable limits what each application cost us.

Interviewer: Do you supply management with any progress report or have meetings to discuss the status of your department?

EDP Director: We don't have regularly scheduled sessions. When we first began to prepare for the computer, we had scheduled meetings with my boss (the controller) and several of the key operating managers. However, I don't think that management could understand what was going on and they didn't seem very motivated to find out. We met for a couple of months but gradually the operating managers dropped out until it was just my boss and me. Since the two of us discuss problems on a day to day basis when any crisis arises, there didn't seem to be any need for a formal status review, so we dropped the regularly scheduled sessions.

Interviewer: Do you think it is possible to utilize a project control method to plan and control a project like a computer installation?

EDP Director: To a certain extent, yes; but you must remember this type of operation is not like a production line process. We are dealing with skilled personnel who are in great demand and who can leave you tomorrow for a better job if they react unfavorably to too rigid a control system. Also keep in mind that systems and programming work is still an art and not a science—as such, it is very difficult to establish a schedule in which one has a great degree of confidence.

Study Questions

1. How typical do you think the situation is?

2. What is your impression of the EDP Director?

3. Do you think the EDP Director is correct in his assessment of the situation?

4. What type of control would you impose if you were the EDP Director? If you were top management?

BIBLIOGRAPHY

BRANDON, DICK H., *Management Standards for Data Processing.* Van Nostrand Reinhold Co., New York, N.Y., 1970, 255 pp.

FISHER, G. H., *Cost Considerations in Systems Analysis.* American Elsevier, New York, 1971, 334 pp.

JOSLIN, E. O. (ed.), *Analysis, Design and Selection of Computer Systems.* College Readings, Inc., Arlington, Va., 1971, 387 pp.

JOSLIN, E. O., *Computer Selection.* Addison-Wesley, Reading, Massachusetts, 1968, 172 pp.

KANTER, J., *Management Guide to Computer System Selection and Use.* Prentice-Hall, Inc., Englewood Cliffs, New Jersey, 1970.

KELLY, J. E., *Computerized Management Information Systems.* The MacMillan Company, New York, 1970, 533 pp.

LOSTY, P. A., *Effective Use of Computers in Business.* Cassell, London, 1970, 148 pp.

ORLICKY, J., *The Successful Computer System.* McGraw-Hill Book Company, New York, 1969, 238 pp.

RUDWICK, B., *Systems Analysis for Effective Planning.* John Wiley & Sons, New York, 1969, 469 pp.

SEILER, K., *Introduction to Systems Cost Effectiveness.* John Wiley & Sons, New York, 1969, 108 pp.

SHARPE, W. F., *The Economics of Computers.* Columbia University Press, New York, 1969.

WILSON/WILSON, V., *Management Innovation and Systems Design.* Auerbach Publishers, Princeton, New Jersey, 1971, 175 pp.

WITHINGTON, F. G., *The Use of Computers in Business Organization.* Addison-Wesley, Reading, Massachusetts, 1966.

Chapter 5

THE TECHNOLOGICAL FOUNDATION

OF MIS

INTRODUCTION

The thesis of this book is that computer technology has not been the limiting factor in the development of management information systems. In the sixties machines were introduced that were bigger, faster, and more powerful than their predecessors. The computing power is available; the major challenge is management's ability to harness the power. Although the technology is secondary in importance to management and system considerations, the cost, complexity, and variety of today's technical offerings make it necesary to assess and evaluate properly the burgeoning list of devices that are being produced by a burgeoning list of companies in the hardware, software, and support services business. This chapter defines what is meant by technology and then proceeds to develop a framework or classification from which to view the total EDP industry. I feel that the thorough analysis and evaluation of these devices is the province of the EDP professionals within a company or of consulting firms if the necessary internal expertise is not present. Top and operating management should certainly have a say in setting the criteria for the selection process and in assisting in any particular evaluations that are pertinent to their area of operation. The EDP personnel making the evaluation should also avail themselves of the legal department and procurement people within the company in writing up the contracts, establishing necessary acceptance tests, and, in general, ensuring that general procurement and business practices are followed. However, the major study and review of technical capabilities should be delegated to the EDP people. A full-time, dedicated effort is required. If top management is not comfortable with delegating this function, it should immediately try to acquire the necessary EDP capability.

Once the classification of the technical EDP world is completed, specific developments that are pertinent to MIS development will be highlighted. Although not its specific responsibility, management should be aware of the overall EDP technical world and the specific elements in it that are necessary for MIS development. The discussion will not attempt to develop an analysis and evaluation procedure for these technological devices, but it will present some of the salient features and explain why they are important to MIS. In other words, the focus will be on a nontechnical exploration of the technical foundation of MIS.

DEFINITION OF COMPUTER TECHNOLOGY

The definition of technology used here covers a broader spectrum of products and services than is usually connoted by the term. Technology not only covers the hardware or physical elements, such as central processors, magnetic storage units, and input–output equipment, it also includes the wide variety of software, application aids, and support services. Figure 5.1 divides computer technology into four elements: hardware, system software, application software, and support services. The last category is viewed as tying together the other three elements. For purposes of definition, the hardware element represents the things you can see, touch, and feel, such as a central processor, a printer, or a card reader. These

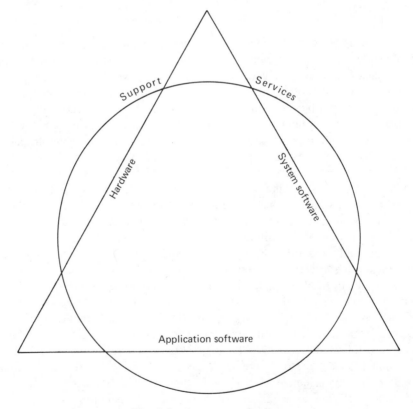

Fig. 5.1 Computer technology

devices are built from a variety of electronic and mechanical parts. I categorize system software as the programs written for a specific computer to aid programmers and operators of that computer. Application software refers to the programs that the user programmers write to accomplish a specific application, like inventory control, payroll, or production scheduling. In so doing, they utilize the software written for the specific computer. Hardware and software are really meaningless unless they can be utilized for the implementation of applications. Thus the three elements of the triangle are required before computer power becomes more than an academic indicator. Support services provide the people power, consulting and educating services, and a whole array of service facilities ranging from the renting of computer time to the subcontracting of a company's total data processing job. Thus the definition of computer technology covers the four major elements in Figure 5.1. I will now categorize the subelements that comprise each of the major elements. This is not an easy undertaking; however, I have checked the classification scheme by reviewing several EDP product catalogs and composite product listings, and although some products and services are a combination of two or more of the categories, the classification holds up.

HARDWARE ELEMENTS

Figure 5.2 lists the hardware elements, beginning with seven general classes of hardware. Bookkeeping machines utilize ledger cards that hold fixed information about customers, employees, or products. The major input device is a keyboard with a serial printer (typewriter) serving as output. An application example is order invoicing where a billing clerk extracts the customer's ledger card from a tub file, places it in the typewriter carriage, and adds the variable data (item ordered, price, and quantity). The machine calculates the extensions and prints the order invoice while updating the customer's order and accounts receivable ledger record.

Tabulating gear is built around the punched-card concept where data is expressed in the form of punched holes in cards. Various machines have the ability to sense the holes electronically and perform predetermined operations on the data represented by the holes and on the cards themselves. Thus punched-card gear can sort, collate, and merge cards; reproduce cards; print on them, as well as calculate and print reports. It is assumed that the reader has had some familiarity with tabulating gear or punched-card equipment.

Desk calculators accept keyboard input, have the ability to store a moderately sized program to process the input mathematically and print out the results on a serial printer or a paper tape (like that found in adding machines).

The foregoing devices are not considered computers in the sense of the term used here and will not be discussed further. Although often found in companies with computerized MIS, these devices usually perform ancillary jobs and are not a significant part of the technology that drives the management information system. The remaining four hardware elements—central processors, peripheral devices, terminal devices, and source data collection devices—are significant technological underpinnings of MIS and will be treated in more depth.

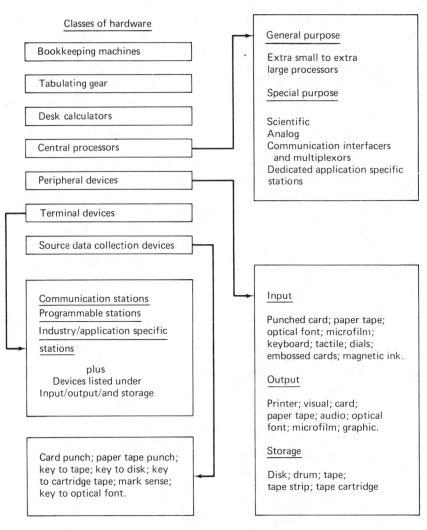

Fig. 5.2   Hardware elements

Figure 5.3 is a schematic of the four basic hardware elements. The central processor is in the center of the illustration; it has the necessary control, arithmetic, and memory components to integrate and tie together the other hardware components. Peripheral devices are shown on the upper-left, upper-right, and upper-middle sections of the figure. They are broken down into input devices, storage devices, and output devices. Source data collection devices are shown on the lower left. The output of these devices (tape, disk, or cassette) can either be inputted to the central processor over communication lines from remote sites or can be accumulated off-line with removable tapes, disk packs, or cartridges placed on the on-site storage devices for processing. In the latter case, the storage devices are acting as input devices, which indeed they are. Although they serve as input-output devices as well as storage devices, their prime purpose is for storage and I have chosen to classify them as such.

Communications hardware is illustrated in the lower-middle and lower-right

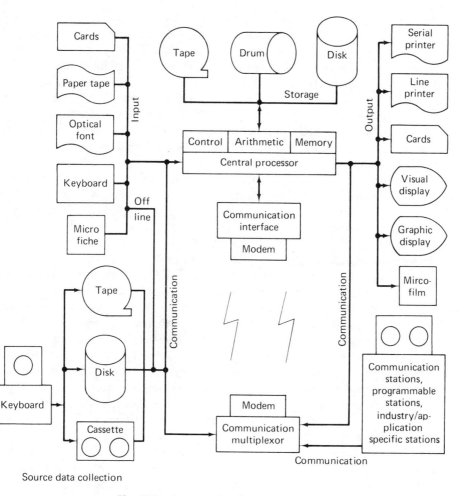

Fig. 5.3 Computer hardware components

portions of the figure. The communication interface to the central processor is shown, as well as the modems (modulator/demodulator) on each end of the communication line that connects the remote site to the computer site (usually a telephone line). The communication multiplexer collects the data from a variety of terminal devices and prepares it for transmission over the communication line. The connecting arrows from the input and output devices to the communication multiplexer indicates that these devices can be utilized as terminals as well as peripherals. In addition, special configurations or combinations of devices, known as communication stations, programmable stations, and industry/application specific stations, are used in particular communication systems. The various hardware elements now will be described in more detail.

Central Processors

Figure 5.2 indicates a breakdown of central processors into general purpose and special purpose. A general-purpose computer is defined as a device that has input-output and storage devices, plus memory and instruction logic, and that is able to process business as well as scientific jobs. Such computers range in size from the extra-small processor renting for as little as $600 per month to the extra-large processor renting for upward of $100,000 per month. Examples of the former are the Burroughs L 8000, Honeywell 58, and IBM System 3, whereas the IBM 195, Univac 1110, and CDC 7600 are examples of the latter. I classify the so-called mini-computers renting from $200 to $1000 per month (though they are usually sold, not rented) as special purpose, for they do not have the requisite hardware and software capabilities to accomplish a broad range of general-purpose business jobs.

Special-purpose processors include the wide range of scientific processors that have fast internal speed and floating-point scientific units which enable them to handle high-precision mathematical calculations. Examples of this category are Wang Laboratories processors, Xerox Data Systems low-numbered Sigma Series, Digital Equipment Corporation's processors, and Honeywell's minisystems. Analog devices are utilized primarily in process control applications where it is necessary to measure temperature or viscosity and to take predetermined action based on the recordings. Continuous-process manufacturers, like chemical, petroleum, or food processors, utilize analog or process control computers to regulate production operations. With the rapid growth of communication-oriented systems, special-purpose processors have been developed to act as communication interfacers which serve as a communication front end to a central processor. When the communication volume and/or number of remote terminals grow to a certain point, it becomes necessary to employ a dedicated processor to handle the transmission as well as the formatting and auditing of messages entering and leaving the central processor. Similarly, at the remote site, volume can reach a point where a dedicated special-purpose computer is employed as a multiplexer or to collect, organize, format, and audit data preparatory to transmission over communication lines. They are also dedicated application-specific special-purpose processors that are directed at a specific job like typesetting or numerical control. These devices are usually special versions of scientific or analog processors. They may have special instructions or hard-wired logic that enables them to do the specialized application more efficiently and economically than a generalized processor.

Peripheral Devices

In one respect input devices have changed dramatically in type and variety, but in another respect they have remained fairly stable. Although there are devices on the market today that can read optical font, magnetic ink, and embossed cards, the main input device is still the punched card. The economics and capability of the former devices have not reached a point where there has been wholesale replacement of the card. Cards come in 80, 90, and 96 column variety and account for about 70 percent of all input to a computer. Paper tape is declining, whereas the other devices are showing slow but steady growth. Magnetic ink is still used primarily for bank checks, while optical font is growing in use over a wide range of industries. Microfiche is a form of punched-card input in that the particular microfilmed document is placed in an insert in a standard punched card. Space remains on the card for punch identifiers of the data on the microfilm. Thus the cards can be read and sorted, and a form of automatic information retrieval developed. Direct keyboard input is increasing in conjunction with key-to-tape and key-to-disk equipment listed under source data collection devices. Dial and embossed card input is characterized by factory data collection devices where the worker places his ID card in a special reader and moves dial settings to correspond to the job, item, and quantity he has completed. This data is then sent directly to the computer. The tactile input device is the most straightforward of all. A display screen provides the input format, such as the following:

Item	1	2	3	4	5	6	7	8	9	10	20	40
Boston Baked Beans												
Bermuda Onions			X							X	X	
Brazilian Coffee												
Florida Oranges												

The program is established to recognize a tactile (finger or stylus) impression and the relative position of the impression such that the impressions designated by the X's are interpreted as an order for 33 cases of Bermuda onions. Subsequent formats on the screen would display the total order catalog.

The major output device is still the printed copy, either a serial printer, which prints a character at a time (typewriter), or a line printer, which has a drum or chain that can print an entire line at one time. Card and paper-tape output have declined to a point where they are used only as a form of returnable media, such as a punched-card invoice where the returned payment can be read back into the system for accounts receivable reconciliation. (However, this can be accomplished as well by printing optically read font on the invoice.) Visual output devices, such as cathode ray tubes, are increasing rapidly as are graphic devices that can produce visual graphs on a cathode ray tube or hard-copy graphic output on a plotter. Also in use are audio devices where a prerecorded message can be selected under computer control and played back to the inquirer. Computer Output Microfilm (COM) devices are growing in number. In a MIS, there is a good deal of historical information that may be required for audit purposes or infrequent information retrieval. If the volume of this type of data is high, it may be economical to put the data on microfilm, which is a cheaper storage medium than magnetic-storage devices, such as tape or disk. COM devices have the ability to transform data from magnetic media to microfilm.

Storage devices consist primarily of magnetic tape, magnetic disk, and magnetic drum. Tape is always removable, whereas drum is always fixed and disks are either removable or fixed. The tape strip and tape cartridge are not primary storage media for computer systems employing MIS. Since the central data base built around tape and disk storage is so important to MIS, storage devices and the software systems that facilitate their use will be discussed as special subjects later in the chapter.

Terminal Devices

All the peripheral devices listed can be used as terminal devices as well. The distinction between a terminal and a peripheral device is that the former is connected to the central processor via a communication line, whereas the latter is located physically at the computer site. Specific combinations of terminal devices are often joined to form a communication data station. For example, a station may have a card reader for batch input, a keyboard for inputting variable data, and a printer to receive output. Other stations may have a cathode-ray-tube visual display or paper-tape equipment. Another class of terminal station is a programmable station. This device is similar to the communication interfacers and multiplexers. It it a small computer with limited capacity having features of both a computer and a communication station. It can do a small amount of application processing by itself; it can act as a terminal, sending and receiving messages; or it can do a combination of the two. For example, an operator may wish to process an order. She inputs the variable data, such as the items and quantities ordered, while the central computer has the inventory status information in its storage devices. By combining the processing capability of the remote programmable station and the file storage facility of the central processor, orders can be prepared locally.

Industry/application specific terminals are offshoots of the terminal and peripheral devices described above, but they are designed and developed for a specific industry purpose. An example of such a device is a computer-oriented point of sale device where credit checks can be made, orders totaled, and by-product sales movement data accumulated, all from a single transaction. Another industry specific terminal is a nurses' data station in a hospital where a specialized keyboard with function keys enables a nurse to update a patient's record with pertinent transactions that serve to schedule lab tests, and doctors' visits, and that provide data for later customer billing. Communication processing will be discussed in more depth because, like storage devices, communication plays a key role in many management information systems.

Source Data Collection Devices

A major bottleneck exists in providing input for computer processing. The computer as yet does not accept verbal input; nor can it comprehend handwritten documents. As a result, data must be fed into it on punched cards, paper tape, keyboards, or optically read documents, and all must be in a rigidly defined format. This process is expensive and time consuming, for it is basically manual in nature. System design has focused on combining and reducing the number of steps in translating human-readable forms into computer-readable media. This is typified by the direct key-to-tape or key-to-disk devices. Formerly data collection was a two-stage process that looked as follows:

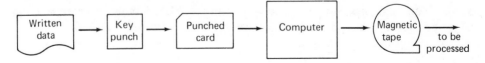

The basic data from some type of written document was keypunched into cards. These cards were then read by a computer and the data edited and placed on magnetic tape. The direct key-to-tape method accomplishes this process in one step.

The logical extension of this process is to read the written data directly into the computer. This is where optically read font comes into being. However, as has been stated, the economics as well as the technological considerations of accurately reading typewritten or handwritten characters have not permitted the wide use of this device. However, the benefits are obvious and the trend is definitely toward optical font.

SYSTEM AND APPLICATION SOFTWARE ELEMENTS

Figure 5.4 combines two sides of the triangle described in Figure 5.1, the system software and application software. Application software is further subdivided into business and scientific. The major distinction between system software and application software is that the former is tied directly to the computer and consists of aids to assist the programmer in translating a particular application into machine language. This class of software also includes aids to assist the computer operation group in scheduling and running the computer efficiently. Applications, on the other hand, are the end product, an order processing or inventory control system in productive operation on a computer. These applications utilize the system software, which in turn utilizes the computer hardware.

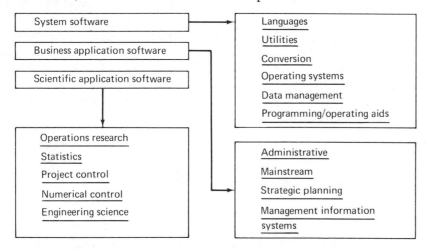

Fig. 5.4 Systems/application software elements

System Software

System software is divided into the groupings listed in Figure 5.4. Languages such as COBOL (COmmon Business Oriented Language) are used by the programmer to express the particular job to be accomplished. Languages are roughly divided into two classifications; (a) machine oriented or those closely tied to the unique characteristics of a particular computer or (b) higher level (i.e., COBOL), which are English-language oriented and standardized such that programs written in the language can be executed on different computers.

Utility programs assist the programmer or operator in performing common functions, such as sorting, collating, and various audit and checking routines that aid in program preparation and testing.

Because of the incompatibilities within a manufacturer's own line of computers, as well as those found between manufacturers' lines, the need exists for conversion software to aid the transfer of data and programs from one computer system to another. These conversion software aids may be required in order to interchange data files from one system to another or to replace one computer with another. The scope of the problem differs, depending on whether the former or the latter is the situation, but the nature of the job embodies similarities that can be materially helped by well-conceived conversion aids.

Operating systems are the internal monitors that reside in computer memory and direct and manage the execution of programs, some sequentially (monoprogramming) and some simultaneously (multiprogramming). Operating systems also help in the economical scheduling and allocating of computer resources in performing a specified job mix. Because of their significance in regard to MIS development, operating systems will be a subject of additional discussion later in the chapter.

Data management software provides the capability of managing and controlling the central data base so important to MIS development. Included in the functions are the ability to organize, capture, update, and retrieve data from the various information files. The data management system works on the storage media described under hardware elements. We will go into more depth on this subject later on.

Programming-Operating aids represent software techniques that enable the programmers and operators to accomplish their jobs in a more expeditious manner. Examples of this category are automatic flow-charting programs that can produce flow charts from written-application descriptions and automatic logging programs that can produce summaries of machine-time utilization. The former is an aid to the programmer, whereas the latter aids the operator.

Business Application Software

Figure 5.5 indicates a projected split in computer time for different application types. These types have been categorized and defined in Chapter 3. According to the figure, administrative applications will account for only 15 percent of total EDP expenditures in 1977 as compared to 55 percent in 1967. Mainstream applications will account for 40 percent of computer running time in 1977 compared to 30 percent in 1967. The major growths will occur in strategic applications and in MIS, which together account for 45 percent of computer time in 1977 compared to a combined 15 percent in 1967. It should be noted that although the circles for 1967 and 1977 are the same size, 1977 represents close to a threefold increase in total computer time compared to 1967.

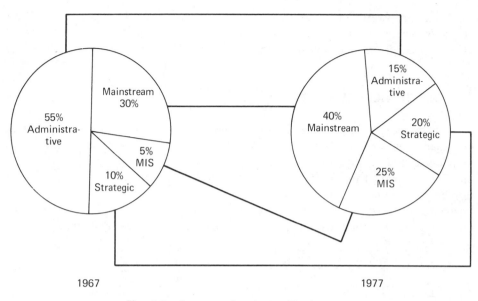

1967   1977

Fig. 5.5 Computer time by application usage

Scientific Application Software

Although this class of software is classified separately, it has elements that are incorporated into both system software and business application software. For example, business application areas, particularly strategic planning, utilize operation research techniques and statistical routines. However, they are listed separately here because the EDP industry treats them as such.

Operations Research (OR) software includes packages like linear programming and general-purpose simulators that can be utilized as subprograms for major applications, such as inventory control, revenue modeling, and forecasting. Statistics are more finite techniques employing specialized mathematical functions, such as regression analysis and curve fitting, which can be used in both business and scientific applications.

Project control include computer-based PERT and Critical Path techniques. PERT (Program Evaluation and Review Technique) and CPM (Critical Path Method) are well recognized and rather standardized approaches to managing complex projects. Generalized computer systems have been developed to facilitate the implementation of these management aids.

Numrical control consists of generalized programs to produce tapes that automatically control a wide variety of machine tools. Packages called APT and ADAPT have been standardized and are available on a broad range of computers. Computerized NC systems have proven extremely beneficial to engineering departments of manufacturing companies.

The category of engineering science completes the list of scientific application software. This category includes such functions as stress and failure analysis, coordinate geometry programs, and programs designed to aid the civil engineering departments of larger companies. The fact that engineering science is better understood and more precise in its measurement facilitates the usefulness of scientific application software. Even though the scope of the application area is greater, the imprecise nature of operations in the business area accounts for the slower evolution of packaged application software.

SUPPORT SERVICES ELEMENTS

As indicated in Chapter 2, support services are rapidly becoming a predominant element in the information services industry. Hardware proliferated and developed very rapidly in the 1960s, and software development began to catch up in the latter part of that decade. What has lagged is the people and support power for an effective merger of hardware and software in order to produce a viable management information system. Figure 5.6 breaks down support services into the categories of computer time, support, application services, and supplies.

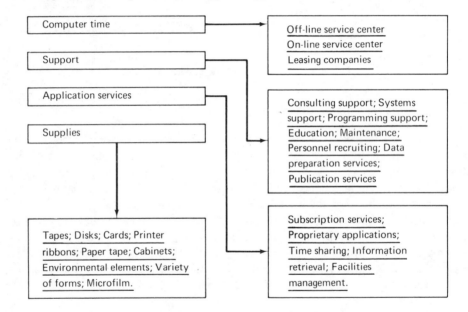

Fig. 5.6 Support services elements

Computer Time

Service centers have been considered by many as necessary only for the smaller companies who cannot afford their own computer. However, the service center is becoming a source of ancillary computer power of both a generalized and specialized nature. Computer users need extra capacity to handle peak loads and also as backup facilities in case of prolonged downtime problems. This type of support is rendered by the off-line service center. The on-line service center is becoming increasingly significant as a source of specialized assistance. A company may have 95 percent of its computer applications devoted to business use, with a 5 percent need for scientific use. It may prove wiser to utilize the facilities of an on-line service center for the engineering department rather than add the necessary facilities and support capability to implement the engineering applications in–house. More and more, medium and large users are availing themselves of the specialized capability offered by on-line service centers.

An additional avenue for acquiring computing power is through a third-party leasing company. The rates can be 10 to 20 percent less than the manufacturer's rental price, depending on whether the lease is short or long term. Obviously the leasing company must charge more for the short-term lease, for it must find a second or third lessee for the returned equipment if a short-term lease is not renewed. The leasing company makes its money by betting that the life of the computer is longer than that reflected in the manufacturer's ratio of purchase price to monthly rental (after the leasing company includes the other cost factors of purchase, such as maintenance, taxes, and insurance).

Support

A wide range of support functions are available to supplement or complement the user's own capabilities. They range from broad consulting help in the areas of EDP organization, long-range computer plans, and top-management EDP orientation to specific areas, such as providing temporary programming assistance or keypunch operators to reduce a backlog of customer transactions. The user can obtain assistance during every step of the application development cycle described in the previous chapter. The gradual evolution of the industry to the separate pricing of support services from hardware and software has been responsible for the proliferation of a wide variety of support services, some offered by sound companies with sound capabilities and others with less noteworthy attributes. In fact, the failure rate of support companies has increased dramatically in the past several years. It behooves prospective users to know what they need and to carefully assess the qualifications and claims of companies offering support assistance.

The list of support includes broad consulting, system, and programming support which can be employed during various phases of the application development cycle. Education is a critical item, and a company may develop the need to enroll key EDP and non-EDP personnel in various classes and seminars offered by companies specializing in educational programs, or it may require the services of a company to tailor a training program to its own particular requirements. The cost and efficacy of outside services should always be measured against the relevant in-house capability.

Computer maintenance, which is usually provided as part of the rental price, can be secured from a third party or separately negotiated with the manufacturer of the equipment if the hardware is purchased. This is true of third-party leases.

Personnel-recruiting services can be utilized to assist in the hiring of in–house system and programming capability. As mentioned earlier, key punchers can be employed or work can be contracted out to handle peak data-preparation work loads. Finally, publication services, which include magazines, periodicals, books, special reports, surveys, competitive product information, researching services, and the like, can be utilized to complement training programs and provide necessary background information for making system and product decisions.

Application Services

Subscription services refer to companies who offer to implement specific application areas for subscribers of the service. The subscription service companies have concentrated on specific areas and have built up expertise in applying computer solutions to these problems. An example of this type of service is a system designed for handling the business applications of small-to medium-sized hospitals. Such a system produces customer bills and the required ancillary accounting reports from input furnished by the hospital's clerical staff. The service can either be off-line such that the input data is delivered to the subscription service company by manual means, or it can be on-line where each hospital has appropriate terminal and communication facilities.

Proprietary applications represent the development of application software described above that is designed to accomplish a particular function, such as sales forecasting, bill of material processing, or inventory control. A variety of packages are on the market today, ranging from basic payroll and accounting applications to advanced-production scheduling systems. As in the case of any support service, the user must carefully evaluate the package to ensure that it is designed properly, is operable, and can be used effectively in his environment.

Time-sharing services have been referred to and can be of significant benefit when focused on specific application areas, as in the case of hospital subsystem services. Another important time-sharing service is in the writing and testing of a company's application programs. Time-sharing services have been established that specialize in remote program building and testing. The one continuing activity that all computer users have in common is the development of new applications. The company's computer can be dedicated exclusively to productive running of programs, while the time-sharing service can be utilized for program writing and testing. This combination often represents a very attractive choice.

Information retrieval services usually center on business areas where there is a need to access data from a common set of files. An example is the National Library of Medicine, which maintains an index of medical research documents cross referenced by several keys. Remote terminals can interrogate the files and obtain the listing and location of reference material pertinent to a specific inquiry. This type of service can be used by public libraries, financial institutions, educational institutions, legal firms, and general business firms.

Companies may not fall neatly into one of the support service categories listed, for many are engaged in a combination of two or more activities. Also, some companies are developing unique approaches by combining these services in different ways. For example, companies have been successful in offering a complete computer package to a prospective user. Such a company will contract for the entire computer system selection and implementation cycle, even running the computer at the user's site when the job is completed. The user states that he wants a system to accomplish order processing, inventory control, and production control; the subcontractor takes it from there. The service these companies offer is called facilities management.

Supplies

The preceding discussion of technical requirements, hardware, software, and support points out the need for a variety of supply items. Removable tapes and disk packs are required for storing a company's data base and for interim storage needs. Additional tapes and disk packs must be purchased as volume and activity increase and as older media wear out. In addition, supplies of punched cards, paper tape, printer ribbons, and printer forms must be procured, as well as microfilm or other specific data medium needed. Cabinets for storing tapes, disk packs, and other supplies, plus environmental elements required in the computer room, such as raised flooring, special cables, raceways, and shelving, complete the list of supplies required for computer operations.

This completes a description of the general technological underpinnings required of an advanced computer system. The remainder of the chapter will focus on the elements of particular significance to a management information system. The key elements are

1. Central data base hardware and software

2. Communication hardware and software

3. Scientific and business application software

CENTRAL DATA BASE HARDWARE AND SOFTWARE

As emphasized in the previous chapter, the central data base (CDB) is most significant to management information systems. In this section the hardware and software technology that are the requisites of a CDB will be discussed. The need for fast access to data has caused the growth of direct access files, which in turn has caused the growth of data base management software systems to manage and control the data within the files.

Data Base Hardware

In designing systems, the designer discovers a hierarchical requirement for formulating data files. Some data requires instant access (seconds)—for example, an inquiry to determine if an item is in inventory or whether a customer's credit is satisfactory. Other data requires medium access (hours), such as the data needed to bill customers for goods ordered or the issuance of a production schedule to a factory. Still other data, such as sales history files or inactive customer accounts, is only accessed periodically (days and weeks). The job of the MIS designer is to balance the system needs for data with the following constraints:

- Capacity
- Speed
- Cost

Figure 5.7 indicates the relative capacity, speeds, and costs of the different storage devices. As can be seen, there are obvious trade-offs between the three elements; for example, main memory is more expensive than a drum, which in turn is more expensive than a disk. These trade-offs usually force a hierarchical storage structure where a combination of storage elements is used.

Main memory is the only true random access device, for every piece of data can be obtained in exactly the same time—there is no minimum or maximum. However, main memory is expensive and has limited capacity. The illustration indicates a purchase price of $264,000 for slightly over half a million bytes of information, or a cost of $503,000 per million bytes. It has a 2-microsecond access time. Bulk memory falls into the same category, although one trades access time in order to obtain added capacity at a lower cost. Drum storage is next on the list and offers more capacity at lower cost per million bytes but with much higher access time than main memory. The average access-time factor in Fig. 5.7 is based on main memory illustrating that bulk memory requires twice the access time of main memory, while high-capacity drum requires 1250 times the access time of main memory. Disk is the principal medium for storing the bulk of today's MIS files. Although the average access time is much higher than either drum or main memory, it is fast enough to satisfy the majority of demands for data file access. Tape is still the workhorse of many computer systems, but its slow average access time (its access time is astronomical when compared to main memory or even disk) limits its use to batch operations and the storage of historical and backup data. Also, disk storage has now come down in cost to where it is about the same cost per million bytes as tape.

Microfilm is another storage media that is not listed on Figure 5.7 but that can be utilized for historical, infrequently accessed data, where machine retrieval is not required. Computer Output Microfilm devices (COM) can produce microfilm from tape records, but once the data is placed on microfilm, there is no way for the computer to retrieve it—it must be done manually.

As the designer matches his data access and capacity needs against the information contained in Figure 5.7, he may see the need for system solutions that are not ideal but that are far less costly than the ideal solution. For example, Pareto's law, which has been defined earlier, has a strong influence in system design. Utilizing the Pareto principle, the designer has the option of optimizing the system toward those transactions that occur most frequently. If the application is credit checking, a drum may be employed to hold the credit status of the 20 percent of the customers who account for 80 percent of the activity (as determined by historical analysis). The other 80 percent may be carried on slower-speed storage or may be printed out each week (since there is minimum activity, a daily status probably is not necessary) to be used on an exception basis. This process is of course slower than being able to access the computer file directly, but it is certainly cheaper and may be a most logical system compromise.

There are obvious advantages in maintaining all files on a single storage medium. Duplication of data and the need to update several files when transactions occur are avoided. The considerations of linking the various files and ensuring that they properly communicate with each other are materially lessened when

Characteristics	Main memory	Bulk memory	Drum		Disk		Tape	
			Low/med. capacity	High capacity	Low/med. capacity	High capacity	Low speed	High speed
Cost (purchase price in thousands of dollars)	$264	$94	$230	$183	$24	$61	$16	$26
Capacity (in millions of bytes)	0.525	1.0	5.4	11.2	30.0	200.0	22.0	44.0
Cost per million bytes (in thousands of dollars)	$503	$94	$42.6	$16.3	$.800	$.305	$.728	$.590
Average access time	2 micro-seconds	4 micro-seconds	2.5 milli-seconds	5.0 milli-seconds	50 milli-seconds	30 milli-seconds	3.2 minutes	1.2 minutes
Average access time	1	2	1,250	2,500	25,000	15,000	1,600,000	600,000

Fig. 5.7 Cost, capacity and access time of data storage media

the single storage medium is utilized. However, the cost considerations of storage devices have precluded the single medium concept. Although one medium usually predominates in an installation, most MIS developers utilize the hierarchical storage concept. The system ideal has always been for billions of characters of direct access storage at the cost of magnetic-tape storage, but this situation has failed to materialize. However, the cost situation has improved dramatically in the past decade and future developments point to a continued improvement.

Figure 5.8 illustrates the storage medium that, historically at least, has been most utilized for the listed system need. System software is usually resident in main memory at execution time, although less frequently used subroutines may be stored on high-speed drums, which can be rapidly accessed when required. Application software, operating the productive programs themselves, must obviously be in main memory when being executed; however, subroutines can be stored and called from drum or even from disk in certain operating modes. Tables and indexes required to locate data on disks are generally stored on drums (sometimes in main memory and less often on disk) because of the frequency of reference. If the tables and indexes are stored on disk, two accesses are required to obtain data. Various files are stored on a combination of disk, tape, and microfilm, depending on the system trade-offs described earlier.

System need	Memory	Drum	Disk	Tape	Microfilm
System software	X	X			
Application software	X	X	X		
Tables and file indexes	X	X			
Fast access time files (inquiry)		X	X		
Fast access time files (transaction)			X		
Medium access time files (batch)			X	X	
Low access time files (batch)				X	
Historical medium/high activity files				X	
Historical low activity files				X	X

Fig. 5.8 Typical media for software and file storage

Data Base Software

The advent of direct access files and storage hierarchy needs pose problems for conventional data processing techniques. Demands of short lead time, one time, or irregularly required reports, requests for data from several files, the need for predicting future management needs all pose quite a challenge, for few managers can look ahead and predict with any degree of certainty what they will need in the way of information. It is difficult enough to get a clear picture of what information management wants today. This uncertainty is often discovered by a system analyst once he develops a system and produces a report that he thought was the one the manager said he needed and then finds that it is not what the manager wanted at all. The only way the system analyst can improve the situation is to follow the precept, "Don't give the manager what he *said* he wanted but what he *meant* he wanted." Needless to say, this situation presents a real problem for MIS designers.

Conventional methods of file design and acquisition have not been responsive (turnaround time for requests for data have been weeks when it should have been days), have not been flexible enough to cope with the inevitable business changes that affect information systems, and have placed too great a burden on the system analyst's time. I would like to make a point about system flexibility. Many systems are built around a file structure that is embedded in each and every program written to process or access that file. This means that each time the file changes, the programs utilizing that file must also be changed. For example, the Social Security Administration had to modify hundreds of existing programs when a change in social security benefits affected the file structure of recipients. The result cost hundreds of thousands of dollars. This situation could have been avoided had the file structure not been embedded in each program using the file. The interleaving of file structure and programs has been a major contribution to high reprogramming costs and inflexibility to changing conditions. Data base software solves this problem by utilizing a common file description interface between the program and the data file as shown in the diagram below.

An example will illustrate how the separation of files and programs facilitates change. A change occurs in the data file; for example, a company's product line may expand to the point where a five-digit item number is needed where a four-digit number previously sufficed. If there is no common file description serving as the link between the many programs that utilize the data (in this case, program 1 and program 2) and the data itself, each and every reference to that file within each program must be altered. Because of the magnitude of the change, and to ensure that all data references are flagged, program retesting and check-out are required. With the file descriptor, only the description itself is changed to indicate that the full size of the item number is now five digits. The data file, of course, must be updated to change the item numbers from four digits to five. Data base software has caught the attention of MIS designers because its purpose is to resolve the problems described. Data base software attacks the problem with two

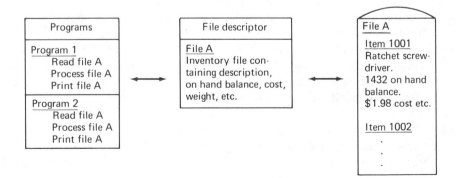

major techniques: (a) file structures to increase the usefulness, flexibility, responsiveness to change, and accessibility of data and (b) data base languages to facilitate ease of access to the data base for managers, system analysts, clerical workers, and programmers.

File Structure

The functions performed on data are shown in the diagram below. Data base software can materially aid the organizing, updating, processing, retrieval and reporting of data; it has little impact on the first two steps of data classification and collection. Data classification involves the establishment of a numbering and coding system for the data. This is an entire study area itself and it deserves

a good deal of attention. The coding system must facilitate the end use of the data and must also provide for an efficient use of the hardware storage devices previously described. Questions of sequencing, alpha versus numeric classification, open or closed identifiers are all factors that must be considered in arriving at the most feasible classification scheme. Acquisition involves the initial collection and conversion of the existing medium onto magnetic media (drum, disk, or tape). It can be a most costly and time-consuming effort. The source data collection devices listed in Figure 5.2 are utilized for this purpose. While continued updating of the file is a recurring cost, the initial gathering, conversion, and buildup of the data base are one-time, nonrecurring costs.

The purpose of the file structure element of data base software is to facilitate the functions of data organization, updating, processing, and retrieval. A key characteristic is to allow cross-indexing or the chaining of related items so that they can be retrieved in a manner consistent with application and user needs. In simple sequential file structures, the information concerning a particular inventory item is stored on an inventory file while the information concerning a particular customer is stored on a customer file. An additional open-order file will list the detail of each customer order that has not been delivered. This file combines information (actually duplicates it) from both the customer file and the inventory file. Although perhaps tolerable under batch sequential approaches, this method is not feasible either from an economical point of view or from a time-demand basis on systems utilizing direct access storage. Features of data base software allow data to be stored once on a direct access file with the appropriate elements linked or chained for rapid access. Storage duplication is thus avoided. For example, Figure 5.9 indicates two files of nonredundant data, one an inventory file indexed on item number and the second a customer file indexed on customer number.

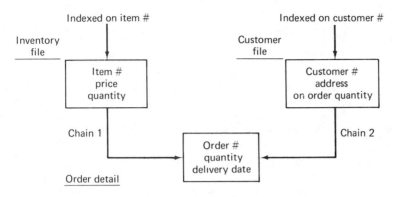

Fig. 5.9 Example of file linkage

The purpose of this example is to give the reader some feeling for the complexity of file design—the need to access information by different keys and indexes and the need to link together files and information. The subject of data base management is a far-reaching one that deserves in-depth study and analysis on its own. This section serves only to point out the degree of difficulty in maintaining, updating, and retrieving information from a central data base.

The data base system establishes a chain that provides a link to all the orders for a particular item while at the same time linking that same order data to the relevant customer record. By utilizing these chaining techniques, the file can be reorganized, alternate chains can be developed, and updates can be made with minimum effort and program reworking. In addition, the system provides the ability to express associations between different files without redundant data storage.

File retrieval is aided by a technique of multiple indexing that allows data access by any of several keys. Figure 5.10 is an example of a payroll file where multiple indexing is desired. The requirement is to set up an employee information file in such a way that data can be retrieved by employee number or by employee with particular job codes or with specified length of service. The illustration shows a sample file with four employees indexed by employee number, job code, and length of service.

The indexes consist of key values that occur in the file, together with record addresses of records containing the values. It is apparent that retrieval by any of the three keys—employee number, job code, or years of experience—is equally efficient. In addition, this file structure can handle multiple-condition retrievals very efficiently. An inquiry requesting all employees who have 2 years experience at job code 12 can be handled by comparing the lists of addresses for job code 12 and 2 years experience and finding equalities; in this case, the record at address 30 is the only one that meets both conditions.

A more pertinent example would be a banking customer file where it is desirable to link savings, loan, and deposit accounts by individual, to be able to access the information by one of several keys, including customer account number

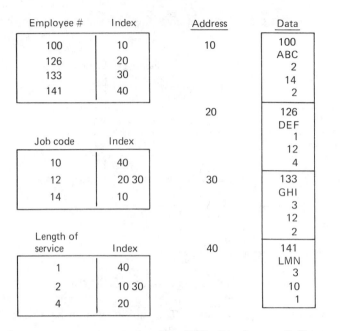

Employee #	Index
100	10
126	20
133	30
141	40

Job code	Index
10	40
12	20 30
14	10

Length of service	Index
1	40
2	10 30
4	20

Address	Data
10	100 ABC 2 14 2
20	126 DEF 1 12 4
30	133 GHI 3 12 2
40	141 LMN 3 10 1

Record format

Employee #
Name
Salary code
Job code
No. years experience

Fig. 5.10 Sample payroll file

or name, and to retrieve data such as savings accounts with over $1000 or accounts with no activity for 60 days or longer. The file structuring element of data base software enables the system designer to accomplish these requirements in an efficient and economical manner.

Data Base Languages

The goal of a computer language can be stated simply. Computers comprehend and respond to the binary numbering system whereas humans comprehend and respond to the English language and the decimal numbering system. The purpose of a language is to allow the human to communicate with the computer in a way that is most efficient for him, as well as being easy to learn. The problem is compounded by the fact that a wide range and class of users of computer processing exist. The scope is increased when management information systems are considered. Users include the following:

- Programmers   Assembly and Compiler Language
- System Analysts
- Clerical Personnel   Free-Form Data Base Language
- Operating Management
- Middle Management   Structured Data Base Language
- Top Management

Each group has different job functions and different skill and capability levels. The manner in which each would like to communicate with the computer differs;

in fact, some would prefer not to communicate at all. Languages such as Assembly and Compiler (COBOL and Fortran) have been developed with the programmer and system analyst in mind. Data base languages have been developed to cut down the turnaround time for information requests. The language has been built in consort with the file structure such that either direct on-line access or batch off-line access can be facilitated. The simplicity of the language makes it feasible for noncomputer people to use, thus breaking down the need to go through a hierarchy of information middlemen to attain a computer report. The free–form language appears to be better suited for clerical people and lower levels of management, whereas the structured version is better suited to upper levels of management.

The free-form language looks as follows:

FILE IS SALES
IF AREA EQUALS 100 AND ON-ORDER IS OVER $1000
SORT ON CUSTOMER—NAME
PRINT CUSTOMER—NAME, ITEM NUMBER, QUANTITY, VALUE

This indicates that the user desires to interrogate the sales file, find customers in a particular geographical area with on-order sales over $1000, and obtain a report showing by customer name, the quantity and value of items on order. The structured form is shown in the diagram. The form is normally a self–instructional one

RETRIEVAL REQUEST FORM				
File: Sales				
Field name	Condition	Value	Connector	Report fields
Area	=	$100	&	Customer Name
On Order	>	$1,000		Item Number
				Quantity
				Value

having a preprinted explanation of the steps required to complete it. The difference between the free form and the structured form is that the former language has a more open format, is more English-language oriented, and requires more training to utilize effectively. The structured language is self-teaching and is better for intermittent or sporadic users who do not have the time to learn a language that, if used often enough, may prove more flexible and powerful.

Chapter 6 will explore the concept of the "keyed-in" executive who employs a remote terminal to communicate directly with the computer. Whether the executive writes the program or pushes the terminal buttons himself, or whether his secretary or a staff assistant does it, will probably be a matter, as it is now, of individual background, education, and management style. It is important, however, to have a system that can respond faster and more effectively. Data base languages tied to data-base file-structure techniques are extremely important tools in accomplishing this end. There is no question that a management information system is built on a central data base that is built on data base software that is built on hierarchical hardware storage devices. Together the data base hardware and software form a vital technological MIS foundation.

A variety of data base software systems on the market today can be purchased or rented on a monthly basis from a computer manufacturer or an independent software house. Although the listing below is not a complete one, it does indicate the major offerings of data base software. The systems differ in capability, basic design, architecture, retrieval language, and cost to the user. The listing itself should indicate the scope and complexity of the data base software field. The reader can refer to the Codasyl System Committee Technical Report of May 1971 (see bibliography at end of chapter) or to the vendors listed below for comparisons of various data base software systems.

IBM
   IMS (Information Management System)
   GIS (Generalized Information System)
   DBOMP (Data Base Organization & Maintenance Processor)

Honeywell
   IDS (Integrated Data Store)
   OS/200 Data Base

Burroughs
   Forte

Univac
   DMS/1100 (Data Management System)

Control Data Corp.
   Mars III
   Mars VI

Xerox Data Systems
   Data Management System

CinCom Systems, Inc. Informatics
   Total
   Mark IV

Computer Sciences Corp.
   Cogent II

Programming Methods Inc.
   (Operation Division of GTE Information Systems, Inc.)
   Score III

COMMUNICATION HARDWARE AND SOFTWARE

An important system design consideration is the degree of communication processing planned now and expected in the future. Viewed in its broadest sense, communication covers the entire area of getting information from computer memory and data storage devices to the ultimate user. In its more accepted sense, it means receiving and sending data over communication lines from remote sites to the central computer site. The broad and narrow sense of communication processing are related because direct input of data from remote sites can preclude or reduce the need for on-site input equipment. This is also true on the output side.

Most companies operate over a geographical area; some have salesmen in major United States cities; others have sales and procurement offices throughout the country; and still others have separate manufacturing plants or warehouses located far apart. In many cases, the people in these outlying offices either supply the crucial input data or receive crucial output data, or do both. Therefore it behooves system designers to broaden their design perspective when considering input and output devices and communication processing. The concept of turn-around time must take this into account. Turnaround time must mean total turn-around time, defined as providing the final document or data in the hands of the user in the time frame he requires it. In the order processing situation, the ultimate purpose of quick order processing is to get the order to the customer when he needs it. The time requirement is not met completely by being able to process the order through the computer in 12 seconds. The order then must reach the ware-house, where physical items comprising it are picked, loaded, and shipped to the waiting customer. If the 12-second order spends 2 days getting to the warehouse, the system might just as well utilize the sequential approach. Similarly, it makes little sense to provide a visual display in a sales manager's office where he can access order, salesman, and customer status in a matter of seconds if the file is updated once a month. Suffice to say, total turnaround time is the crucial element, and communication processing plays a key role in determining total time.

Similar to on-site management information systems that are directed mainly at lower levels of management, most communication–oriented MIS's are directed at logistic systems that support operating and, less frequently, middle manage-ment. Thus remote order processing systems, inventory control systems, savings bank systems, and hospital accounting systems are the rule. Relatively few middle and top executives see printed computer output directly, much less utilize on–line terminals. Their subordinates utilize computer output but add further analysis and summary content before information is reviewed with the top executives. This subject will be covered in more detail in Chapter 6 when the influence of MIS on management is explored.

It is my opinion that the hardware technology is available to transmit data to a manager's office in a format suitable for his comprehension. The lagging ele-ments have been the software and system know-how required to put the hardware and software elements together. Another reason why management-directed com-munication systems have lagged is because of the rather intangible benefits when compared to the benefits offered by high volume, repetitive, and well-understood applications built around customer, inventory, and sales files.

Communication Hardware

Communication processing takes many forms and shapes. The proliferation of communication equipment and devices makes this area a rather difficult one to comprehend. There are many stages, ranging from the very simple remote sales office that transmits sales orders on paper tape by means of a teletype station, to the nation-wide network of hundreds of remote stations in two-way communica-tion through visual and audio display units direct to manager's offices.

Two stages of communication systems, direct access inquiry response and direct access on-line processing, will be described.

Direct Access Inquiry/Response

Having data in random storage facilitates immediate access to the data and the development of a fast response system. Examples of inquiries are credit checking, order reservation, inventory status, or a customer request for information. A salesman in a remote spot wants to know if he can fill an order for a particular item. He queries the computer and, in a matter of a few seconds, the computer interrogates the direct-access inventory file and reports back the answer. Similarly, a person's credit can be checked from a remote spot. Normally the computer is processing the daily work load, is interrupted whenever there is an inquiry, processes the inquiry, and returns to its main-line function. The inquiries can have two levels of priority: those that must be handled now and those that can be handled later. The nonpriority items can be batched and processed later.

The direct access approach affords a programmed dialogue between the inquirer and the computer that can have significant benefits. The following interchange indicates the advantages of this approach:

Inquirer: My customer wants a 4387A gauge.

Computer: Please recheck the order number. I don't show such a number.

Inquirer: My customer wants a 4378A gauge.

Computer: Out of stock. Order can be filled in two weeks.
          Can I suggest a substitute?

Inquirer: Yes.

Computer: How about a 4378B gauge? It differs only in color.

Inquirer: Customer will accept. Please reserve.

Computer: Order accepted.

The computer is programmed to check for the routine types of error, such as the preceding inversion of numbers, and to suggest alternate solutions to problems, such as the substitute item that is similar to the one ordered. The substitution logic must, of course, be preprogrammed. Programmed instruction in schools is patterned after this type of dialogue; the student answers questions and, based on the answer, the computer either moves on to the next question or looks back to display an additional series of questions emphasizing the concept the student has missed. This tutorial method of instruction is a sound approach provided (and this is a big proviso) that the instruction logic is properly programmed. This point is also true in using this method in a business environment. If the programmer developing the decision logic suggests a substitute item that has completely different characteristics than the one ordered, the system soon will fall apart.

Direct Access On-Line Processing

This stage in communication processing may seem similar to the previous one but there is an important distinction. The previous stage involved two separate independent job streams; the inquiry programs were not linked to the production programs taking place in the background. In this model, the inquiry program and the background jobs are interdependent and operate on common files. This stage of development is distinguished from the previous stage by its greater degree of implementation complexity. Prior to this step, an inquiry entered the system and was answered; however, it did not simultaneously trigger the processing. For example, the salesman wanted to know the inventory status of a gauge, but this did not initiate the order processing cycle for that particular customer. However, with direct access on-line processing, the order can be initiated by the remote point and the inventory record reduced by the order amount, so that other systems now using the inventory file will receive the adjusted balance. Thus the programs are interdependent. This appears a most desirable development but serious implementation problems must be overcome. Because one of many remote sites can initiate action that can affect other applications, the proper interfacing and control techniques must be utilized. It is possible for a salesman to enter a large order (possibly in error) that triggers the immediate scheduling of a large production lot. Because of the high priority placed on this order, the production schedule is changed to accommodate the order. The snowballing effect of erroneously entered transactions in an interdependent on-line communications system becomes painfully evident. Needless to say, the proper checks and balances must be established before embarking on such a system approach.

Although the problems are difficult, this stage of communication processing represents the high point of information systems. A well-planned and implemented direct access system embodies the flexibility and dynamic nature required by fast-moving companies. It represents a paper-work business system that indeed accurately reflects the physical operation of the company. Here is the way such a system works.

1. A worker reports the completion of a particular job by means of the data collection network.

2. He is told the next job (Job 43) on which to work.

3. Job 43 was substituted for the previous one (Job 86) in the work queue because the foreman inputted to the system, just a minute ago, that the machine needed to accomplish Job 86 was out of operation.

4. The system indicates a maintenance work order that is printed on the remote printer in the plant engineering department.

5. At the same time, an important customer indicates that an alternate supplier has failed to meet a delivery and he needs a particular part within

a week. An inquiry from a remote site checks the availability of raw materials and tools to machine the particular part, receives an affirmative reply, and initiates the order at that point.

This interaction of subsystems is the key to a responsive and dynamic management information system. It is a goal to shoot at, but it cannot be instituted overnight. The old cliché of "too many cooks spoil the broth" is valid here in that a system of this type involves the interaction of many people representing different functions of the business. If not properly controlled, these cooks can indeed have a material effect on the resultant product. Consequently, most companies instituting such a system have utilized a phasing approach that recognizes the normal learning curve in which the company gradually builds the technical capabilities and the working environment to implement the direct access on-line system.

Communication Software

Communication-oriented operating systems are needed to implement the type of systems described above effectively. A computer can be viewed in its basic form as being similar to a production-line machine center in a manufacturing plant. The objective of the machine center is to turn out a quality product in the most economical manner, and a computer center has the same goal. The product (finished goods) of the computer is meaningful printed or visual output, while the input (raw material) consists of cards, paper tapes, keyboard input, and the like. The computer center also has in-process inventory in the form of intermediate data tapes or transactions stored on disk. Thus there is an analogy between the production center and the computer center. To expand on the analogy, the computer operating system is similar to the production scheduling system and the computer operating staff is similar to the machine tool operators who feed the machine and ensure that it remains in productive operation with minimal interjob interruption or down time. Just as the production center operator is assisted by numerically controlled machine tools that automatically position and direct the machine's actions, so the computer operator is assisted by a computer operating system that automatically runs a series of programs without manual intervention. The computer operating system has two major functions: (a) to provide an optimum schedule of computer program operation based on the job to be run and the resources available for its operation, and (b) to monitor the execution phase, ensuring that the resources continue to be properly allocated, based on priority of job execution, and that changes that were unforseen at scheduling time can be added and handled on a dynamic basis.

An operating system consists of several parts. Figure 5.11 illustrates six operating system modules. It also indicates a program or job stack, usually stored on a drum or disk, from which programs are loaded into memory as called upon for execution as operating programs. The six modules perform the following functions:

1. *Job scheduler.* Given the available peripheral and storage devices and memory, the job scheduler allocates these resources to particular programs based on a stated priority.

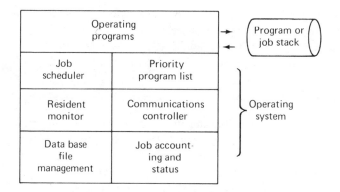

Fig. 5.11 Operating system modules

2. *Priority program list.* The list of active programs or jobs to be executed. Whenever an additional program is added to the active program stack, the job scheduler recalculates program priority and resource allocation.

3. *Resident monitor.* The real control center of the operating system, the communications link between all elements of the system; initiates the loading of programs into and out of memory from the program or job stack.

4. *Communications controller.* Provides control over communications functions and the flow of data associated with the functions.

5. *Data base file management.* Functions as the interface between the active programs and the data utilized by the programs.

6. *Job accounting and status.* Provides facilities to account for the resource time utilized by each program and to present a dynamic status of resources being utilized.

Figure 5.12 shows how an operating system would work on four specific jobs. This example shows memory being partitioned into four segments. In reality, there could be *n* number of segments, depending on the memory size and peripheral/storage/terminal resources. Program A is a sales forecast program that employs a good amount of mathematical processing. It utilizes a sales forecast or sales history file; calculates trends, past forecast errors, and mean absolute deviations; and builds a new forecast file. Program B is a communication program in which a number of remote sales offices can interrogate a direct access file and get the latest status on particular open orders in which the customer is interested. Program C involves printing an inventory analysis report from magnetic tape that has been produced in a previous run. Program D is an executive action program that allows executives using remote terminals to interact and initiate reports based on an analysis of the central data base. They may well be utilizing the data base language described in the previous section.

Thus we have four independent computer programs, each using its own peripherals but sharing the power of the computer's memory and processing unit. This is a most efficient and economical way to operate. It is a practical way to operate even if you do not have a communication application. In this type of computer processing, the operating system allocates resources to obtain the most efficient peripheral mix and job schedule. It then facilitates and controls the simultaneous time sharing of the central processor's memory and processing unit.

Design Considerations in a Communication System

As mentioned, the real limiting items in the use of communication systems are the software and system know-how necessary to utilize the hardware and software. Communication systems are complex, whereas on-site systems utilize a manageable array of input–output devices. A multitude of additional elements must be considered in a communication system. For example, the system designer must decide what type of communication line service and what speed lines are required. Here is a listing of the basic Bell System offerings:

Common user services (dial network)
Low speed   TWX
Medium speed   Voice
                    Data Phone
                    WATS
                    Data Access Arrangement
                    Communication System Interconnection
High speed   Picturephone
                    Data Phone 50
Dedicated (private line) services (channels and terminals)
Low speed   Private line teletypewriter
Medium speed   Voice
                    Alternate voice/data
                    Data
High speed   TELPAK using 5000 Type channels and terminals
                    48 KC using 8000 Type channels and terminals
Dedicated (private line) services (channels only)
Low speed   1000 Type channels
Medium speed   2000 Type channels
                    3000 Type channels
High speed   None

Considerations that must be reflected in selection of transmission media are as follows:

1. Line characteristics
   Noise, both "natural" and man-made (impulse)
   Distortion of signals
   Switch elements
   Fading
   Propagation delay

2. Error rates
   Error-detection procedures
   Error-correction procedures
   Check digits and parity bits
   Retransmission
   Redundancy checks

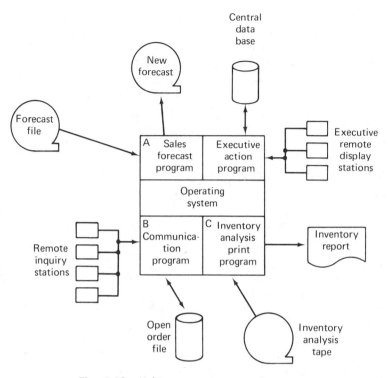

Fig. 5.12 Multi-programming operating system

3. Line speeds
   1200, 1800, 2000, 2400, 3600, 4800, 9600 bits per second

4. Modem speeds
   45.5, 110, 150, 300, 1000, 1200, 1400, 1800, 2000, 3600, 4800, 5400, 19,200, 40,800, 50,000, 230,400.

5. Data transmission codes
   8 bit EBCDIC
   7 bit USASCII
   6 bit BCD
   5 bit Baudot
   4 of 8 bit code
   2 of 5 bit code

6. Fallback and recovery procedures

7. Test plan and systems cutover

8. Volume, peaking, and queuing considerations

9. Relative costs: switched, leased, half-duplex, duplex

10. Regulatory considerations

This list is by no means exhaustive, but it should indicate the complexities of installing communication systems. Management should precede with caution in installing such systems. The payoffs are there, but there is a high requirement for experienced and capable system designers who know the communication area, are aware of cost versus benefit analysis and who can apply the technical, economic, and operational feasibility criteria discussed in Chapter 4. If the capability is not present, it may be wise to forego communication processing in favor of improving and enhancing the on-site management information system—to build and refine the central data base so that when communication is added to the system, the data it accesses is meaningful and worth transmitting in real time.

SCIENTIFIC AND BUSINESS APPLICATION SOFTWARE

Management information systems have long gestation periods. It has been stated that they take from 3 to 5 years to get going and then the system is never really completed; demands for additional reports and new applications continue to exceed the supply of competent system analysts and programmers to implement them. Consequently, it is almost mandatory to utilize techniques and system approaches that others have successfully pioneered and installed. The "not-invented-here" syndrome has no place in MIS development. Practical MIS designers continually study and analyze the scientific and business application software available from computer manufacturers software houses and other support companies. Although it takes a skilled eye to judge whether a particular application package or scientific system can be applied and made part of a company's MIS, the benefits in cost and time savings can be quite significant. For example, several excellent sales-forecasting systems that cover various proven and accepted forecasting techniques are on the market. It would seem unwise for a company to expend the effort to develop its own forecasting system, for it is a complex mathematical process and the degree of improvement probably would not justify the cost of implementation. This section will discuss the potential benefits from utilizing (a) scientific or operations research type of software aids and (b) general business application software.

Scientific Software Aids

The need for utilizing operations research techniques to aid in the important strategic planning applications has already been discussed. This category of application has been elusive to computerization, but the benefits and potential are such that it warrants serious attention from the MIS designer. The know-how required to implement effectively Operations Research (OR) applications is usually developed over a long period of time; there is necessary learning curve. OR is usually most valuable where decisions that require manifold interrelationships among voluminous elements of data must be made, where there is a high degree of uncertainty of market or production activity, and where there are competitive and business pressures for timely decision and action. It is true that many OR problems can be solved without a computer, without MIS, and without a central data base. However, as someone has stated, this assertion is similar to someone stating that the problem of traveling from Los Angeles to Boston can be resolved by traveling on horseback, and that the advent of jet planes is merely adding a frill. What this assertion fails to recognize is that the objective of most people traveling across the country includes such factors as speed, safety, comfort, and cost, which are as equally or even more important than just getting there. The analogy holds for OR and the application of the computer-to-problem resolution.

The employment of scientific software can materially aid the solution of OR problems. However, it should be remembered that just as a software system does not help in the design of systems, so scientific software aids cannot establish application priorities, select these problems that represent the highest payoff area, or even formulate the problem to be solved. However, with experience has come the analysis and categorization of different classes of problems. Scientific packages have been developed that help structure the problem and facilitate problem testing, simulation, and eventual solution. Figure 5.13 describes six classes of operations research techniques. The function, effect, and software tools available are listed for each technique. The important point is that this class of software is highly mathematically oriented and foreign to system designers and programmers of business-oriented applications. The user is generally obliged to utilize the software written by a computer manufacturer or software house or else he must tie into a time-sharing facility that specializes in scientific problem solving. The latter route may be the most feasible when costs and capabilities are considered.

For illustrative purposes, a brief description will indicate the benefits of simulation in solving a business problem. Although the use of OR techniques is not widespread, the particular problem shown is typical of OR application. Figure 5.14 illustrates the general steps that are necessary to solve an OR problem. The first step is to analyze the problem, whether it be the balancing of production machine centers, the location of a new warehouse, or the optimum sales mix of products. The next step is to isolate the key elements or those factors that are significant in optimizing or minimizing a function. Optimizing usually involves increasing profits, while minimizing usually involves reducing costs. Next a mathematical model is constructed that expresses the interrelationship of the variables (elements) and simulates the effect of different combinations of them. The model is then tested (using computer simulation software) and the results measured against desired standards or against previous simulations. If the results are not satisfactory, the model (variables) is modified and resimulated. This iteration continues until the model's performance is satisfactory. Actual conditions and facilities are changed to conform to the model. The model is thus reflected in actual operation; and if the computer model was a mirror of the real world, the results should equal those obtained by the simulation.

The following example depicts the application of these steps in OR to a problem involving warehouse dock facilities.

The Problem

A prominent Midwest department store chain supplies its retail outlets from three warehouses located in the greater Chicago area. A series of changing conditions (including increased traffic) led management to question whether the trans-

Operations research technique	Function	Effect	Software tools available
Mathematical programming	Utilize complex mathematics for solving engineering/research problems.	Computational processing is performed at electronic speeds. Special languages and subroutines facilitate expression and solution of problems.	Fortran — language for expressing mathematical equations and formulas. Basic — fortran like language optimized for remote inquiry and problem solving. Math library - precoded routines e.g., numerical analysis, interpolation, exponential and log functions and matrix analysis. Statistics library e.g., media, variance, T-ratio, standard deviation, binomial distribution, random number generator and curve fitting.
	Analysis of quantitative and statistical data for such applications as market research, sales forecasting, inventory control, research and quality control.	Improves accuracy and validity of decision-making by providing more sophisticated mathematical analysis.	
Linear programming	Mathematical technique for solving problems of competing demands for limited resources where there are a great number of interracting variables.	Resolves complex problems that can only be approximated or guesstimated by conventional means. Increases accuracy and improves decision-making in broad class of decisions.	Linear programming (LP) packages assist in problem structuring and formulation and then provide high speed computing power to efficiently produce solutions based on alternate decision rules.
Network analysis	Scheduling, costing and status reporting of major projects.	Improves planning, scheduling and implementing of complex projects comprised of multiple events and activities. Permits continuous evaluation of projects progress to increase probabilities of on-time, on-cost performance.	PERT (program evaluation and review technique) and CPM (critical path method) - software systems for processing large networks of events and activities producing a variety of computer reports to pin point schedule slippages, critical events and action needed to get back on schedule.
Queuing Theory	Solving problems where it is desirable to minimize the costs and/or time associated with waiting lines or queues.	Improves management ability to improve operations like check out counters, receiving docks, machine centers or turnpike toll stations.	General purpose simulators aid the construction and development of complex simulation models. The simulator has the ability to produce random numbers to test various activity patterns and optimize the use of resources.
Simulation	Determines the impact of decisions using hypothetical or historical data in lieu of incurring the expense of risk of trying out decisions on line data.	Business managers can test and project the effects of decisions on a wide variety of operational areas thus ensuring optimal results when the decisions and policies are out into practice.	General purpose simulators as above.

Fig. 5.13 Operations research techniques

portation and warehousing situation could not be handled in a more economical manner and still maintain (or improve) the delivery cycle.

Problem Analysis. A study was initiated to analyze the existing traffic flow at the three warehouses and the results projected to that expected with increased volume. The study involved a sample 7-week period in the spring. The effect of seasonal variations was projected from the basic data using historical company records. It was discovered that the number of trucks increased only 5 percent during the Christmas rush but that the number of pieces handled increased 50 percent. In addition, truck-servicing time was studied and found to vary within certain bounds, depending on factors such as size of truck and type of merchan-

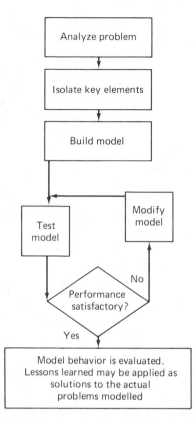

Fig. 5.14 Steps in operations research

dise. A service time pattern was found to be a combination of a fixed-time interval and a variable-time interval, depending on the number of pieces being handled.

Isolate Key Elements. An initial consideration was the addition of dock facilities necessary to handle the increased truck traffic. The additional dock facilities could be realistically planned if three factors were known: the number of trucks, their arrival time, and the time to service each truck. In addition, economic considerations were involved in the problem. The trucks were leased so that waiting time had a definite cost associated with it. However, additional dock facilities, although cutting down waiting time, necessitated a considerable monetary investment. The problem of cost factors in economic conflict with each other and the waiting-line principle is a classic case for the application of simulation and queuing theory.

Building the Model. Although the number of truck arrivals had certain patterns and frequencies—for example, an average of 105 trucks arrived in the morning while 65 arrived in the afternoon—there was a chance relationship that precluded a simple arithmetic solution. A new wrinkle was added to the simulation and queuing theory solution—the use of the "Monte Carlo" method. The word Monte Carlo implies the presence of chance. Using the frequency distributions produced by the studies as boundaries, the Monte Carlo technique randomly selected a time of arrival and a service time for each of the arriving trucks. This is where the power of the computer comes into play. The computer simulates a day's operation by totaling the waiting time and length of queue of each truck serviced that day. The computer runs through a full-year's operation, pulling off random numbers to simulate actual conditions while assuming a varying number of docks. These iterations are repeated to the point where computer output indicates to management the trade-offs of waiting time and investment in new dock facilities. This then forms the basis for the most economical solution to the problem.

Solution. There was a strong predisposition that five warehouse docks were required because of the increase in volume that occurred in the last two years and the delay in loading trucks that was being experienced. However, various simulation showed that if the company could improve the time to load trucks by 20 percent, four docks would handle the volume increased expected over the next 2-year period. Automatic palletizing equipment was installed to increase loading efficiency. As a result, waiting time was reduced and the added capital expenditure for a fifth dock (a very expensive proposition) was avoided.

General Business Application Software

As mentioned, a management information system consists of a multitude of application subsystems, which in turn consist of other subsystems. It is like a set of building blocks all coming together and fitting into the overall framework. If an MIS designer can obtain certain of these subsystem building blocks and use them as "prefab" components, then he is that much ahead. However, he must ensure that they do indeed fit into the framework. An MIS is built around a central data base. Thus the "prefab" modules selected must be flexible enough to operate or be modified to operate from the company's own central data base. There comes a trade-off point when the effort to modify equals the work to build from scratch. A careful analysis of general-application software offerings must proceed an intent to incorporate them into a system plan. Application software can provide design concepts and, in some cases, actual coded systems based on the know-how gained in working with companies involved in applications similar to those being implemented. However, they are not a substitute for determining system goals and objectives, nor do they automatically make data processing operations successful. Figure 5.15 presents a sample listing of the types of application systems that can be purchased in today's market. Each of the packages listed is offered by one or more computer manufacturers and/or software houses.

The benefit of application software can be viewed as follows:

50 days	30 days	20 days
Application analysis and design	Coding and testing	Blending and modifying
50%	30%	20%

General accounting systems

  Accounts receivable
  Accounts payable
  General ledger
  Payroll
  Inventory reporting
  Fixed asset accounting

Banking systems

  Magnetic ink character reading routines
  Proof and transit
  Demand deposit accounting system
  Savings bank data entry system

Hospital/medical

  Patient accounting system
  Personnel administration
  Payroll and general ledger
  Inventory control

Printing/publishing

  Subscription fulfillment
  Computerized typesetting

Utilities

  Customer billing
  Maintenance accounting
  Facilities planning

Retailing

  Sales forecasting
  Retail inventory control
  Credit checking
  Customer billing

Manufacturing systems

  Numerical control
  Bill of material processing
  Net requirements generation
  Inventory control
  Inventory simulator
  Production scheduling
  Sales forecasting

Insurance

  Life insurance new policy issue
  Life insurance daily circle processing
  Life insurance estate planner
  Life insurance reserve calculation
  (above also applies to Fire and
   casualty insurance)

Education

  Student scheduling
  Student administration
  (test scoring, grade reporting,
   placement)
  Computer assisted instruction

Distribution

  Sales order processing
  Inventory control
  Truck scheduling
  Sales forecasting

Government

  Utility billing
  Payroll, personnel administration
  Municipal accounting system

General

  Hotel/motel customer accounting systems
  Legal/medical/education information retrieval system
  Law enforcement systems (stolen auto checking, etc.)
  Stock portfolio analysis

Fig. 5.15 Business application software

Experience has shown that the analysis and design of a system take close to 60 percent of the total job, whereas 40 percent of the job is coding and testing. If we assume that the acquisition of an application package from a third party necessitates 20 percent of the total job for tailoring the package for a specific need, the breakdown becomes 50 percent for analysis and design, 30 percent for coding and testing, and 20 percent for blending and modifying.

Broken down by days, if the total implementation effort is estimated at 100 days, the split would be 50/30/20 days. The break-even analysis for package acquisition involves a refinement of the blending and modifying percentage. If the designer feels that it will take 20 days in this instance versus 80 days if he starts from scratch, he can weigh the 60 days against the cost of buying the package.

An example of a business-application offering is the system called SCHED-

ULER for truck dispatching described below. Note the comment that it can be tailored to suit a particular situation. This factor is most important in application evaluation.

SCHEDULER (see Figure 5.16) is a computer technique for maximizing the efficiency of shipment deliveries. It facilitates the scheduling and routing of trucks from a single point to many destinations—for example, from factory to warehouses, warehouse to stores, or store to homes.

As input, SCHEDULER uses order data consisting of weight and volume of shipment, destination, and the requested time of arrival of the shipment at its destination, plus constraints such as available trucks, travel time, and unloading time. Applying mathematical techniques to this data, SCHEDULER yields assignment sheets that list sizes of trucks to be employed, orders that are to be grouped together, routes to be followed, and times of departure from the shipping terminal. Among the benefits to be derived from SCHEDULER are more profitable use of truck space, reduction of mileage, and, as by-products, improved customer service and more efficient assignment of employees.

SCHEDULER is designed to be linked with existing computerized order processing systems, so as to provide computer efficiency from order to shipment. It has been written as a general-purpose program that may be tailored to the specific requirements of any shipping activity, ranging from those of small independent delivery services to large manufacturing firms.

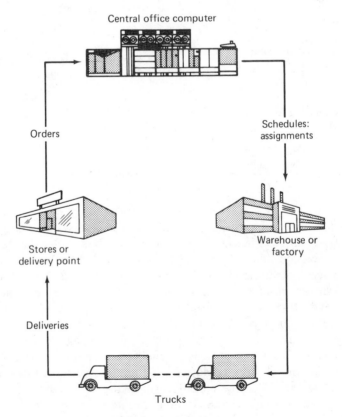

Fig. 5.16 Truck dispatching system

SUMMARY

The chapter began with a definition of computer technology, dividing it into four elements: (a) hardware, (b) system software, (c) application software, and (d) support services. This classification was used to analyze the various elements that provide the technological power of today's management information systems. Three major technological factors were singled out as having prime significance for MIS: (a) central data base hardware and software, (b) communication hardware and software, and (c) business and scientific application software.

The data base hardware included a discussion of the various hierarchical storage elements, including main memory, bulk memory, drum, disk, tape, and microfilm. Data base software centered on a file-structuring subsystem that facilitates data organization, updating, processing, retrieval, and reporting, together with a data-language subsystem that utilizes free form or a structured language to enable various users of the data to access the data base.

Next, the fastest growing segment of the EDP marketplace, communication processing, was discussed. Communication hardware centered on those devices required to support inquiry/response and direct access on-line processing systems. Stress was placed on the important software element, communication–oriented operating systems, which are required for multirun communication applications as well as for conventional batch applications using common memory, central processing units, and storage devices. Considerations in communication system design and implementation concluded the discussion of communication hardware and software.

The third technological factor explored was scientific and business application software. Scientific software aids were classified and defined. Simulation was used to illustrate the basic steps in adapting this technique to solve a typical operation research problem. The potenital benefits of utilizing business application software were then explored. General types of available application packages were listed and a description of a particular package was presented.

Chapters 3 and 4 explored the horizontal and vertical subsystems of MIS. This chapter developed the technological elements that are available to implement the various subsystems. As mentioned, there are three major feasibility elements in establishing priorities for subsystem development—technical, economical, and operational. The reader should now have a better grasp of the considerations in determining technical feasibility. We now focus more directly on management considerations in MIS, the impact of MIS on management, and, conversely, the role management must take to gain maximum benefit from MIS.

STUDY CASETTES

SCHOTTEN MACHINE TOOL

John Roberts, EDP Director for Schotten Machine Tool was pondering what his next move should be. Roberts was appointed director of EDP some two years ago, having had a reputation as an experienced professional who possessed imagination and creativity and was considered one of the real comers in the company and in the EDP industry. He was written up as one of the "bright young men of information" in a prominent business magazine. Roberts gained his reputation by always being in the forefront of technology; the installations he managed always installed the latest equipment on the market. He was a pioneer in on-line disk storage, optical scanning, remote terminals, data base systems, management information systems and had even installed the first graphic terminal for his previous company.

Roberts experience included two year stints with Univac, IBM, RCA, and NCR as well as two to three year assignments at three different companies. Roberts was 40 and grew up with the EDP industry joining Univac in 1952 as a design engineer. His experience ran the gamut from engineering to marketing. He held product planning positions for computer vendors and system management positions for computer users.

Schotten had hired a consultant to review the progress of their EDP operation, because the president and members of top management recently showed concern for the lack of progress in certain crucial application areas. Through a friend of his, Roberts had found out the report to be presented to top management was quite critical of his department. It pointed out that while Schotten had the latest equipment, their use of the equipment was limited and their cost effectiveness left much to be desired. In comparing EDP operating costs with those of similar sized companies with same types of businesses, the analysis indicated Schotten spent 30% more than the next highest cost operation.

Study Questions

1. What do you think Roberts should do?

2. Do you think top management will concur with the report?

3. What are the reasons for the existing EDP situation?

4. What action would you take if you represented Schotten's top management?

RUTGERS ELECTRONICS

The following conversation takes place in the office of the Vice-President of Marketing of a medium-sized electronics company. MM (Modern Manager) in the dialogue below represents the VP of Marketing while TT (Technical Type) represents the Manager of Data Processing.

MM: Let's review the situation briefly to put the problem in perspective. It was a year ago today that I told you I wanted a Cathode Ray Tube display in my office. We're in the electronics business, and I think we should be in the forefront of the people using our products. I indicated I wanted to be able to make inquiries of our customer file to find out the current status of customers, shipments, on order and the like. I asked you when you thought you could have this set up for me and you said six months. Is that correct?

TT: I would have to say that your recollection is basically correct, but I think there are some real mitigating circumstances underlying the problem.

MM: Before you get into that, let me continue for a minute. The terminal was not installed in six months as you indicated but three months later than that. The terminal was hooked up and could communicate with a local time-sharing company's computer and also with an educational institution in the area, but it didn't communicate with our own data base. You indicated we could be ready on a week-to-week basis, but the fact of the matter is that another three months has passed and I still don't have any results. It's quite embarrassing to have people come into the office, ask about the CRT and what I can do with it. Frankly, I usually tell them what I wanted to do with it, and try to mix the tenses so they don't realize it's what I'd like to do and not what I can do. I usually have to make some kind of excuse if they ask me to demonstrate it.

TT: What you say is true and I apologize for the lack of results, but I would like to review the circumstances. You remember when we started out with this project, I told you the terminal itself was the simplest part of our problem—like the iceberg analogy, 10% is visible above the surface (that's the terminal), while 90% is below the surface (that's the customer data base and communications software that provides the data to the terminal). Frankly, we've had one heck of a time developing the customer data base. That's where the problem lies. We had a tape file, and we've had to go to disk to facilitate on-line inquiry. We've also had problems keeping the file current and incorporating the information you wanted as well as the information desired by other parts of the organization.

MM: Are you saying that my demands have been given low priority?

TT: Not exactly, but I think you would agree that the first thing we must do is bill our customers accurately for the products and services they get from us, and then setting up the accounts receivable so that we get the cash.

MM: That may be so, but it seems we should be able to do that type of thing with no trouble at all. When can I use my terminal the way you and I talked about it?

TT: I want to be frank with you because I'm well aware of your impatience and disappointment—I assure you I share your feelings. It's still difficult, despite our experience, to predict when we can have the system operable. You know our business has been growing and changing very rapidly and the minute we think we've got the situation under control, something else breaks that impacts the system—a new sales division is added, or we add a new product line and so on. I've discussed the matter with my systems people, and I think we can reasonably promise you that your CRT can be hooked on-line three months from today.

MM: If that's the situation, take the device out of my office. It's stupid to pay rent on a machine I'm not using. It's an expensive office play toy when you get nothing from it. This time you tell me when you're ready to go; I've lost confidence that we'll ever make it.

Study Questions

1. Do you think this situation is typical?

2. Do you feel TT's explanation of the delay is reasonable?

3. Do you think MM bears some of the blame for the problem?

4. How do you think TT should have handled the situation from the outset?

5. What should be TT's plan of action now?

6. Does MM really need the terminal or is it just an office toy?

BIBLIOGRAPHY

ACKOFF, R. L., and P. RIVETT, *A Manager's Guide to Operations Research.* John Wiley & Sons, New York, 1963.

ALLEN, B., Time Sharing Takes Off. *Harvard Business Review,* March–April, 1969, pp. 128–135.

APPLEBAUM, S., What Does It Take To Go On-Line? *Computer Decisions,* January, 1970, pp. 21–24.

CANNING, R. G., Creating The Corporate Data Base. *EDP Analyzer,* Vol. 8, #'s 2, 3, 4, 5. February–May, 1970.

CANNING, R. G., Using Shared Data Files. *EDP Analyzer,* Vol. 8, #11, November, 1970, 14 pp.

EMSHOFF, J., and R. SISSON, *Design and Use of Computer Simulation Models.* The Macmillan Company, New York, 1970, 302 pp.

FRY, J. P., Managing Data is The Key To MIS. *Computer Decisions,* January, 1971, pp. 6–10.

GRUENBERGER, F. (ed.), *Critical Factors in Data Management.* Prentice-Hall, Inc., Englewood Cliffs, New Jersey, 1969, 146 pp.

HAYES, R. M., Information Retrieval: An Introduction. *Datamation,* March, 1968, pp. 22–26.

JONES, C. J., At Last: Real Computer Power for Decision Makers. *Harvard Business Review,* September–October, 1970, pp. 75–89.

LICKLIDER, J. C. R., *Libraries of the Future.* The MIT Press, Massachusetts Institute of Technology, Cambridge, Mass., 1965.

MARTIN, J., *Telecommunications and the Computer.* Prentice-Hall, Inc., Englewood Cliffs, New Jersey, 1969, 470 pp.

MARTIN, J., *Future Developments in Telecommunications.* Prentice-Hall, Inc., Englewood Cliffs, New Jersey, 1971, 413 pp.

MEIER, R. C., W. T. NEWELL, and H. L. PAZER, *Simulation in Business and Economics.* Prentice-Hall, Inc., Englewood Cliffs, New Jersey, 1969, 369 pp.

MILLEO, E. C., *Advanced Techniques for Strategic Planning.* American Management Association, New York, 1971, 174 pp.

WAGNER, H. M., *Principles of Management Science with Applications to Executive Decisions.* Prentice-Hall, Inc., Englewood Cliffs, New Jersey, 1970, 562 pp.

Chapter 6

THE EFFECT OF MIS
ON MANAGEMENT AND
THE MANAGEMENT PROCESS

INTRODUCTION

The different levels of management were described in Chapter 1. The principal job requirements and responsibilities of top management, middle management, and operating management were delineated. The reason for the breakdown is to avoid lumping together all of management when questions arise pertaining to the impact of MIS on management that is discussed in this chapter. We start by presenting two opposing views of the impact of MIS on management, one stressing the major influence that MIS has had on management, the other strongly stating that MIS has had little if any influence. These positions will establish the framework or at least the poles of the subsequent discussion. The impact of MIS on each of the three levels of management will be explored. It will be apparent that there is a considerable contrast in the role of MIS at the three levels and herein rests a good deal of the MIS confusion. The chapter concludes by focusing on the effect of MIS on company organization. Particular emphasis will be placed on the centralization-decentralization issue and the shifting of departmental boundaries and organization as a result of the integration of heretofore unintegrated functional operating areas of a company.

TWO POINTS OF VIEW ON THE IMPACT OF MIS

People get quite violent when discussing the impact of MIS on management and on business organization. It is a pertinent subject that arouses the emotions of a wide range of academicians, business managers, and EDP professionals. Two extreme positions exist, and it is useful to review them in order to gain perspective on the subject.

The focus of discussion usually centers on the following matters: the effect of the new information technology on middle management, the impact on organizational centralization/decentralization, the impact on top management, and the emergence of an information-processing elite corps. The proponents of the radical stand-point (I will call them futurists) feel that the availability of accurate, reliable, comprehensive, and timely information in the hands of top management, and the ability of the computer to process data under predefined decision rules, will enable top management to control a greater part of the business. Much of the work of middle management will be programmed and performed by the computer, thereby drastically reducing the number of middle managers required by a business. At the same time, simulation models of the company's operations will give the top executive a far more realistic picture of the cause and effect of policy decisions and enable him to test strategies to ensure maximum return on investment, thus avoiding the costs of unsuccessful and abortive programs and projects. These models will also take into account the competitive environment in which a company operates, thereby facilitating the optimal return from initiating programs, such as introducing new products or initiating national advertising campaigns. The futurists foresee the day when executives will communicate directly to a computer via remote consoles, getting snapshot pictures of current sales movement, production variances, and profitability. Executives will be able to ask a series of "what if" questions; for example, what if I increased sales 10 percent, would our factory be able to handle it or would the resultant overtime and/or inventory problems counterbalance the added revenue? Thus top management can participate in real-time organizational simulation.

The futurists see the evolution of an information elite who will assist top management in formulation of the computer models and will develop the technical aids to facilitate the direct communication between the manager and the machine. The information elite will be trained in the top business and engineering schools and will be well versed in the use of management science and the application of advancd mathematical techniques to the solution of business problems.

Finally, the futurists see the computer and the erosion of middle management as the vehicles for a major shift to recentralization. The new information technology will enable management to view an operation as a single entity whose effectiveness can only be optimized by making decisions that take into account the entity and not the individual parts. Centralized control with rapid access to information gathered locally, as well as information that emanates from computer models, is the most advantageous way to operate. The centralized company utilizing advanced information technology will have a decided edge on its competition. Although I do not ascribe the following quotation to the business futurists, a West Coast professor has allowed his mind to run far beyond the on-line, real-time executive. The executive gets his information from a remote console that unscrambles a stream of pulses passing over a telephone line into alphanumeric characters. The professor carries this type of communication a step further in the following quote, taken from an article entitled "21st Century: A World of Artificial Men." *L. A. Times* and *Washington Post*.

> It may be possible by 2067 for man to travel by "teleportation"; that is, the cells of the human body, and even its personality and memories, will be transmitted from one place to another by radio. This could be done by feeding an individual's entire genetic code into a computer, and sending the information to another computer perhaps on the moon or Mars. The information then would be used to reconstruct the individual out of the essential materials in storage at the destination. This would amount to creation of exact replicas.

The proponents of the more-conservative point of view (I will call them institutionalists) are skeptical of the rather grand things predicted by the futurists. They see the prime role of middle management as motivating and directing the workers under them to achieve prescribed goals. The institutionalists feel that there is little the computer can do to aid in this process. Furthermore, they point to the fact that the futurists have been claiming that computers will replace managers for over 10 years now and little if any headway has been made. The responsibilities of top management are to plan the long-range activities of the firm and to ensure that the necessary resources are available to reach long-term revenue and profit objectives. With this longer-range outlook, the idea of a top executive needing instantaneous real-time data on current operations and being hooked on-line to the computer represents fadism rather than the result of a careful business cost versus benefit analysis. The on-line, real-time executive is a business anachronism, so say the institutionalists.

The more conservative point of view is distrustful of the so-called information elite that will set tomorrow's important business policies and strategies. Simulation models do not take into account the myriad of intangible psychological and motivational factors that are so important to a successful enterprise. Furthermore, the information specialist had better have a good grounding in the operation of the business he is modeling, besides possessing solid business perspective, or else his model will not reflect the real world at all. Institutionalists facetiously point out that these new techniques will enable management to make wrong decisions faster than they ever did before.

The institutionalists see nothing the computer can offer to change the basic concept of decentralized organization. If the decentralization concept made sense before the advent of information technology, it still makes sense. The rationale of decentralization—that of providing an entrepreneur environment and a profit motivation to divisional managers—is not altered because of the availability of a central computer. It is possible that the data processing function can be centralized with cost savings and an ability to provide more accurate summaries and reports, but the basic decision making should be decentralized in order to obtain the best performance from local managers.

The following is an excerpt from an article called "The Passing of Old Business Methods" that I found while rummaging through some old copies of the

Saturday Evening Post. It is dated May 2, 1903, and supports the institutionalist's point of view that people have been talking about replacing middle managers for years.

> Perhaps the keynote of the modern office—aside from accuracy and dispatch—is the elimination of expensive help. Where, under the old system, five good accountants at twenty-five dollars a week were required, now the same labor is more easily and efficiently done by one good man at thirty-five dollars and four cheap assistants at four dollars to ten dollars. This is not a pleasing prospect from a strictly humanitarian viewpoint, but it is business, and we cannot circumvent the laws of progress, however much we may be puzzled in deciphering its compensations and its final relation to universal justice.

This, then, represents the extreme positions of the futurist and the institutionalist. There is validity in both standpoints, but, like most polarized positions, the truth probably lies somewhere between the poles. With this background, let us take a look at the relative impact on the various levels of management.

EFFECT OF MIS ON TOP MANAGEMENT

Before speculating on what future influence MIS might have on management, let us take a look at the situation as it appears today. Figure 6.1, which is based on several computer surveys and verified by my own experience, indicates that MIS has had far less impact at the top management level than at the middle or operating management level. MIS has had scant influence on the decision-making process, has hardly impacted the job content, and has had no influence on reducing or increasing the number of top managers required. The major responsibilities of top management involve long- and short-range planning, resource and capacity analysis, setting of profit and budget goals, and, in general, establishing the business objectives of the company. There is a heavy planning content as opposed to a heavy control content at the lower-management levels. Information systems have been more effective in the control area than in the planning field. A look back at Chapter 1 and Figure 1.3, which summarizes the job content of

	Decision making process	Job content	Job numbers
Top management	Scant influence	Scant change	No influence
Middle management	Moderate influence	Moderate change	Scant influence
Operating management	Major influence	Major change	Moderate influence

Fig. 6.1   Effect of MIS on management

the different management levels, illustrates why this is so. Control functions tend to be more structured, more programmable, and more straightforward and, therefore, more receptive to automated information systems.

Survey after survey indicates that few if any members of top management actually receive print-out directly from a computer. Thus, if the automated system has an effect on their decision-making process, it would have to be an indirect one through information gathered by members of middle management. The decision-making process consists of the following six elements:

1. Identify Areas of Improvement

This involves either the uncovering of a new opportunity that will produce increased revenue and profit for the company or the resolution of a problem that has been detracting from profitability. The introduction of a new product is an example of a new opportunity area, while a competitive price weakness in a particular product market segment is an example of a problem area.

2. Analyze These Areas

There are a host of potential solutions to improve the areas that are identified. This step in decision making analyzes the situation in more depth in order to develop the scope and range of possible solutions and to give priority to the solutions in accordance with predetermined criteria, such as resource availability and time to resolve. In the preceding example, the introduction of a new product could be focused on filling a gap in the existing product line or could open up an entirely new market. Possible alternatives to the competitive price weakness could be the development of new pricing contracts or a heightened merchandising program that stresses specific product features and advantages.

3. Develop Alternate Solutions

Each of the potential solutions must now be developed. The specifications of each solution are identified so that they may be evaluated in the next step. If a new product is to be introduced, its characteristics must be determined, specific market targets for the new product described, and the necessary marketing support, training, and sales plans developed.

4. Evaluate Alternate Solutions

This step involves projecting the potential profitability and company impact of each of the alternatives. Although there are many quantitative factors in the analysis, many factors will be qualitative in nature and will involve an analysis and weighing of relative risk. For example, the introduction of a new product may be 2 to 3 years away such that the marketplace at the time of product introduction is the significant element. This may be difficult to predict in a rapidly changing industry.

5. Make the Decision

This involves the selection of the course of action that best matches the company's short–and long–range goals. This is obviously the culmination of the decision-making process.

6. Implement the Decision

Although carried out after the decision is made, implementation considerations must be a strong element in the decision. In some instances, a pilot or test model is necessary to validate the final decision. Thus the implementation effort serves as a feedback loop to the decision-making process.

In reviewing several studies on this subject, such as the *Harvard Business Review* article entitled "Computers in Top-Level Decision Making," the *Wall Street Journal* survey of computer usage, and through my own personal contact with executives of medium and large companies utilizing computers, I view the impact of MIS and computers on top management decision making as illustrated in Figure 6.2. Since top management does not receive computer print-out directly except in a few cases, the effect of MIS on decision making is negligible. However, this is not to say that their decisions have not been influenced by MIS through the intercession of middle management.

Although computerized performance reports may indicate areas of improvement, these areas are usually pertinent to a specific operational entity. For example, reports may show production variances of material and labor are reaching

	Top management	Middle management
Identify areas of improvement	None	Scant
Analyze these areas	None	Scant
Develop alternate solutions	Scant	Moderate
Evaluate alternate solutions	Scant	Moderate
Make decision	None	None
Implement the decision	Not applicable	Heavy

Fig. 6.2 Effect of MIS on the decision-making process

alarming proportions or that the order backlog is growing because of inability to fill orders from inventory. The areas for improvement are generally not of the scope that require top management decision. Similarly, the areas of improvement that represent new opportunities (as opposed to problem resolution) do not come from computerized reports. New opportunities emanate from a variety of sources, including staff-planning departments, executive committee meetings, "brain-storming" sessions, attendance at seminars and trade shows, outside consultants, and so on; they rarely if ever emanate from the computer.

The steps most influenced by computer systems are the development and evaluation of alternate solutions. The degree "moderate" does not indicate that the majority of companies are utilizing computers for this purpose; it indicates that a good number (possibly 25 percent) represent the leading edge in the use of techniques like simulation that are required to develop and evaluate solutions to problems. Although a few top managers utilize these techniques directly and review computer output, most often the middle managers and/or staff departments act as the information middlemen between the computer and top management.

I have never encountered a company where the computer analysis provided the final decision on an issue that was the exclusive province of top management. The writers who state that computers are making decisions for top management usually are referring to operating decisions that happen to be made by top management. These decisions should rightfully be delegated to middle management and even to operating management. Important elements that are subjective or nonquantifiable in nature bear heavily on decisions of this type. Therefore, although the computer may have accomplished a good deal of the analysis and testing of alternatives, the final decision was not tied directly to the automated information system. Automated management information systems can make decisions on lot sizes and length of production runs, but they cannot make final decisions on the introduction of new products, the site of a new warehouse, or the need for an additional factory.

MIS plays a prominent role in the implementation of decisions once made. For example, the entire introduction cycle of a product from initial design to its availability in the marketplace is materially aided by automated information systems. Indeed, the overall schedule and resource allocation for the new product can be controlled by a computerized PERT or Critical Path system.

REASONS FOR LIMITED MIS IMPACT ON
TOP MANAGEMENT DECISION MAKING

There are three basic reasons for the limited effect of MIS on decision making to date. The first is the external and general unstructured nature of the data required for the type of issues faced by top management. The second is the lack of general understanding and rather slow acceptance of management science or operations research techniques as described in Chapter 5. The third reason is the element of intuition, executive sensitivity, "gut feel," nonquantifiable data, or whatever one wishes to call it involved in management decision making. Although more and more of the data elements are being quantified and more of the management process understood and programmed, there is still a factor of intuition with which the computer is incapable of dealing.

Unstructured Nature of Data

Chapter 1 (see Figure 1.4) discusses the business dimension of data. It indicates that the data required by top management is unstructured, nonprogrammed, future oriented, inexact, and external. The information matrix in Chapter 1 (Figure 1.5) shows that the type of information required by top management is the most difficult to acquire, update, and process, and therefore few computerized systems exist in this area. Another factor restricting the development of MIS for top management is the lack of definite cause-and-effect relationships of data. An example is a sales forecast for a new item that is planned by a company in a future period. In order to project a reasonable forecast, the company must know such factors as the market in which the product will compete, the market saturation for the particular product, and the impact on existing products in the line. Whether the most reasonable basis to forecast is an extrapolation of how similar items have behaved in the past or a competitive share of market analysis, is open to question. The basis selected is obviously quite crucial to the forecast. Even if the necessary data is available—for example past sales history by item—there may be no proven or logical basis by which to show the effect on sales of the introduction of a new item. There are many other examples where management decisions must be made in the absence of quantified cause-and-effect relationship of data. This is not to say that these relationships will never be known. However, the problem of obtaining the type of data required for top management decisions when combined with the questionable decision rules of how to analyze the data meaningfully presents a formidable obstacle for computerized information systems directed at the strategic planning area.

Management Science Techniques

Management science or operation research techniques were described in Chapter 5. Although there are many cases where these types of methods have been used with a good deal of success in aiding top management decision making, the companies that utilize management science are still in the minority. Assuming that the proper technique has been selected for tackling a particular problem, there are still some major barriers to overcome. A communication gap exists between management and the operation research analyst who is responsible for preparing the set of linear equations if, for example, the problem is one that can be handled by linear programming. Management is skeptical of making a decision based on a set of ill-understood equations and often the OR specialist is incapable of explaining in manangement terms just what the mathematical processing will accomplish. Furthermore, if a manager realizes that the data used as input to the model does not have a high degree of accuracy, he is suspicious of the results. Although the only alternative may be a complete "seat of the pants" decision, the manager somehow feels more secure doing so than depending on the model. At least, it is cheaper, he rationalizes. What he fails to realize is that although there are certain probabilities that neither the OR solution nor the "seat of the pants" solution will prove accurate, the odds on the OR solution (if the technique is properly used) are a good deal better.

The Element of Intuition

Many top managers feel that good strategic decisions are made more by intuition than by a quantitative analysis of the available data. They do not ignore the data completely but believe that there is a strong intuitive factor, particularly when little or no data is available. An interesting article ["Question: What Do Some Executives Have More of? Answer: Intuition, Maybe." *Think,* Nov.–Dec., 1969.] by Professor John Mihalasky of the Newark College of Engineering points out the fact that the higher a man is in the organization, the more incomplete is the data on which he bases decisions and the more he relies on someting called intuition, hunches, or instinct. Professor Mihalasky feels that we may be putting too much faith on machines and data, on the logical decision maker versus the so-called nonlogical decision maker. He further points out that studies suggest that some managers have more "precognitive" ability than others and that this ability gives them a better batting average in making decisions intuitively as opposed to logically. The study involved dividing 25 chief executives into two classes on the basis of their proven performance based on profitability. The tests included things like matching a series of numbers (0 to 9) printed out randomly by a computer. An average score is 10 percent. The successful executives outscored the nonperformers in 22 out of 27 tests. Statistically the chances of this happening by accident are fewer than 5 in 1000.

This study does not claim to answer conclusively the question of the role of intuition in decision making, but it does raise some interesting questions. If there is such a thing as intuitive ability and if the ability can be tested, to what degree should the intuitive decision be valued in contrast to the logical decision based on advanced management science techniques? Granting that the logical decision is the preferable one when the data is known and quantifiable, what degree of data reliability is the break-even point where the logical decision becomes the preferred one? One need not answer these questions to realize that management is well aware of the somewhat illusive quality called intuition or precognitive power. Many have extended the thesis suggested by Professor Mihalasky (beyond what the professor has intended) and used it as a rationale for ignoring quantitative and logical approaches to manangement decision making.

COMPUTERIZED DECISION MAKING BY THE LEADING EDGE

Despite the problems referred to above, there is no question that there are companies (they can be called the leading edge) who are making effective use of manangement science methods. A prominent paper company has developed a computerized model of their timber and wood products division to aid them in gaining the most efficient use of timber land and site location for new plywood plants. The model consists of 8000 equations and 15,000 variables. A major chemical company uses a computer model to simulate an industry segment and the company's potential for a share of market and profitability. A glass company has a corporate financial model that allows executives to test the impact of ideas and strategies on future profitability and to determine the needs for funds and physical resources. Other examples described in business periodicals and trade publications indicate where companies, in addition to simulation, have utilized the computer-risk analysis, gaining a composite picture of the key factors involved in implementing a new policy, and determining the probabilities of each event occurring on time and the composite odds for success. Another area is sensitivity analysis or the measurement of the effect of the variation of individual factors to final result (for example, in certain instances the leverage of an individual factor is high—a 5 percent increase in sales may trigger a 30 percent increase in inventory and may have a major impact on the overall result of a program, whereas in another case a 50 percent fluctuation in one element has minimal effect on the final outcome). Replies from more than 300 members of the Planning Executive Institute indicate that 63 have corporate models in operation while 39 others say they will begin developing one within a year.

George Gershefski, manager of the Corporate Economic Planning Division of the Sun Oil Company, developed a corporate financial model which he states may be the largest and most complex corporate model yet developed. The computerized model takes into account the production, transportation, manufacturing, and marketing operations of the company. It is significant that the working version required 13 man-years to complete and an additional 10 man-years to familiarize manangement with the operation of the model, to solicit comments and suggestions for improvement, and to incorporate some of the suggestions into the model. It is rather interesting to note that it took almost as much time to get the model into effect as to build and implement it in the first place. This supports the discussion in the previous section emphasizing the need to reduce the skepticism that managers have toward sophisticated computerized decision-making aids. Gershefski sums up what models can do by stating that the model puts pertinent information into an analytical famework which aids the management decision-making process. He points to the following benefits of the model:

- An accurate forecast (within 1 percent) can be made of net income for one year.
- Preparation of short-term profit plans and long-range projections (10 year).
- Provides preplanning information in budget preparation.
- Calculates variances between budgeted and actual results.
- Triggers revised forecasts if not proceeding in accordance with plan.
- Acts as early warning system for monitoring activities and signaling necessary reactive plans.
- Indicates effect on income and cash flow by following alternate investment strategies.

- Assists in planning the addition of new facilities and a host of special studies.
- Can accomplish all the preceding items with great speed (for example, the computer processing time to simulate one year of operation is 14 seconds).

Gershefski (in his article, "Building a Corporate Financial Model," *Harvard Business Review,* Jul.-Aug., 1969) feels that the corporate model is the first step in building a management information system. There may be disagreement on that point, for the model obviously depends on data fed into it by other information systems within the company. Therefore the model cannot be the first step. If the model is the first step, then there will be few management information systems because few companies possess the capability or will invest the monetary resources necessary to develop a model of the scope of that developed by Sun Oil. However, there is little doubt that if MIS is going to have a major impact on the strategic planning process of top management, the corporate financial model of the type described is a key element.

Although the effect of computerized information systems on top management has been limited to the leading edge, there is no question that the trend toward using them is rising; in this case, the leading edge is an indicator of what the majority of companies will be doing in the next 10 to 15 years. I firmly feel that advanced information systems can materially aid the six-step decision process described previously. A basic example will illustrate the point. Over 32,000 stocks are listed on the various stock exchanges. The job of the investment counselor is to develop a stock portfolio that best meets the requirements of his client. A computerized information system can materially aid in this process (in fact, such systems are in use at several investment firms). A three-stage system development plan produces the required portfolio. The first stage is the determination of what characteristics or indices are pertinent to evaluating stocks. An analysis of this area introduces such elements as price-earnings ratio, dividend record, and price performance during recessions. Those elements that are considered pertinent to predicting future value are captured and put in machine-readable format. A system to update and keep current the data that is collated must not be overlooked.

The second stage involves the categorization of the stocks based on a predetermined classification scheme. Thus the stocks are ranked according to such categories as high yield, growth, and volatility, categories that are pertinent to the requirements of investors. It is obvious that a good deal of professional judgment and expertise is needed to establish the key stock indicators in stage one and the classification scheme in stage two.

Stage three involves the categorization of the investor based on a predetermined classification scheme. The salient elements of such a categorization include current and anticipated income level, current cash position, investment objectives, and so on. There may be some seemingly intangible but necessary personal criteria; for example, the stocks must be in certain industries and the companies must not be doing work for the war effort. These criteria must be considered beforehand so that the necessary information is contained within the system to make this classification possible.

With the completion of the three developmental stages, the resulting model is now able to aid the decision-making process of the investment counselor in selecting a portfolio individually suited to his client. The model permits the counselor to develop a wider range of alternative solutions and to test them out under a wider variety of circumstances. The computerized system widens the scope of potential stocks and minimizes quick and premature decisions which are often resorted to because the counselor lacks the time or the knowledge and which are unfavorable to his client.

The example illustrated here aids steps 3 and 4 in the decision-making process (Figure 6.2). There are many parallels in the use of this type of approach to business operation. A direct parallel is an investment decision when many alternative choices are available. Market models and revenue models are extensions of this technique. It is obvious that the type of information analysis does not give the complete answer and thus allow the decision to be made by the computer. Certain subjective, external factors must also be reflected quantitatively or, if this is not possible, qualitatively. However, the development of this programmed type of analysis in an ever-expanding variety of business operations will give the manager more time to explore the intangible subtleties of problem solving and thus reach better man-machine-based decisions.

MAKING DECISIONS UNDER CONDITIONS OF UNCERTAINTY

The preceding discussion has assumed a "black-and-white" world; that is, either something is known or it is not. However, in actual business operation, obviously there are certain risks or probabilities that a certain course of action will be successful. The technique of risk analysis is called decision theory and is being linked to a computer system in a growing but still selective circle of companies. A basic example of the technique and its benefits to decision making may help qualify the future use of this type of analysis.

The problem to be solved by the use of decision theory is the evaluation of sales prospects who are considering the purchase of a high-value durable goods item with a good deal of necessary presale effort. The problem of selecting the prospects that hold greatest profit potential is of prime significance in order to focus a limited sales force on an expanding marketplace. Considerable selectivity must be exercised, and the importance of the judgment underlying this selectivity is extremely important.

In analyzing the situation, the following questions must be tackled one at a time and an economic evaluation made of each.

What is the payoff or profit potential of each prospect?

What are the costs involved in bidding for the account?

What are the odds on getting the account?

The profit potential is based on the revenue that can be expected over a 5-year period. A 5-year period is selected because a customer can be expected to contribute add-on business after the initial sale. If installation is not anticipated before 12 months, the profit potential must reflect this factor. For example, a multidivision company expecting to sign a contract for one machine ($110,000 revenue) to be installed in 12 months with two similar machines to be installed 2 years after the first would have a 5-year revenue potential of $880,000 ($110,-000 × 4 + $220,000 × 2). The revenue potential must then be viewed in light of its profit contribution (based on the company's accounting methods) and must be discontinued in light of the fact that revenue does not all accrue the first year. The resultant discounted contribution margin for the above sale might be $170,000.

The next question to answer is the presale effort that must be expended in an attempt to sign the account. This figure covers the cost of special engineering, system analysis, special training courses, demonstration programs, proposal preparation, and other support needed to bid for the business. For example, if an elaborate proposal, plus considerable special engineering, is required, the costs might be as follows:

2 engineers for 4 months (8 man-months × $2000)	= $16,000
2 illustrators/designers for 4 months ($1500 man/month)	12,000
Supplies and proposal material	1,000
	$29,000

The next step is the determination of the betting odds or the probability that the business can be closed. This is a rather subjective evaluation, but an analysis of competitive factors, plus past experience, can be used to establish the odds. The result is stated in terms of a percentage probability.

To see how decision theory works, assume that there are two prospects and that it is desired to rank them according to priority, for it is not possible to expend a major sales effort on each.

	Account A (the account described above)	Account B
Revenue potential	$880,000	$560,000
Profit potential	170,000	90,000
Sales cost	—29,000	—6,000
Net profit potential	$141,000	$ 84,000

DECISION TABLE STATEMENT OF PROBLEMS

Alternatives	Bid on Prospect A	Probability	Bid on Prospect B	Probability
Get the sale	+$170,000	20%	+$90,000	40%
Lose the sale	—29,000	80	—6,000	60
Expected monetary value	+10,800		+32,400	

The decision table indicates that prospect B holds the greater profit potential. It brings this out by comparing the expected monetary value of the two accounts. Prospect A has higher potential but with less probability of realizing it and with a greater selling expense. If prospect A is signed, a profit return of $170,000 will result, whereas a loss of $29,000 will be incurred if the prospect is lost. If prospect

B is signed, a profit return of $90,000 will result, whereas a loss of $6000 will be incurred if the prospect is lost. The expected monetary value of B is $32,400 as compared to $10,800 for A. These figures are obtained by multiplying the probability of getting the sale (20 percent in the case of A) times the profit if the sale is made ($170,000) and subtracting the amount obtained by multiplying the probability of losing the sale (80 percent) times the sales cost or loss if the sale is lost ($29,000).

Decision theory is a systematic method of facilitating decision making under conditions of uncertainty. The example used here has but a few variables and there are only two alternate courses of action. As the variables and alternatives are multiplied severalfold, as is the case in most business decisions, the need for techniques like decision theory becomes more apparent.

Decision theory analyzes the factors underlying a decision and allows the decision maker to quantify the major parts of the problem so that he is free to concentrate on those factors that cannot be readily quantified. The human mind has a difficult time handling multidimension problems. Decision theory divides a problem into its logical parts, analyzes each part separately, and then puts the parts back together in their proper prospective in order to reach a decision. Decision theory follows the philosophy of "divide and conquer"; that is, divide a problem into its logical components, analyze and quantify each component, and thereby conquer the overall problem.

Thus the examples of computer-aided portfolio analysis and choosing between two sales prospects by use of decision theory illustrate in a simplified manner the way information systems are impacting top management decision making. Although it is only the leading edge of companies who are effectively utilizing such approaches today, the success that the relatively few are experiencing augurs well for greatly extended use in the future.

THE KEYED-IN TOP EXECUTIVE

It is 8:00 A.M., and Harris P. Updike enters the executive offices of the Thirston Manufacturing Company, moves quickly past the receptionist, and presses '8' on the executive elevator. Moving briskly down the oak-paneled hall, he enters the sanctuary of his office. The feel of the thick mauve carpeting is comforting and exudes a sense of substance and security. He quickly buzzes his secretary and tells her to summon the management information specialist, Calvin Sharp, to his office.

Calvin is 26 years old, a graduate of Beckett College where he majored in computer sciences, and holds a master's degree in information technology. He has been with the Thirston Company for 3 years.

Updike presses the button next to his desk, thereby opening the drapes on the far side of the room and revealing a remote tele-interrogation station. Updike requests Sharp to give him a review of last night's operations. Sharp picks up the electronic stylus and writes the proper code on the screen in the proper position.

Through an on-line hookup to a remote computer, the screen indicates in three columns the scheduled production, the actual production, and the coded reasons for the variances. The screen also displays standard costs and actual costs, by item and by department. Updike then asks Sharp to give him a report of yesterday's sales activities. A touch of the electronic stylus in the proper location lights up sales by item, variance from plan, and reasons for the variances.

Updike now wants to look at the financial situation. Another movement of the stylus indicates Thirston's cash position as of 8:00 A.M. that morning. While all this activity is taking place, Updike is intermittently speaking into his dictation machine and asking further questions of Sharp.

It is now 8:20 A.M., and Updike has dictated orders to his production and sales manangement people, as well as to the treasurer and controller. He tells Sharp to return at 10:00 A.M. so that he can review the early morning activities and take the necessary action. He calls for his secretary to order him a cup of coffee (light cream, no sugar).

Today's fast-moving business world has produced the keyed-up executive who works under the constant pressure of mounting job responsibilities and decision making. Harris P. Updike is an example of what might be termed the keyed-in executive. If one believes that the computer can aid an executive in the way it aids Updike, the keyed-in executive might take much of the decision-making burden off the keyed-up executive.

However, as stated at the outset of this chapter, there is a dichotomy of opinion as to whether tomorrow's top executive will deal directly with the computer. Richard Sprague, a prominent EDP spokesman, bases his thesis that managers can benefit from an ability to communicate directly with a management information system on research that was stimulated by members of the continuing seminar on management information systems of the American Management Association. Sprague has written several articles over the past years, one predicting that by 1984 we (not just programmers or managers) will all be communicating directly with a computer system; a second foretelling the coming of the browsing era when a manager can browse through computerized information or decision alternatives pertinent to his responsibilities, and a third postulating a Personalized Data System (PDS) where the personal data a manager deals with can be computerized and made a facet in improving the way he carries out his job functions. [See "Personalized Data Systems," *Business Automation,* October 1969; "Electronic Business Systems—Nineteen Eighty-Four," *Business Automation,* February 1966; "The Browsing Era," *Business Automation,* June 1967. All by Richard Sprague.]

The opposing point of view emphatically states that there are factors in the way business and business managers operate that cast aspersions on the future for the keyed-in executive. John Deardon in an article entitled "The Myth of Real-Time Management Information" [*Harvard Business Review,* May/June 1966] describes the functions of top management and concludes that instantaneous real-time information is not pertinent in accomplishing these functions and, therefore, that attempts to do so are a waste of money. Professor Deardon would say that Harris P. Updike is not really performing in his role as top executive of Thirston Manufacturing but is making operating decisions that are the prerogative of middle management. Updike should be concerned with the longer-term and strategic planning aspects of the business. In this capacity, real-time information is meaningless and unnecessary. Other business and EDP experts point out that a top executive and a computer terminal are incompatible; that the direct dialing system did not stop the executive from asking his secretary to place a call. In a like manner, the executive will have an information middleman, someone like Calvin Sharp, as a computer intermediary.

I believe that the keyed-in executive will not become prominent in the next 5 to 10 years. However, as business schools continue to expand the use of computer terminals and computer-aided instruction to a wider range of students and over a wider range of business problems, the use of terminals will become commonplace. Tomorrow's executive will not use a secretary as much, he may dial his own calls, and, similarly, he may not use a Calvin Sharp as much; he may be communicating directly with the computer. I do not believe that he will be writing his own programs as Sprague suggests in his personalized data system concept, but the manager will be able to call on previously written programs and communicate with them via a simplified inquiry and response language. The manager will not be using the computer to give him the current status of the day's production operations; while the top executive has indicated to corporate management that he will earn $3,600,000 this year, he did not tell them that he would earn $10,000 each of 360 days. Rather, he will be using the computer as a kind of interactive mental jogger or memory extender to stretch his vision and problem-solving capability—to improve his ability to experiment and innovate. He will be able to calculate quickly rates of return and effect on profitability of different strategies. He will use the computer to assess quickly the implications of an idea while the idea is still fresh in his mind, similar to the way an engineer uses a slide rule. Waiting until an information specialist can obtain an answer will lessen the enthusiasm and the motivated mental framework that are necessary ingredients to creative problem solving.

In closing this section on the impact of MIS and the computer on top management, I am reminded of that portion of the book *The Peter Principle* [by Laurence J. Peter and Raymond Hull. New York: William Morrow & Co., Inc., 1969, pp. 157–159] which applies the principle to computers. The Peter Principle satirically states that, in a hierarchy, every employee tends to rise to his level of incompetence. In the last chapter of the book, the thesis as applied to computers is that the computer, like a human employee, does good work at first, but the initial success creates a strong tendency to promote it continually to higher-level and more responsible tasks until it reaches its level of incompetence. Some would say that the use of computers to aid top management is the application of Peter's Principle. Certainly some results in this area bear this point out. The prerequisites to success are a proper appreciation of the role of the computer, a comprehensive understanding of business operation, the employment of the required system and operations research (OR) talent, and the necessary executive understanding and commitment. If these elements are not present, it may be preferable to maintain the focus of the computer and MIS at the middle and operating levels of management.

IMPACT OF MIS ON MIDDLE AND OPERATING MANAGEMENT

As indicated in Figure 6.1, MIS has had greater effect on middle and operating management than on top manangement. MIS has had moderate influence on the decision-making process and on the job content of middle managers, whereas it has major influence on operating manangement. The computer has had scant influence on top management. The reason for the greater impact on middle and operating management is the nature of the job responsibilities performed by middle and operating management. Figure 1.3 of Chapter 1 indicates the heavy control content of the middle manager's job, while Figure 1.4 points out that the information middle management deals with is more programmed and structured and, therefore, more susceptible to computerization. However, although a good deal of the job content is programmable, it must be kept in mind as well that a good deal is not structured. The latter fact is why the computer has had a negligible effect on the number of jobs at the middle-management level. Because middle management is so crucial to management information systems (indeed it is often the starting or focal point of MIS), it is significant to analyze the job content in greater depth.

THE MANAGEMENT PROCESS

Figure 6.3 is an abbreviated illustration of the management process as described by R. Alec MacKenzie. ["The Management Process in 3-D," *Harvard Business Review,* November/December 1969.] I am most impressed with the framework that Mr. MacKenzie has developed; and as I compared it with my own management role and those above and below me, I realized how much thought went into what appears to be a rather simple schematic. My purpose here is to explain the elements of the manager's job in enough depth to ascertain the effect that a management information system can have in helping the manager carry out his job responsibilities.

Figure 6.3 indicates that the manager basically deals with three elements— *ideas, things,* and *people*. These elements are reflected in the *tasks* of *conceptual thinking,* where one formulates new business ideas and opportunities, *administration,* where the details of the management process are handled, and *leadership,* where people are motivated to accomplish business objectives. The functions of *analyzing problems,* where facts are gathered and alternate solutions are evaluated (much like the steps in decision making discussed earlier), *making decisions,* and *communicating* the decisions to the people who must implement them are termed *continuous functions,* for they occur repeatedly throughout the management process rather than sequentially, as is the case with the items that will now be described.

The *sequential functions* consist of *plan,* where a course of action is selected, *organize,* where the work is arranged for accomplishing the plan, *staff,* or the selection and allocation of the work to the people who will perform it, *direct,* the commencement of purposeful action on the work at hand, and *control,* where the plan is carried out and satisfactorily completed.

The activities indicate what constitutes the five sequential functions of the management process. In order to develop a *plan,* one must *forecast* or determine the effect on future sales, costs, or profit; *set objectives,* the end results; and *develop strategies* on how to achieve the end results. One must *program* or establish a priority and sequence of the strategy, *budget* or allocate resources, *set procedures* or arrive at standardized methods, and, finally, *develop policies* ensuring that rules and regulations exist to govern significant recurring matters.

An example might serve to bring the plan function into perspective. My experience as a planning manager in developing a product business plan follows the seven listed activities. In planning the introduction of a new item, a forecast of the future marketplace and impact of the product in the market are important starting points. Then objectives, such as desired market share and revenue and profit goals, are established. The strategies of how to achieve these goals involve statements like the following ones: we will go after new markets, we will offer the lowest price products, we will offer the best quality product, or any combination thereof. The programming involved is to indicate what products with what features will be offered first and why. The budget for the project must be established at this point, and it must be consistent with what it will take to carry out the objectives and strategies, and yet it must not affect on-going programs to any great degree. The procedures and policies begin to blend into the *organize* function because they involve statements stating, for example, that PERT will be used as a project control technique with monthly status reports prepared for top management.

The organize function is more straightforward and, following the example above, includes *establishing the organizational structure* for the production of the

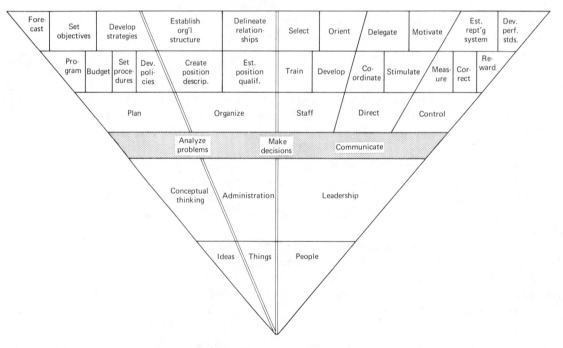

Fig. 6.3 The management process

new product. If the product is to be produced by the existing line organization, this point will be determined, or it may be that a new operational unit is organized to design and produce the new product. If a new organization is set up, top management must *delineate relationships* between the new and the existing structure and define communication and liaison points. The *creation of position descriptions* and the *establishment of position qualifications* will indicate whether the plan can be carried out by the existing organization or whether additional people with specifically required skills are needed.

This leads into the *staff* function, where the qualified people for the required positions are *selected, oriented* to the plan objectives, strategies, policies, and so on, *trained* in the necessary tasks to be performed, and *developed* to the extent of making them feel a part of the company and the project on which they are working.

The *direct* function involves the steps that are normally associated with "getting things done through people." These steps include *delegating* or assigning responsibility and accountability, *motivating* to persuade and inspire, *coordinating* to ensure that the efforts of one group are consistent with the efforts of others, and *stimulating change* when differences occur, conflicts arise, and it is necessary to resolve these differences before proceeding with the task.

The *control* function completes the cycle and involves the *establishment of a reporting system* that is consistent with the total reporting structure but that reflects pertinent milestones and progress against a schedule, the *development of performance standards,* to set the conditions that will determine if the job is properly completed, a technique to *measure results* to ascertain if the desired quality was attained and the extent of variance from the goal or standard, the taking of *corrective action* to get the task back on schedule and up to standard when deviations occur, and, finally, to *reward,* whether by praise or remuneration for the accomplishment of the job and the meeting of goals.

Having analyzed the management process, it is appropriate to assess the relative impact of management information systems on the various functions and then to overlay the categorization of top, middle, and operating management that was developed in Chapter 1 to get a clearer idea of how MIS can be expected to influence management.

I feel that MIS can be expected to influence the five sequential functions in the next 5 to 10 years in accordance with the following percentages:

$$
\begin{array}{rr}
\text{PLAN} & 30\% \\
\text{ORGANIZE} & 15 \\
\text{STAFF} & 25 \\
\text{DIRECT} & 5 \\
\text{CONTROL} & 80
\end{array}
$$

It has been shown that planning, or the decision-making process, can be materially influenced by MIS; the 30 percent may be considered conservative by some. MIS will not have a great deal of influence on the organize function, although job and skills inventories will assist in the process. The computerized skills and job inventories can materially assist the staffing function, but I still feel that a strong qualitative element will remain. The direct function is people and motivation oriented, and I see little if any impact of MIS in this area. The big area for MIS is in the control function, and it is here where more experience in analyzing business operations and in experimenting with programmed decision rules will bring more functions under automatic programmed control.

It is obvious that the categorization of management into three levels is an oversimplification because the nature of the work within the same category differs greatly and there does not exist a definitive line separating the top from the middle and the middle from operating management.

For example, a job of managing a group of forecasters whose job it is to project the sales, shipments, returns, and so on, differs dramatically, depending on the nature of the product. If the product is a stable one that is influenced by competitive and other external factors to only a minor extent, the job of fore-casting is much more receptive to computerization than if the product is highly unstable and subject to external forces. Similarly, a job shop manufacturer deal-ing in one-of-a-kind specials has a different problem than a repetitive, assembly-line operation. In order to ascertain the impact of MIS on a management job, the percentage of time devoted to the five functions described can serve as a general indication. For example, Figure 6.4 indicates a MIS quotient of 29 percent for top management, 43 percent for middle management, and 61 percent for operating management. It must be stressed again that this figure is a gross oversimplifica-tion; it is presented only to indicate a relative evaluation rather than an exact one.

However, I feel that the framework is a valid one for projecting what the future impact of MIS will be. In order to determine if a computer can replace you as a manager, analyze the proportion of your time spent on the described func-

	% Susceptible to computerization	Top management		Middle management		Operating management	
		% Of job devoted to	Weighted value	% Of job devoted to	Weighted value	% Of job devoted to	Weighted value
Plan	30%	70%	21%	20%	6%	5%	1.5%
Organize	15	10	1.5	10	1.5	5	1.0
Staff	25	10	2.5	10	2.5	5	1.5
Direct	5	5	—	20	1.0	20	1.0
Control	80	5	4	40	32.0	70	56.0
Computerization quotient			29%		43%		61%

Fig. 6.4 Computerization quotient

tional activities. Next, determine the percentage of that function you feel is susceptible to MIS and computerization and develop your personal computerization quotient. If it is high, you might give some thought to learning new skills.

EFFECT OF A MIS ON OPERATING MANAGEMENT

Figures 6.1 and 6.4 indicate that the impact of MIS on operating management is far greater than the impact on top and middle management in all three listed categories. This is true because the operating manager's job is directed more at the control functions which Figure 6.4 show are highly receptive to computerization. The focus of this discussion will be on the nature of the changes in job content caused by computerization. The nature of the job changes is the reason for predicating the need for fewer operating managers to accomplish the same amount of work. An analogy to automated factory machinery will be used to illustrate the changes in job content occurring because of computerized management information systems.

There are lessons to learn from analyzing the accelerating trend toward numerically controlled machines. In numerical control, a machine like a drill press or lathe is controlled by a paper tape. The holes in the paper tape are interpreted by a control unit attached to the machine tool, which generates the necessary impulses to control the drilling of a hole in a specific spot in a piece of metal. The reason that the process is called numerical control is that the movements of the drill and the work to be drilled are controlled by numbers representing the shape of the desired finished part. It is more accurately called symbolic control, because the actual machining process is described by symbols, some of which happen to be numbers.

Figure 6.5 represents a schematic of the process. (A) and (B) in the schematic will be explained later. The paper tape can be generated by an individual with a conventional paper-tape keyboarding device or by a computer that has the necessary intelligence to accept instructions describing the finished product and translate these instructions into holes in the paper tape. The more complicated the product being produced, the greater the dependence and benefit offered by the computer. Also, the introduction of the computer offers other benefits. Because a computer is adept at mathematical calculations and data interpretations, the individual can

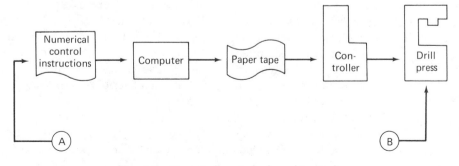

Fig. 6.5 Numerical control of machine tools

describe the part being machined in a language that is more mathematical and system oriented and less machine-tool oriented.

It is interesting to analyze the ramifications of numerical control. This type of control can be considered an evolutionary stage in automation in which the machine assumes a job previously performed by man. In this instance, the machine usually can accomplish the work more economically and accurately than man. Before the advent of the drill press, the worker drilled holes in metal by hammering a boringlike device of prescribed size through the metal. Later he used a hand drill with an adjustable bit. Then he used a drill press to position the work piece under the drill and pressed a button to lower the drill through the work piece. These evolutionary drilling developments removed the physical portion of the job from the worker and reduced his direct contact with the machine. The advent of numerical control removes him still further from the machine, indeed almost all the way. However, one should not overlook the continuing human involvement; the significance is that it occurs at a different part of the work cycle and the type of involvement has been changed markedly.

It is appropriate now to discuss the job of the middle manager in an information system, keeping in mind the parallel to the effect of numerical control on the drill press operator. Figure 1.1 indicates that the manager of inventory control reports to the vice-president of production. The inventory control manager has reporting to him two assistant managers who in turn have buyers reporting to them. The buyer controls a number of inventory items and supervises a clerical staff that prepares stock requisitions and purchase orders. For illustrative purposes, the effect of a computerized inventory control system on the job content of the buyers and assistant managers will be analyzed. Although it may be stretching things to call a buyer a manager, he is in effect because he supervises a group of people and manages the procurement and stock control of a group of inventory items.

Operating management has an initial advantage because it has been dealing in symbols for quite some time. The assistant inventory manager or buyer looks at an inventory status report, sees that there are 25 fuel gauges in inventory, and orders 50 more even though he has not seen a fuel gauge in some time or perhaps has never seen one. The buyer is dealing in a symbolic world. This is no earth-shaking revelation. Of more significance is the level of symbolism being employed —to what extent the buyer uses symbols to control his operation.

A computer that merely records the status of inventory for the buyer is one level. Here it is using internal reported information. But when the computer automatically produces a purchase order or schedules a new lot of an item when it reaches a predetermined minimum, then we have another level. Here it is using internal processed information and using it in a most meaningful manner. Figure 6.6 represents a schematic of this process. (Again, Ⓐ and Ⓑ in the schematic will be explained later.) The automatic inventory system changes the character of the buyer's job just as numerical control changes the character of the worker's job. It dictates that the buyer shift to a new symbolic plane.

First, what effect does an operating-type management information system have on the number of operating managers involved? It is apparent that operating systems of the type discussed can reduce the number of buyers and assistant man-

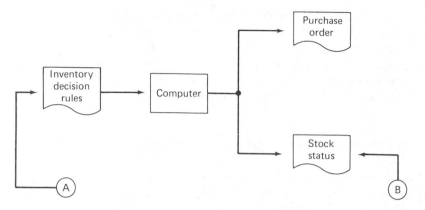

Fig. 6.6 Computerized inventory control

agers required for a specific function. Fortunately, because of the shortage of both skilled machinists and skilled managers, and because of the growth of industry in general, reduction does not present a problem. Buyers still will be required, but automated information systems have extended their reach to the point that perhaps two will be needed where five are needed now; thus the computer has not replaced operating management, it has reduced the number involved. In the inventory control department, it is possible that a well-conceived and comprehensive computerized inventory control system can reduce the number of buyers by three and the number of assistant inventory control managers by one. The management, by exception principle, is being followed. A machinist is still needed to handle exceptions and to determine when the symbolic control system has gone awry. Similarly, the buyer or assistant manager is needed to handle exceptions where the computer system cannot handle the situation with preprogrammed logic.

Second, what effect does an automated information system have on the job content of the machinist and the buyer? In addition to the exception control required by the machinist and buyer, both must play a significant role in developing the symbolic systems that control the operations. Their input is needed, but it is now at a different stage in the operation cycle. Their participation is now more toward the front end. In referring to Figures 6.5 and 6.6, the contact point with the system is now *A* rather than *B*. (Point *B* is now resorted to only on an exception basis.)

Does this mean that the machinist and the buyer will become computer programmers or system analysts? Although it is true that this change may occur in certain cases, it is not true on a wholesale basis. The nature of the job is changed and the skills or, more important, the aptitudes that make good buyers and machinists are not necessarily those that make good programmers or system analysts. This is not to say that their participation is not needed; it most certainly is. A part programmer (the person who describes in symbolic terms the part to be machined) and the system analyst or programmer (the person who writes the computer program to make automatic inventory decisions) must know the operations of machine tools and the physical characteristics of the symbolic world in order to represent accurately the real operational world. The inaccurate representation of the real world is a serious inherent danger in symbolic control. It is easy to believe that one is reflecting the real world when actually the model is not even a reasonable facsimile. The machinist and the buyer are the only ones who can ensure that the symbolic model is an accurate one. They must also audit and check to see that any changes in the real world are immediately reflected in the model. This last step is of prime concern in symbolic control, for the model may be a good one when first instituted but subsequent change may outmode it.

IMPACT OF COMPUTERS ON ORGANIZATIONAL STRUCTURE

MIS has been viewed from the standpoint of its impact on top management, middle management, and operating management. The conclusion is that its influence differs markedly, depending on what management level is being analyzed. Another important subject to which we now turn is the impact of MIS on organizational structure.

A common philosophy on the subject of computers and organization is that computers are responsible for a trend to centralization in many business enterprises. It is appropriate to explore the decentralization concept to determine the principal advantages companies have found in adopting the concept. In order to establish a framework for discussion, Figure 6.7 depicts the organization of a sales division of a company that markets its product nationally. The principal sales unit is the branch office. The branch is treated as a profit center such that the title of branch sales manager has been changed to branch business manager. The branches have zone offices reporting to them. The branches themselves report to one of four areas: the western area in Los Angeles, the central area in Chicago, the eastern area in New York, or the southern area in Atlanta.

The company in question has gone through four distinct phases, which can illustrate the role of computers and MIS on the centralization-decentralization concept. During phase 1, the company was small and had only two major sales offices, the headquarters office in Chicago and suboffices in Minneapolis and Detroit. Almost all major sales decisions were made out of Chicago, for the marketing area was concentrated in the Midwest. A computer system billed customers and handled accounts receivable. In addition, it provided various sales analyses. No attempt was made to break out costs or profit by the suboffices, or even by product. The top executives controlled matters from the headquarters office and had a good grip on how they were going.

Sales grew rapidly, and during the next 5-year period a national sales force was hired and organized to cover the entire eastern part of the country. It was about the same time that a newly hired EDP director convinced the vice-president of sales that a comprehensive marketing information system should be established. He argued that activity was expanding at such a rate that they were already operating by the seat of their pants and it was going to get worse. At the same time, the sales division launched a program of decentralization. It was decided that profit centers would be established in the major cities. Each city would be a branch office with the branch manager responsible for sales, costs, and profit over his geographical territory. Certain home office expenses would be allocated and charged to his branch to reflect those costs that could be directly associated with

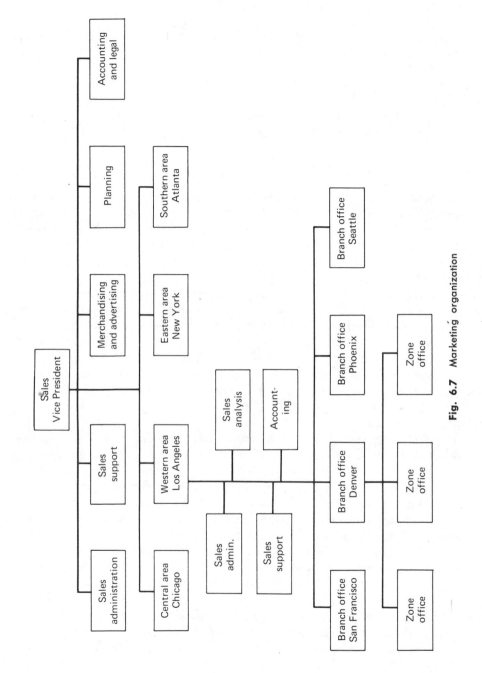

Fig. 6.7 Marketing organization

a branch, such as shipping charges and telephone services. Data processing for the branches would still be handled centrally, but reports on the branch's monthly operation (profit and loss, etc.) were processed and sent to the branches. This marked phase 2.

As sales continued to grow, the branches grew in numbers as well as in revenue per branch; there was a definite decentralization shift. The marketing division's top management was convinced that decentralization was working out. This belief was heavily influenced by the strength of the branches and the growing pressures applied by branch managers who wanted more authority to make decisions in their geographical area. Three regions were carved out, with offices in Chicago, Denver, and Los Angeles. These regional offices were headed by a marketing director who gradually built his own administrative and support staff. The regional offices became critical of the centralized marketing information system. They claimed that it was not responsive to their needs, the reports were late, the analyses were in error, and the response time for requests for new reports was 4 to 6 months if their requests were satisfied at all. Since the regions and the branches under them were profit centers, the decision was made to install three smaller computer systems, one each at the three regional offices, with the central computer maintained for consolidation purposes and manufacturing applications. This characterized phase 3.

The results of phase 4 are illustrated in Figure 6.7. It was during this phase that the EDP director recommended that a large computer be installed to run an expanded version of the marketing information system. The centralized computer would replace the three regional computers. Branch offices would be connected on-line to the computer via communication terminals. The EDP director claimed that his setup would allow management the flexibility of continuing its decentralized mode of operation or of developing a central data base that would allow more decisions to be made at headquarters, thereby returning to a greater degree of centralized control.

The preceding history of sales expansion and marketing organization change is true of other companies, particular those in "growth" industries. The key question to be explored is the role played by the computer and MIS in the organizational evolution of the subject company. Did the computer have any impact on the decision to decentralize or the recommendation to recentralize? The decentralization approach can be defined as the one in which the authority for decision making is delegated to the lowest point in the organization where the required information and capabilities can be brought together. The benefits accrue from the development of an environment where individuals are motivated to apply their maximum effort and talent to reach or exceed stated goals. The motivation usually comes via increased remuneration and the prospect of promotion to more responsible positions. These are the reasons companies decentralize. Does the advent of the computer, communication equipment, and the like influence these reasons? First, can the information necessary to make decisions be made available at the headquarters office? The answer is that it can. In fact, it may be combined or correlated with other information available at headquarters in order to produce an improved information base. However, in many cases, decision making, particularly the important decisions, of the type made at the branch office is more a matter of how to use the data rather than of the kind of data used. There are still many qualitative factors in making sales decisions; a decision to buy is often based on such intangibles as feeling "comfortable" with the salesman. For this reason, it is doubtful that the required capabilities can be made available at the headquarters office. There is still truth in the old refrain, as applied to the computer, "but he doesn't know the territory." Therefore, although the data can be made available, the required capabilities to use it most effectively are only available at the local level. As stated, motivation is a strong factor in the decentralized approach, and this element is not influenced by the computer at all. The conclusion is that the computer does not affect the major reasons for adopting the decentralization concept. Thus it does not have a major impact on whether a company centralizes or decentralizes.

However, the advent of communication processing enables the branch manager to have rapid access to local as well as headquarters information and therefore to make better decisions. Thus the centralized marketing information system can favorably influence the decentralization concept.

There are certain instances where a marketing information system can also abet the centralization approach. In situations where the stable nature of products permits the modeling of consumer buying habits, a centralized marketing information system might be connected to the point-of-sale devices at each store. The system knows at the end of each day what items were sold. Also, knowing the items shipped to the store each day, it can plot sales trends from historical movement tempered by external information, such as expected promotions, holidays, and seasonal elements, and can produce automatic orders and reorders. Under these circumstances, the centralized marketing system might be able to do a better ordering job than a store manager, thus taking over a major decision-making area. As computerized models are improved, it will be possible to expand this process to a wider range of marketing activities, but not all by any means. The point is that computerized marketing information systems, in the case of a sales organization, offer organizational alternatives that were not available previously. Although not the major determinant of whether a company centralizes or decentralizes, the computer is an aid in proceeding along either route. This is true of most of the organizational restructuring occurring within a company. The computer is an aid and a catalyst but not the reason (and it is illogical to assume it is) for the organizational change.

SUMMARY

There is no question that computers and MIS have had and will have progressively more impact on management. Existing systems have influenced lower levels of management, particularly operating management. The effect on middle management has been slight, while the impact on top management has been almost nonexistent. However, a review of the decision-making process indicates that key steps in the process can be materially aided by computerized decision making. A better understanding and quantification of external data, accelerated development and acceptance of management science techniques, and the proper distinction between qualitative logical facts and intuition are important elements in facilitating computer-assisted decision making. The type of change in job content illustrated by the numerical control analogy can be expected gradually to creep upward to higher levels of management. Whether tomorrow's executive will be of the "keyed-in" variety is open to speculation. However, the information middleman will continue to play a strong role even though the gap between the manager and the machine will be materially lessened.

A phenomenon first mentioned in Chapter 4 and one that has already appeared on the scene as a result of the ability of computers to gather, accumulate, and turn out information rapidly and effectively from its data banks is a syndrome called "information glut." This debilitating by-product of the computerized era is described by a company president in comparing the computer, which operates in pico-second speed (less than a billionth of a second), to man, an electronically primitive mechanism who operates according to a 60-second schedule: 30 minutes to drive to the office, 40 minutes at a meeting, 90 minutes to eat lunch. He goes on to state:

> Yet sixty-second man—and his management—will soon find themselves in a pico-second world. Like the business traveler who constantly flies great distances and complains of "jet stomach," his desk-bound colleague may one day suffer from both information indigestion and a blighted ego—simply because he does not know how to communicate with the computer, has not kept current with developments in the field, and has not learned to digest and use its output or to identify his role as manager clearly and quantitatively enough to avail himself of the EDP—electronic data processing—help that awaits his summons.

(From "Sixty Second Man in a Pico-Second World" by R. E. Slater, July, 1967 *Management Thinking,* Harvard Business School Ass'n.)

The president of Volkswagon puts it this way:

> We think that the jet aircraft with its high-speed comfort has made our life easier. Instead, we now find we spend more time traveling—not less. We go greater distances, but in doing so may accomplish less.
>
> Thirty years ago, a trip from London to Frankfurt was carefully planned. It was not an easy trip and, therefore, was made only after proper preparations. Today, the trip is so quick, so easy, that we tend to do it without planning. . . .
>
> As a result, we often come back without accomplishment; and because the trip was so easy and so quick, we are less disappointed when it is not productive. Many times a thoughtful letter or an intelligent and well-prepared telephone conversation could have accomplished more.
>
> Before the arrival of the electrostatic copier we thought carefully about the distribution of documents. A great deal of work was necessary to make extra copies and, as a result, only those who really could use the data were given copies. Today, we push a button and 20 copies come out in an instant. . . .
>
> My greatest problem is not lack of information, but rather a surplus

of it. There is no surplus of what I need to know, but there is a surplus of what others think I should know. We must return to concise and economical communications. . . .

(From "Business Communications" by Dr. Heinz Nordhoff. HBS Executive Letter, Sept. 1967, Harvard Business School Ass'n.)

STUDY CASETTES

EXPERIENCE OF A SMALL INTEGRATED STEEL COMPANY

[From "A Small Company Turns to the Computer" by Daniel A. Roblin, Jr. *Management Thinking,* Harvard Business School Association, October 1968]

Several years ago, we came to the conclusion that any company big enough to afford a computer that does not have one either functioning or in its planning for the immediate future is not going to grow in the competitive business world of today. Everything we've learned during our first year as a computer user has served to reinforce that conviction.

If we were willing to spend the money, we could manually prepare most of the reports our computer is giving us today.

Five years from now this will not be true. We will then have a management information system pervading all phases of our corporate activity, and we will be achieving the growth and earnings objectives we have set for ourselves, which we could not hope to achieve without the computer.

A small company dedicated to growth thus can utilize the benefits of a computer more fully and in a shorter period of time than a large complex corporation. The complete management information system we are installing here, for example, will be accomplished in five years or less.

To ensure that the computer has no adverse effect on the company and to hasten its full utilization, it is necessary to properly indoctrinate all of the management group to its use. The procedure is the same as the indoctrination program after the purchase of a new piece of sophisticated machinery. You have a training program for those who are to be involved with it. The only difference is that in this case the computer is a tool that is used by the whole management group, not by just a handful of operating people, so the whole management group is included in the educational programs.

Prior to the installation of the computer we began our indoctrination program with a three-day seminar at Cornell University for our whole management group to discuss what we hoped to accomplish with our new computer. We then formed a committee of operating people who analyzed every piece of paper in use in the entire corporation. After the committee completed its work, we held a second seminar to talk about what we had accomplished in the course of that year—but no longer were we talking about just a computer. We were talking now about our business, its progress, and its goals. At this second seminar, we introduced the management information system concept, explaining that such a system had always existed, but in a very crude form. All of those pieces of paper we had worked with every day were part of this system; for that matter, information written on a paper napkin would be part of it.

We try to manage this business by objectives. In order for us to do this, management people must make commitments on how they are going to operate each unit of the company. The computer is beginning to play a big part in helping them to set these goals and to reach them.

For example, one new plant manager faced with setting his standards for the year was able to make a massive analysis of past operations to secure some particular data he felt he needed that would have been impossible to get with our old tab equipment. Furthermore, with some corrections and revisions, this same system is helping him now to attain his objectives by supplying him with a weekly status report. Soon he may be able to have updated information on a daily basis as part of our complete management information system.

In another instance, the sales department was able to use a very detailed sales analysis of past performance provided by the computer to predict what they will sell to each customer this year, not just in dollar volume, but by product, broken down by specific chemistry and size. This in turn permitted our manufacturing people and purchasing people, who formerly had to base their cost objectives on groups of products, to determine more accurately the specific alloys they will require and the amount of material they will have to produce in various sizes, and therefore to forecast more accurately what the cost of sales will be. The more accurately you can predict, the more effectively your costs can be reduced.

Because we do measure management people by their performance relative to the objectives they themselves have set, they also determine what information they want and what the computer can do to help them. Manufacturing applications, for example, are developed by manufacturing people assisted by the people in the computer department—and not the other way around.

I do not know what possibilities we will uncover in the future, when more data becomes available. We are contemplating a complete random access system, with terminals in all of our operating departments. I foresee people, for example, in order processing, production scheduling, or sales, with a computer inquiry station at their desks being able to press a button when a customer calls and have instantly displayed all information needed to give an immediate answer to questions about delivery, pricing, and so on.

I can envision a computer-controlled continuous steelmaking process in which a scrapped automobile will go in at one end of a plant and a finished steel product will come out the other end. It is possible that this kind of thinking eventually will cause a complete revision of the operating systems we have now.

As my function is more planning and looking to the future, I do not need information in the detail or with the frequency that people involved in making our day-to-day decisions do. But I would like to have on my desk each morning a summary report of corporate activities up through the day before—cash balance, accounts receivable, accounts payable, shipments, production, and the like—for each segment of the business. This can not happen for a long time, of course, but eventually it will be possible.

Study Questions

1. How important is an information system that can grow along with the company— will it take five years to develop?

2. Do you think it relevant that members of the management group drifted from just talking about a computer and started discussing business goals and objectives?

3. Do you see indications that the computer is becoming woven into the basic fabric of the company's operation—is this the correct approach?

4. Do you think the view of the future is realistic in light of the company's experience and viewpoint to date?

THE MANAGER LOOKS AT MIS

[This material originally appeared as part of the article "The Manager Looks at MIS" by Franz Edelman. *Computer Decisions,* August, 1971]

Every management information system, to be of any value, should be designed for and by the managers who are to use it. In order to be involved in the creation of an MIS, there are certain elements of an information system, and certain relationships between these elements, that the manager should understand.

There are two "Laws of Relevance" which should govern the modern manager's style in his use of MIS technology. The first is:

"No manager with responsibility for a business—or a part thereof—will base important decisions on the outcome of a process which he, himself, does not adequately understand."

In other words, regardless of the manager's confidence in his "management scientist," he should never stick his neck out unless he fully understands the reasons for doing so.

This first law of management systems and sciences deals with the art of managing. The second law is concerned with the methodological content of the management task:

"Genuine management information consists of the quantitative (numerical) and the qualitative (relational) descriptions of the business issues at hand."

An example of the quantitative aspect of management information would be the fact that a company has sold 10 million widgets during the first half of 1971. The number 10 million is a piece of purely numerical information which is of significance even if it is out of context with regard to the economic environment, company marketing objectives, and any other factors which imply a relationship.

Qualitative information, on the other hand, defines relationships. A good example of this sort of relational or structural information is provided by the example:

After-tax proceeds = (1—tax rate) × (revenues—expenses other than depreciation) + (tax rate) × (depreciation).

This too is information even though it contains not a single numerical value. It expresses a relationship among a number of variables. It is a piece of purely relational data without regard to numerical content.

Another such example is the formula:

$$y = ax + b$$

To most people, this immediately suggests a straight line relationship between the two variables x and y regardless of what these variables happen to be.

It is important to clearly define these two different types of information—

numerical and relational. To be effective, an MIS must be capable of managing two different and separate repositories—the first containing the numerical data and the second containing the relationships. The data repository is called the data base and the relationship repository is called the model.

In discussing the significance to management information systems of the data base and the model, there are three facts which should be kept in mind:

1. It takes both numbers and relationships to produce results that are useful in decision-making.

2. Numbers change faster than relationships.

3. It is easier and more economical to change numerical inputs to a system (its data base) than it is to change programmed instructions (its model).

With these facts in mind, it is logical that the model should not only be devoid of numerical content (in order to avoid expensive program changes every time a numerical value changes) but, conversely, the data base should be devoid of structure (except that which is required by the system for retrieval). This will avoid the necessity of reorganizing a massive data base every time you decide to reorganize your business.

Study Questions

1. Can you expect managers to adequately understand some of the complex processes embedded in advanced computer systems as stated in the first "Law of Relevance"?

2. What do you think of the author's explanation of the data base and the model?

3. How would you go about explaining complex mathematical models to management?

BIBLIOGRAPHY

BRADY, R. H., Computers in Top Level Decision Making. *Harvard Business Review,* July–August, 1968, pp. 67–76.

BRINK, V. Z., *Computers and Management: The Executive Viewpoint.* Prentice-Hall, Inc., Englewood Cliffs, New Jersey, 1971, 172 pp.

KRIEBEL, et al. *MIS: Progress and Perspectives.* Carnegie Press, Pittsburgh, Penn., 1971, 497 pp.

Management and The Computer. A *Wall Street Journal* study of the management men responsible for their companies' purchases of computer equipment and services. Dow Jones & Co. Inc., 1969.

Management Information Series. Reprints from *Harvard Business Review* (14 articles).

MORTON, M. S. *Management Decision Systems.* Harvard University Press, Cambridge, Massachusetts, 1971, 216 pp.

MYERS, C. A. (ed.), *The Impact of Computers on Management.* The MIT Press, Cambridge, Massachusetts, 1967, 310 pp.

NEWMAN, J. W., Management Applications of Decision Theory. Harper and Row, New York, 1971, 210 pp.

SCHODERBEK, P. P., and J. D. BABCOCK, The Proper Placement of Computers: Organizational Location Affects Efficiency. *Business Horizons,* October, 1969, pp. 35–42.

SCHRIEBER, ALBERT N., *Corporate Simulation Models.* University of Washington, Seattle, Washington, 1970, 614 pp.

TOMESKI, F., The Executive Use of Computers. Collier Books, New York, 1969, 146 pp.

WITHINGTON, F. G., *The Real Computer: Its Influence, Uses and Effects.* Addison-Wesley, Reading, Massachusetts, 1969.

Chapter 7

MANAGEMENT INVOLVEMENT
AND INFLUENCE IN MIS

The previous chapter discussed the impact of computers and MIS on management. The conclusion was that although the impact varied among the various levels of management, MIS affected all levels to some degree. The trend most definitely is that MIS will have an accelerating influence on management. The typical manager's job has not shown a revolutionary change up to now, but most would agree that computer–powered MIS provides enough potential to affect his job and the business environment surrounding his job materially. It is time for the manager to become more involved and to gain a comprehensive understanding of EDP and related activities. No longer do managers feel that computer applications and system development are activities that can be delegated exclusively to the technical people who are expert in these areas. They do not argue the point of *whether* they need exposure and involvement; the issue now is *what kind* of involvement. The former point has come to be an accepted fact.

Two major issues will be discussed in this chapter. The first is the level of involvement required of management. As we shall see, this criterion depends on such factors as the particular level of management, the immediacy of the impact of EDP, and the degree of company-wide computerization. The level of involvement is also closely related to the computerization quotient discussed in Chapter 6. Once the role is recognized, the second issue is how the manager proceeds to gain the necessary training, education, and practical EDP experience.

The supposition is that management will not be programming computers on a wholesale basis. Nor will the majority be communicating directly with computers via on-line inquiry-oriented languages. For the most part, management will work with the machine through a system analyst or information middleman. MIS is a combination of inanimate objects like a computer and animate objects like system analysts and programmers. Management will have to deal mainly with animate objects. Thus management involvement is tied directly to the system analysts and to the managers of data processing. For this reason, I will discuss the roles of both general management and EDP management and the vital interaction required between the two groups. The involvement of one group without the other is meaningless. It is the proper blending of the two groups that produces effective and successful management information systems.

MANAGEMENT'S ROLE IN SYSTEM DEVELOPMENT

Figure 7.1 establishes the framework for discussing the type of involvement required of different levels of management. The middle triangle is similar to that used in Chapter 1 to describe the various vertical stages of system and subsystem development. Reading from bottom to top, it lists seven major elements in putting an information system in operation. It starts with the overall business objective and goals and then proceeds to a definition of external and internal business and product strategies required to meet these general goals. These elements were described more completely in Chapter 4. The integrated system specification establishing the overall MIS framework leads into the design criteria for the integrated system. The former describes the *what* of MIS while the latter describes *how* it is to be accomplished. The cycle next proceeds through individual subsystems specification and design and, finally, to the programming and operation of each application area selected for implementation.

The inverted triangle on the left of Figure 7.1 comes from Chapter 1 and illustrates the three levels of management; top management setting the overall company goals and strategies, middle management interpreting the goals and strategies and planning their implementation, and operating management actually carrying out and performing the work to implement the plan. The EDP management on the right of Figure 7.1 is a microcosm of general management in that top management within EDP develops the overall EDP goals and objectives in the same way that the top management of the total company does for the company. The various system analysts and project leaders are the middle managers of EDP who interpret EDP top-management policy and take charge of pertinent subelements or subsystems. Programming and operating management make certain that the individual computer programs are consistent with the established system specifications and that, once programmed and tested, they are operated in accordance with predetermined procedures.

Figure 7.1 establishes the relative management-involvement levels and the interface points between general management and EDP management. It indicates that the top management is concerned with the first three system development elements. Overlapping exists in the involvement of different levels of management, as can be seen from the chart.

Middle management is concerned with the establishment of external-internal strategies through subsystem specification, while operating management's involvement in the various systems elements can be seen on the right of Figure 7.1. The interface points between general and EDP management are through the common system elements with which each is concerned.

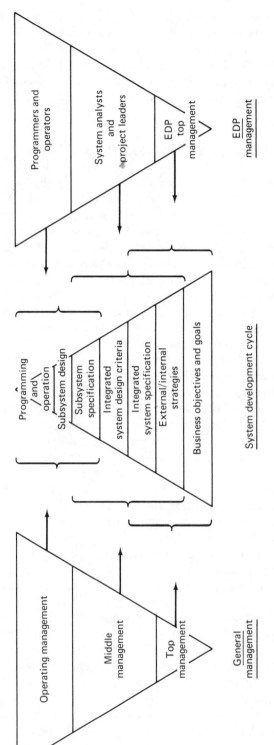

Fig. 7.1 Management's role in system development

Figures 7.2 and 7.3 define general management and EDP management's involvement in MIS by particular management level. It becomes clear, in viewing the respective roles, that there are common areas of concern. It is necessary for both sides to come together and mutually discuss these areas. Unilateral resolution of particular system problems has been a major cause of system failure. This point is particularly true of MIS where the interaction of middle-and top-management levels is extremely important. Conventional system approaches that attack lower-level subsystems on a department basis while underplaying the integration aspects of systems require interaction at the operating management level only. MIS, with its emphasis on integration and automatic decision making, requires interaction at the middle-and top-management level.

ISSUES OF IMPORTANCE TO MIS PROFESSIONALS

The founding conference (in September, 1969) of the Society for Management Information Systems, of which I am a charter member, was attended by EDP consultants, members of professional agencies, educators, developers of MIS, would-be developers of MIS, and non-EDP management of companies installing MIS. Thus the group consisted of 125 individuals who represented a high level of MIS experience and know-how. It is interesting to look at the relative importance these professionals placed on potential MIS research projects. Figure 7.4 ranks these projects in order by a computer-ranking score.

I have indicated, next to each project, an M if the item is concerned with a managerial problem, B if the item is concerned with a behavioral problem, and T if the item is concerned with a technical problem, or can be resolved exclusively by EDP management. It is interesting to note that 10 of the first 15 projects are management considerations, whereas 2 are behavioral in nature. Only 3 of the first 15 projects are technical in nature, whereas the remaining 11 are technical. The indication is that the experienced MIS people have found that the toughest problems to solve are such management problems as determining the content of information, the needs of decision makers, economic considerations in MIS, and the selection of application areas. The two behavioral areas listed are related to overcoming the problems of user-designer interface and managing problems associated with system changes. This result further emphasizes the need for management involvement in MIS. More often than not, it is the non-EDP element that has caused the greater problem in MIS design and implementation. Yet educational programs continue to concentrate on training the technical EDP people. The result is a serious dilemma that must be resolved if MIS is to serve management and operating personnel outside the EDP department.

This discussion has described the role that various levels of general and EDP management should take in developing an MIS and the importance of management involvement. The next question to explore is how one obtains the proper involvement level. It is pertinent that a discussion of *what* precedes the *how*. Too often management is talked into some type of specialized executive computer course or system course without knowing if it is the right level or type of exposure. In order to determine whether it is, one must know beforehand what role he will be playing

Top management

-- Concern with business objectives; explain what is essential for EDP; ensure an understanding; monitor to see that the understanding and awareness are present.

-- Ensure that external/internal strategies are understood, e.g., production scheduling system must take into account the level employment of skilled workers; all application areas must take into account the financial and capital requirements; applications must be built on the assumption that business conditions will change.

-- Participate in establishing and reviewing integrated system spec; this is overall game plan — the framework or road map — and is very important. Should have opportunity to review any major system changes.

-- Participate in establishing over — all schedule. Review major milestones and project status.

Middle management

-- Awareness and participation in establishment of external/ internal strategies. Middle management is cognizant of the effect of these polices on actual operations.

-- Participate in development of the overall integrates system spec.

-- Representation on steering committee. Involvement in the sub-systems that affect the manager's department or affects those departments with whom he inter-faces.

-- Obtain proper people involvement by setting the proper example. Middle management is not concerned with specific system design but the issues discussed and reviewed at steering committee meetings will impact design.

-- Assign analysts within a particular area or at least provide contact point, an individual who can speak for the department or has perspective to know when middle management should be called in to approve a major issue.

Operating management

-- Develop and produce procedure manuals. Train people in use of system. Make necessary preparations for the conversion and transition period. Should be on call to handle detailed questions or respond to specific issues

-- Help establish psychological atmosphere for acceptance and co-operation of operating people involved. Develop outlook that emphasizes that system benefits will offset the effort of change and transaction.

-- Explain where the individual parts or roles of operating people fit into total MIS picture. Maintain positive motivation.

-- Ensure that system operates according to specification — feed back any discrepancies or problems.

Fig. 7.2 General management involvement in MIS

EDP top management	EDP middle management (System analysts and project leaders)	EDP operating management (Programmers and operators)
—Aware of over-all company business goals, EDP goals and the relation of the two. —Aware of company strategies as they affect the overall system planning and MIS design. —Major participant along with general management in setting specifications, schedules and milestones for MIS. Must take leadership role and ensure proper level of management involvement. —Complete responsibility for the design of the overall integrated system (MIS and integrated system are used synonomously in this context). The selection of the particular computer system with the required input/output and storage devices rests with EDP top management. —Must be knowledgeable in EDP state of the art — what other users are doing, what computer manufacturers, software houses and service companies are doing.	—Work with EDP top management and general management counterparts to aid in the development of the integrated system spec. —Project leaders are responsible for developing individual subsystem specs in conjunction with key management of the affected departments. Must ensure that spec is what using department wants and sees as its requirements. —Responsible for subsystem design. Design must satisfy specifications. Must review and seek resolution of and spec change or on major trade off decision. —Work with programmers to effect adequate translation of system design into coded programs.	—Develop individual programs consistent with subsystem specs. —Check out and fully test resulting programs. —Review questionable areas with system analysts and project leaders. —Establish operating procedures for productive execution of programs. —Execute and monitor productive programs in daily operation. —Develop detailed conversion and cutover plan for new applications. —Provide feed back loop to system designers for incorporation of new features in subsequent re-writes and modification of applications.

Fig. 7.3 EDP management involvement in MIS

Rank	Project	Computed score	Problem classification
1	Development of methods for determining what the content of an information system should be	4.07	M
2	Investigation into the characteristics of decision makers which affects MIS system design	3.95	M
3	Investigation of means for overcoming user-designer interface problems	3.76	B
4	Development of methods for evaluating in an economic sense a computerized MIS	3.70	M
5	Development of computer assisted planning models	3.63	M
6	Determination of the factors contributing to success of failure of EDP projects	3.57	M
7	Development of data management software systems	3.56	T
8	Development of improved methods for time and cost estimating of system design projects	3.45	M
9	Development of improved methods of establishing data security in on-line systems	3.32	T
10	Investigation of the value of CRT's in displaying MIS output	3.32	T
11	Investigation of the relationship between a centralized MIS and a decentralized management organization	3.31	M
12	Development of improved methods for EDP project control	3.31	M
13	Determination of ways to manage behavioral problems associated with new systems or systems changes	3.25	B

Fig. 7.4a   Importance ratings of potential MIS research projects

in his company's computer program. A top executive requires a different type of exposure than a middle manager, and a middle manager of a department that is to be immediately impacted by EDP requires a different exposure than a manager of an unaffected department. Thus the discussion of the various management roles in MIS sets the stage for exploring the question: How does one get involved in MIS?

ESTABLISHING THE PROPER INVOLVEMENT LEVEL

As in learning any new skill, there are several ways to acquire the necessary EDP knowledge. The first way is to learn by doing, by participating in the actual system and/or programming activity during some part of the implementation cycle. This, of course, can either be full-time or part-time participation. For classification

Rank	Project	Computed score	Problem classification
14	Development of methods for the selection of EDP applications projects	3.20	M
15	Investigation of methods for accomplishing feasibility studies on EDP proposals	3.18	M
16	Exploration of methods for measuring response time requirements for information from an MIS	3.17	T
17	Improvement of program documentation methods	3.16	T
18	Development of a bibliographic file for MIS literature	3.15	T
19	Investigation of uses of graphic plotter equipment in displaying MIS output	2.99	T
20	Development of methods for selecting and placing EDP personnel	2.91	T
21	Exploration of methods for improving EDP personnel evaluation	2.83	T
22	Definition of the function of an information specialist	2.76	T
23	Development of methods for costing shared use of an organization's centralized EDP system	2.74	T
24	Development of programs to audit other applications programs	2.73	T
25	Design of specialized simulation languages	2.69	T
26	Development of improved methods for debugging computer programs	2.64	T
Key:	M = Managerial B = Behavioral T = Technical		

Fig. 7.4b Importance ratings of potential MIS research projects (*continued*)

purposes, I have chosen to divide the participation method into (a) direct and (b) indirect, depending on the level of participation. Another method of acquiring computer knowledge is by formal training or education. In reality, knowledge is usually acquired by a combination of (a) direct participation, (b) indirect participation, and (c) education. Since many of today's managers attended college when computer courses were either nonexistent or inadequate, the education has to be acquired after college. I will now discuss each of the three methods.

DIRECT EDP PARTICIPATION

Looking at the EDP picture from an operating-department point of view, we list several assignments where one can acquire computer and system know-how.

- As an in-department system analyst.
- As an out-department system analyst.
- As part of a special task force.

In the first instance, the department whose activities are being computerized assigns an individual(s) to devote full time to the effort. This person works as the in-department system analyst, analyzing and defining the department's information needs, assisting in developing the system spec, the design of the system, and the necessary preparatory work before turning the application over to the programmers. This is an excellent way to become involved in the computer project. The individual learns about computers and systems by practical experience while, at the same time, he represents the interests of his department. He usually remains organizationally in his current department but has a dotted-line relationship to the EDP department. He works full time on the project and produces periodic status reports for his department's management. Often, after a period of time, the system analyst becomes so interested in computer systems that he requests transfer to the EDP department. This is a heatlhy situation, for there is a shortage of good system analysts and experience in general company business operations is excellent background. The EDP staff that has business-based system analysts generally is more responsive to operating needs and is better able to bridge the user-system designer gap that exists.

The out-department system analyst operates in a similar manner except that the individual is transferred from his current department to the EDP department. This move may be required for budgetary reasons or for control purposes. The man is on loan to the EDP department but is responsible for reflecting the interests of the department from which he transferred. This situation has some advantage over the in-department setup, but the risk is that the individual loses the user orientation that is so important to good system work.

Finally, a member(s) of the operating department may be placed on a special task force that is established to computerize a specified application area. The participation can be part time or full time with preference on the latter if the budget exists for it. The individual, who may be a manager if the participation is part time, does not act in the role of a system analyst but rather in the role of a fact finder, system reviewer, sounding board, control point, or whatever you wish to call it. Again he represents the using department and works with the system analyst to provide him with the necessary background information about the department's operations and requirements. It is obvious that in either one of the three cases mentioned some type of formal training should supplement the practical experience. However, the major focus is on learning by doing, by working with experienced system analysts and EDP personnel in actual implementation of an application.

INDIRECT EDP PARTICIPATION

There are other ways to become involved in EDP without the full time or direct participation just described. The following represent assignments that can indirectly involve people in the EDP process:

- Steering committee
- Department-coordinator
- System spec developer
- Application selection committee

These are more passive approaches, but they can still be quite effective in providing proper operating-department involvement. The steering committee is a group established at the outset to act as a higher-level management review board. The group normally meets weekly, or less frequently, to go over progress, review the key problem areas, and recommend solutions. The group controls people and budget assets and can recommend that additional resources be utilized if the program is behind schedule. It then has the authority to assign the additional people. Weekly review meetings are commonly supplemented by periodic tutorial sessions to equip the committee with the knowledge to assess progress more accurately.

The department coordinator continues to work full time on his assigned tasks within the operating department. However, he is assigned the role of coordinator to the system group working in an applications area that affects his department. He is available to answer any questions or to set up sessions with pertinent people in the department if he cannot answer the questions directly. This approach is more passive and relies on the ability of the full-time system analysts to ask the right questions.

The system spec developer is also a part-time participant who works with the EDP staff through the development of the system spec. He signs off on the spec for his department. Since the spec specifies the objectives and purpose of the application, as well as the detailed input, output, and storage requirements, a sign-off at this stage is an important consideration. However, the risk is that the implemenation may proceed counter to the spec in certain areas or that subsequent system design may force system spec trade-offs. If the individual is available only up to system spec sign-off, too much reliance may be placed on the EDP staff.

Finally, an individual of an operating department can participate in EDP activity by being a member of the application selection committee. As has been mentioned, one of the key considerations in successful EDP is the procedure for giving priority to the implementation of applications. There are always many more potential computer applications that can be handled by the existing staff. The steering committee must review the economic, technical, and operational feasibility on an application by application basis and select those that have the highest composite value to the company. This is usually a management job, so that the steering committee consists of key managers from the major operating departments. Generally they meet monthly to review the overall status of application development and to select additional applications if resources are available. As in the case of the steering committee, periodic tutorial sessions build the knowledge base of committee members.

As stated at the outset, the direct and indirect EDP participation routes must be supplemented by both formal and informal training programs. It is time to take a look at this most important subject and to discuss the pros and cons of the many training methods available today. Perspective is extremely important in this area.

MANAGEMENT EDUCATION AND TRAINING

Computer education has been a major growth area within the EDP industry. The number of computer installations has grown faster than the number of trained people who can run them. The picture has been complicated by the fact that until recently, colleges and universities were not equipped to train students properly in EDP. Figure 7.5 lists the types of educational facilities available today. It breaks down the facilities into (a) schools, including elementary and preparatory schools, but primarily colleges, business schools, and universities; (b) internal on-site company training, which includes training by the company's own EDP department or training furnished by the computer vendor, a consultant, or private educational institutional but accomplished on the company's own premises tailored especially for its own personnel; and (c) external training accomplished off the company site by EDP professional societies and educational agencies, seminars, and business meetings devoted to EDP, continuing education programs of colleges and universities, and, finally, self-study in the form of correspondence courses or merely home reading of EDP texts and publications. I will now discuss each category in turn. The key consideration in the discussion of education is the importance of establishing educational objectives of each class of personnel being trained. The significant question that should continually be raised is: What does the particular individual have to know about EDP to do his job better or to direct the jobs of others?

Schools	Secondary schools
	Colleges
	Business schools
	Graduate schools
Internal on-site company training	EDP department
	Computer vendor
	Consultants
	Private educational institutions
External training	EDP professional societies
	EDP educational agencies
	Seminars and business meetings
	University continuing education programs
	Self study courses

Fig. 7.5   EDP education facilities

EDP Education in Schools

There has been a great deal of misunderstanding concerning the teaching of computers in schools, from the elementary and high schools to the business colleges and postgraduate universities. The basis of this misundertanding is a confusion as to the role the computer plays, first, in a business and scientific sense and, secondly, in the daily lives of each of us. Computers have come on the scene so quickly that educators as well as businessmen are still confused as to the computer's place in society. On the one hand, the computer seems to be simply an extension of the computing power of business equipment like calculators, accounting machines, and other business paper-work processors, whereas, on the other hand, the computer and EDP can be viewed as opening up an entirely new functional area of business operation called information technology or something similar. The business-school educational proponents of the former attitude establish a computer fundamentals course, usually within the accounting department, and then treat computers as an adjunct to other functional course areas. For example, the financial department discusses computers as they apply to the financial operations of a company, while the marketing area touches on the use of computers in sales forecasting or market analysis. Those who believe that the computer has ushered in a new science of information have established special departments and course curricula leading to advanced degrees in management information systems. For example, the school of business administration at the University of Minnesota has established a program that grants a master's or doctorate degree in management information systems. The school has also established a MIS Research Center to focus research efforts in this area of study. The MIS field of study recognizes information as a resourse parallel to land, labor, and capital that should be subject to managerial planning and control. The course is aimed at providing both (a) a knowledge of the management process and the functional areas of business and (b) a knowledge of computer technology hardware, software, and programming, plus its application to the analysis, design, and administration of management information systems.

An analogy might help bring computer education into better focus. A student learns a foreign language in school for several reasons. First, like most educational processes, it is an intellectual logical exercise that stretches the mind and forces the student to think of the subject as a series of grammatical rules and relationships. Secondly, learning a language can help a student achieve a better understanding of the history and the economic, social, and political workings of a particular country or culture. Finally, a foreign-language skill can provide the necessary preparation for a career as a translator or interpreter, or for one in the field of international business.

I see the teaching of computers in preparatory schools, and in many colleges as well, as being primarily in the mind-stretching capacity. Most students will not be computer system analysts or programmers in the future, just as most will not be accountants or salesmen. Why should preparatory schools devote time to the former if they do not devote time to the latter? Computer programming is an excellent mental discipline that forces the individual to think logically and rationally and to focus on solving a specific problem. Furthermore, it can be an enjoyable educational experience and an educational motivator to many students. In addition, it should be noted that the basic computer programming courses given in secondary schools, particularly those schools with terminals that can communicate with a remote computer, also aid in the understanding of information processing and data communication in general. The students gain an awareness that data, like voices, can be transmitted over telephone lines and that the computer at the other end will act in accordance with prescribed rules. For example, if you describe a complex equation and wish to solve the equation based on a series of alternate values, the computer will accomplish the mathematical processing and return the solution(s) to you in a very short period of time.

Many parents are blaming the computer for the new math that is taught in the elementary schools because it introduces a new teaching method which parents find difficult to comprehend. However, the computer is not the real culprit. It is true that computers utilize the binary system for representing members, but it is not necessary for humans to know binary to program the machine. Learning that there are numbering systems other than decimal is useful, but not because a computer uses the binary numbering system. My conclusion, therefore, is that computers and EDP, if taught in the elementary schools, should be viewed as mind stretchers and educational motivators and not primarily for practical application later in life. If the latter is the primary goal or if there are better alternatives for mind stretching, then it might be well to reduce the emphasis on computer training in the elementary schools.

Computer usage and education are growing in liberal arts colleges. Since colleges do begin to specialize students for particular jobs, there is more reason for teaching computers as a skill to be utilized in business or science. However, I feel that the main focus should still be on a computer as a mind stretcher and as a device to facilitate a better understanding of communication and information processing. Dartmouth College has been a pioneer in the use of computers in its educational curriculum. The Spring 1970 *Carnegie Quarterly* quotes John G. Kemeny, father of the Dartmouth computer system and developer of a specialized language that facilitates direct communication with the computer and now president of the college: "Learning to use a high-speed computer should be an essential part of a liberal education." The article goes on to say that

> Not only will this give Dartmouth alumni an idea of the multitude of problems computers can be asked to solve and how to ask the right questions, but as lawyers, businessmen, doctors, engineers, they will also have a sophisticated understanding of how to use social science data in creative ways. The result of this special approach is not to use a computer instead of a teacher or a book to give students information and to answer student questions. Instead, students must learn to teach the computer, by programming it to sort stored information in useful ways.

["The Computer and the Liberal Arts: A Compatible Relationship." *Carnegie Quarterly,* Spring 1970.]

Dartmouth, as well as Dr. Kemeny, has gone further than most colleges in the use of computers. Some might disagree with his statement that computer education should be an essential part of a liberal education. I would tend to agree more with an amended statement, which reads "Computer education can prove a most beneficial part of a liberal education." There is no question that having access to a computer in college can extend the range of problems that can be tackled; for example, access to a computerized simulation model adds a new dimension to a mathematics or physical science course. I believe that it should be pointed out to students, however, that a cost benefit justification process is necessary to assess the value of remote terminals and computer processing in a profit-making organization. One gets the feeling, particularly at Dartmouth, where remote computer terminals are in such profusion, that this is an accepted way of life and is as easy as using the telephone. Although the educational benefits may justify the costs, the justification is different in business, and it is true that remote data processing has not as yet assumed the ease and reliability of the telephone.

Several years ago, I was invited to Dartmouth's Tuck School of Business as a guest lecturer. The professor asked if I would direct my remarks to the cost/benefit and business considerations underlying the installation of time-sharing systems like those at Dartmouth; he was concerned over the spreading "fadism."

Business and graduate schools present a different problem because it is here that students are trained for business and professional specialization. A distinction must be made between training (a) the student who plans to be a specialist in data processing and (b) the student who plans to pursue a general business career, specializing in a field other than data processing. I feel that the business schools may be guilty of following the secondary and college educational objectives of computers as mind stretchers and educational motivators. This practice may be desirable, but it should be viewed in perspective to the major educational objective of giving students the proper computer background to accomplish either of the two roles described above. In my opinion many business schools lean toward the exciting, exotic, and new, at the expense of accomplishing the key educational objectives. Remote terminals and on-line communication processing have been overemphasized in business schools. Several prominent business schools indoctrinate business students in information processing with an extensive programming course that enables them to use remote terminals. Although this activity may have merit, I think the sequence is wrong. It is the thesis of this book that system analysis begins with a thorough understanding of business information needs and of the functional subsystems that underlay a management information system. I think training in EDP should begin with this orientation rather than with the premise that all of tomorrow's business managers will be keyed-in executives, to borrow a term from the preceding chapter. There is too much emphasis on on-line, real-time, scientific processing (Fortran or BASIC are almost always the software languages that are taught) and communication networks at the expense of sound business data processing emphasizing the economic, technical, and operational feasibility of computerization.

I think that this situation arises from a general confusion over the computer's role in business and from the educational gap that has occurred because of the rapid proliferation of computers. The computer instructors in business schools are chiefly young business school graduates who have been trained as computer specialists. They have an unbalanced view of the technical aspects versus the general business aspects of computer training. They stress the former. This situation is accentuated by the fact that they are most familiar and comfortable with the technical. Furthermore, the technical aspects are easier to teach. The educational gap exists because the older faculty, who are more experienced in general business requirements, did not learn computers in school and did not encounter them much in their business careers. They have handed over computer training to the computer specialists and now suffer the same communication and interface problem that exists between the general manager and the EDP specialist within a company. Until this situation is rectified and programs have been established to "teach the teachers," the technical educational emphasis will continue to exist. I have taught a variety of computer courses in several business colleges and I realize the tendency of an instructor to teach what he is comfortable with, which usually means shying away from the subject matter of the type found in Chapters 1, 3, 4, 6, and 7 of this book. A basic Fortran programming course or the use of a terminal is more specific and straightforward, besides being easier to teach.

My recommendation is to establish two study programs, one for the would-be computer specialist and one for the would-be general manager. The objectives of the study curriculum would be to prepare individuals for the type of computer involvement described in Figures 7.2 and 7.3, respectively. There would be common educational modules but the emphasis would be different for the two programs. Later in the chapter an education matrix will illustrate the variety of course offerings for each group. The major focus should be on basic system analysis and the various interlocking information subsystems within a company. I feel that the management information system concept is an important cornerstone to the training of both the computer specialist and the general business manager, particularly the latter. Professor R. I. Tricker of the University of Warwick in England, states "from the study of systems in the firm has come the study of the firm as a system." I think this statement is extremely important and puts the proper perspective on the teaching of MIS in business schools. I would also make a plea for holding off the Fortran and on-line communication sessions until after the student has a firm foundation in information systems in general. He will be able to approach this phase of his education with far-greater perspective and understanding of where communication and remote problem solving fit into the total information system.

Internal On-Site Company Training

Since most business managers went to business schools before computers were properly brought into the curriculum, a need to train today's management exists. It is also apparent that those managers who did receive EDP training need continual refreshening and updating. A common method of obtaining this training is for a company to conduct its own on-site education program tailored around its individual requirements. The larger, more experienced users of MIS may have a training department for this purpose. In most firms it is a by-product responsibility of the EDP department. Training is so important that it is beneficial to establish a training group or possibly a training steering committee consisting of non-EDP people as well as EDP people. Doing so makes sense because the majority of the people being trained are not part of the EDP department.

Most companies look to the EDP department as the primary source of educators. Although it is quite possible that talent of this type exists within the department, the company must guard against too technical a focus. As has been illustrated, the general manager requires more than a basic hardware and software course. Other sources of on-site training are computer vendors and consultants. The major computer vendors have been in the education business for many years and have the talent and the course material to assume a good deal of the training burden for a company. However, like the business schools, they, too, have specialized more in technical training, and their basic system and computer management courses may be weak. Most vendors will tailor a course or an entire educational program for a particular company. With the growth of separate pricing for vendor services, a company will generally have to pay for this service. The computer vendor has the advantage of having a full set of instructional aids, complete course outlines, and educational documentation, all of which is extremely important. However, a company should carefully review the course objectives, course content, and instructors to ensure that the course is suitable for the company's own individual requirements.

Consultants and private educational institutions can provide the same type of services offered by the computer vendor. These two sources usually have the advantage of not gearing the education around a specific piece of hardware, as might be the case with the computer vendor. However, normally they do not possess the experience or course documentation of the vendor. These courses can be given on company time, in the evening, or a combination of both day and evening sessions can be utilized. It is important to state clearly the objectives and background expected for each course and to have a group with roughly the same background and interests in the sessions. Management's enthusiasm for computers can diminish quickly if they attend technical sessions with highly technical people. If the company resorts to the use of consultants or private educational institutions, course objectives and capabilities should be thoroughly evaluated before a contract is signed.

External Training

A wider variety of course offerings and educational opportunities exist if the company is willing to go outside for its training. EDP professional societies, such as the American Management Association, Data Processing Management Association, and Systems & Procedure Association, either present courses on a variety of EDP subjects or can help organize and arrange outside training sessions. EDP educational agencies can be utilized for training outside the company just as they can be for internal training. The outside courses offer the opportunity for managers and personnel to mix with their counterparts from other companies, to exchange ideas and broaden their appreciation for EDP. Most of the sessions put on by these agencies are well constructed and tested and clearly state the objectives and purpose. Many are aimed at management-level people. However, a caution is in order, because some courses are not what they look like on paper. It is wise to spend time in evaluating the offerings before signing up. Several telephone calls to prior attendees in a position similar to your own might help qualify the particular session. It is also desirable to discuss the seminar content with someone from the company's own EDP department to qualify it further.

In addition to the paid courses discussed above, there are good opportunities to attend seminars and business meetings devoted to specific EDP subjects. Special interest groups on either an industry or functional basis (sales, finance, etc.) are adding EDP and MIS as subjects at their regular business meetings or are holding periodic seminars on these subjects. These sessions offer excellent opportunities to further one's EDP education and have the added benefit that the people attending are in the same line of work and have similar EDP background.

Most universities have credit and noncredit courses as part of their continuing education program in computer and computer-related subjects. These courses are presented in the evening and can offer an attractive method of acquiring EDP background. Again, one should be aware of what he is getting into, and a call to previous students or to the instructor himself is often a good idea.

Finally, the executive should not rely completely on organized classroom study. Outside reading of books and periodicals should be used to supplement the formal training. A subscription to one of the EDP journals may prove a good investment, or the occasional reading of a management-based computer book. There are firms like the International Accountants Society, Inc., who offer home-study courses. For the most part, they cover fundaments and programming, but management-oriented courses are being developed as well.

EDP EDUCATION MATRIX

Figure 7.6 presents a listing of EDP courses and a ranking of courses by priority of need (first, second, or third) for several classes of business people. The courses are divided into the following seven categories:

1. EDP technology

2. System design

3. Applications (functional

4. Applications (general)

5. Applications (specific)

6. EDP management

7. General managment

The classes of people correspond to the breakdown used earlier in the chapter. I have added "aides" to the various levels of general management, for they are often appointed to work directly with the EDP department.

EDP technology includes both introductory courses on EDP and more sophisticated subjects, such as hierarchical storage devices and advanced programming. Most of these subjects are top priority for EDP people, but, except for the introduction to EDP course, are secondary or tertiary for general management or their aides. System design courses are first priority for EDP top management and system analysts, but of lesser priority for programmers and operators. The system approach is a basic and important module highly ranked for general management as well as EDP management.

The next three course areas cover functional, general, and specific applications. The functional applications are those that focus on a particular area, such as marketing or production. The general applications cover categories or broad classes of computer application like communication or direct access systems. They focus on specific hardware or software use rather than on a particular functional application. The last class of applications covers specific areas, possibly within a functional application area, such as forecasting or numerical control. Generally

1 = First priority 2 = Second priority 3 = Third priority * First priority if you are a member of the department utilizing the specific application	Top management	Middle management	Operating management	Aides to top management	Aides to middle management	Aides to operating management	EDP top management	EDP system analysts	EDP programmers	EDP operators
EDP technology										
Introduction to EDP	1	1	1	1	1	1	1	1	1	1
Hardware components	3	3	3	3	3	2	1	1	1	1
Software components	3	3	3	3	3	2	1	1	1	1
Operating systems						3	1	1	1	1
Hierarchical storage devices						3	1	1	1	1
Basic programming			3	2	2	2	1	1	1	1
Advanced programming					3	3		2	1	3
Programming exercise	2	2	2	2	2	1				
Machine operation							2	2	1	1
System design										
The system approach	1	1	1	1	1	1	1	1	2	
Basic system analysis and design	3	3	3	2	2	2	1	1	1	
Business-based information systems	2	2	2	2	2	2	1	1	1	
Optimizing system design		3	3		2	2	2	1	3	
Interviewing and evaluation techniques							1	1	2	3
Conversion and transition procedures	3	3	2	3	2	2	1	1	2	1
Application (functional)										
Marketing information systems		*	*		*	*		*		
Financial information systems		*	*		*	*		*		
Personnel information systems		*	*		*	*		*		
Planning information systems	2	*	*	1	*	*		*		
Production information systems		*	*		*	*		*		
Applications (general)										
Communications systems		2	2	2	2	2	1	2	2	2
Management science	2	2	2	1	2	2	2	2	3	
Direct access systems		3	3		2	2	1	2	2	2
Remote time sharing		3	3	2	2	2	1	2	3	2
Management decision making	2	3	3	1	2	2	2	2	3	
Application trends	3			3	3	3	2	2	2	
Data base oriented systems		3	3		2	2	1	2	2	2
Applications (specific)										
Forecasting		*	*	*	*	*		*		
Inventory control		*	*	*	*	*		*		
Project management	2	2	2	2	2	2		*		
Numerical control		*	*	*	*	*		*		
Computer aided design		*	*	*	*	*		*		
EDP management										
Managing programmers and system analysts							1	1	3	2
Project control applied to EDP		3	3	2	2	2	1	1	2	2
Operational efficiency and EDP							1	1	2	2
Design considerations in MIS				2	2	2	1	1	2	
General management										
The role of management in EDP	1	1	1	1	1	1	1	1	3	
Using MIS effectively	1	1	1	1	1	1	1	1	3	
	2	2	2	2	2	2	1	2	3	
Feasibility and profitability of computer applications	2	2	2	1	1	1	1	1	3	3

Fig. 7.6 EDP education matrix

these courses are specialized in nature and are required only for those people whose department and work function are directly impacted by the computer.

The last two course areas are directly aimed at EDP management and general management. Both areas have lagged behind the others in quantity and quality. Although there are numerous programming and system courses, there are few on how to manage a computer department. As can be seen, these courses are top priority for EDP management.

The general management courses are top priority for both general management and EDP management; in fact, it is desirable if these course modules can be presented concurrently for both groups. Doing so will be a big step forward in alleviating the conflict that exists between general management and the EDP specialist, a conflict to which we now turn. Before leaving this discussion of education, it should be pointed out that education is an obviously vital and significant part of a successful MIS. Education is not a one-shot deal where a big push is established to upgrade everyone on computers in a month's time. It is a continuing job that must be considered more as a way of life than a specific isolated activity. Above all, education must be flexible and modular to serve the varying needs within a company. The educational matrix serves to accentuate this point.

OPERATING PERSONNEL AND EDP PERSONNEL—
THE CONFLICT

A case study will illustrate the problems that system people can meet when dealing with operating personnel. This case is a typical one that has occurred often in my experience. I feel that it is a rather classical situation. The case study will form the framework for discussion of the conflict areas and point to a review of the specific action that should be taken on both the operating and system side to alleviate the problems.

Paul Foster is a system analyst for the Brown Manufacturing Company, manufacturer of a wide range of paper products. Foster has been with the company for 2 years, serving in the EDP department. Prior to this job, he was a programmer and system engineer for a prominent computer manufacturer. He was considered an intelligent, hard-working individual with creative ideas. There was no question that he was a most competent system analyst.

Foster's major system job was to install a statistical forecasting system to aid the sales, inventory, and production departments. His primary focus was to enable the company's procurement department to base ordering policy on an exponential smoothing type of forecasting which formed the basis of automatic calculation of reorder points, economical order quantities, and quantity discount analysis. The system would automatically produce a purchase order that needed only the buyer's initials before release to the vendor. Foster incorporated several new ideas in the forecasting and ordering algorithms. He used an advanced seasonality analyzer and also was able to include the effect of known external events like special promotions and holidays. He was quite proud of the system he had developed and was determined to see the successful implementation of his approach. He was sure it would materially aid the Brown Company by better balancing inventory, reducing ordering costs, and eliminating expensive stock outs.

At the outset of the implementation phase, Foster conducted a special seminar for the procurement department. He brought in a leading expert on exponential smoothing from a consulting company. Although the session was quite technical in nature, he detected an enthusiastic response from several of the buyers. He thought they were quite impressed with the degree of sophistication in the system they were installing. Foster followed up the seminar with individual discussions with two of the buyers who appeared rather passive to the new system. He had an additional briefing session prior to productive running. A disturbing element to Foster was the fact that, although he tried, he could never make contact with A. L. Metcalfe, director of purchasing. Metcalfe was a busy man and was either on the road or tied up when Foster held his seminars and briefing sessions. He did speak to Metcalfe briefly during the implementation phase and was assured of the director's endorsement of the system.

Foster was somewhat concerned that his system was a little difficult to comprehend because of the nuances that he had incorporated. However, he was convinced that the techniques were well conceived, had been proven at several companies in other industries, and would work at the Brown Company. He felt that the significant benefits produced by the sophisticated system were well worth the risk. The forecasting and ordering system would put Brown in the leadership position in its industry; the system would be superior to any system then in use.

The system was installed on schedule. A conversion seminar was held prior to installation in order to explain the different forms and operating procedures employed by the new system. Several instructional sessions had to be cancelled in order to maintain the schedule and cut-over schedule that had been established. A postinstallation audit was conducted 3 months after the system was put into operation. The audit indicated that only two of the ten buyers were utilizing the order forms emanating from the system. The majority had reverted back to the old method of utilizing a manual card index file for ordering. They used the computer print-out on weekly movement to post and update their manual records but chose to ignore the ordering methods. Most buyers were utilizing the same techniques they had used in the past but were comparing their decisions with the computer's suggested ordering strategy. However, when there were significant differences, they followed the techniques that they knew.

The foregoing case study illustrates a typical reaction of operating people to the advent of a new and sophisticated system. The well-intentioned Paul Foster failed to establish the proper relationship with the operating people who were to use the system. It may have proven wise to proceed a little slower and to have spent more time with Metcalfe and his buyers. It is possible that a less-sophisticated system or a phased approach would have worked better. The following discussion will shed more light on the conflict between the system analyst and the user.

REASONS FOR EDP-USER CONFLICT

A most provocative thesis was written by Thomas Barnett for his degree from MIT's Sloan School of Industrial Management Thesis by T. O. Barnett. (*The Relations of Organizational Relationships to Computer Planning Effectiveness.*

Jan., 1970, MIT). Barnett was an experienced EDP professional before returning to MIT for his master's degree. I had worked with him on the design of an advanced computer system. His thesis focused on the EDP-User relationship under the premise that the lack of a good relationship and communication between these two groups has been a major deterrent to successful system implementation. This premise was also the conclusion of several in-depth surveys on the experience of leading medium and large companies with EDP. What makes Barnett's study unique is the fact that his is the only work I have seen that probed the reasons for this conflict. Barnett interviewed both EDP people and EDP users in a variety of companies. He approached the conflict from the behavioral science point of view. The analysis is particularly pertinent if one keeps in mind the case study of Paul Foster and the Brown Manufacturing Company. The points listed are findings from Barnett's thesis. I agree with the points raised and have added personal comments from my own experience to support them. Thus the points or considerations are his; the elaboration represents a good deal of my own thinking.

The Place of EDP in the Organization

Although not the crucial element, the place of EDP in the organization was an important factor in the conflict that existed in several of the companies. The EDP function has historically been the province of the accounting or controller's department. Since most of the initial applications focused on applications like payroll, accounts receivable, sales-order processing, and inventory reporting and accounting, it seemed a logical extension of the controller's responsibilities. However, since applications under the MIS concept have expanded to include functions like production scheduling, sales forecasting, and requirements generation, the sphere of the controller's responsibility has become enlarged. A common view of the accounting or controller's department is that it is an auditing and control organization that checks up on the work of others. This view may not be a detriment when EDP focused on accounting applications, but it has proven a problem as EDP has delved into the main-line functions of the operating departments. There is resentment on the part of some. Furthermore, there is a question of whether the controller's department enjoys enough stature to win the support of the operating departments it serves. The controller is often a staff level below the managers of the other line departments. This places the EDP department, which reports to the controller, even lower in the organizational hierarchy.

EDP Viewed as a Threat

The users interviewed commonly referred to EDP as a potential threat. They saw the EDP department playing a power game to assume more and more control over operations. Although the EDP department was not significant from an organizational standpoint, it was evident that the EDP group had the president's ear and therefore enjoyed added significance. The operating department management had already experienced the influence of other staff groups on the conduct of their business, some of it not altogether satisfactory. They viewed EDP in this light. Some considered it a personal threat influencing their own job function and future with the company, particularly since they had scant EDP knowledge or background. However, in most cases, it was not a personal threat but a threat to the control of department operations. They feared a detrimental impact on the way they were accustomed to doing business. They were concerned over more complications, more confusion, more foul-ups.

Broad Charter of EDP

The charter of EDP was viewed not only as being very broad in scope but very vague as well. This attitude was tied into the feeling that EDP had the president's ear. These factors together would extend the influence of EDP into areas where it perhaps did not belong. The operating department personnel worried that the company might get carried away by this new "toy" or gadget. They saw an organizational centralization taking place where the charter of EDP would include more and more functions formerly performed by the operating departments. Although they could see the benefit in having the computer assume certain clerical and record-handling duties, they were concerned about its role in decision making. This was no doubt a factor in the case of the buyers at the Brown Manufacturing Company. They could not understand the new system and therefore objected to the computer creating purchase orders that went directly to vendors.

Distorted Viewpoint Concerning EDP

As might be expected, not all the feelings about EDP described above are based on a valid and true understanding of the department's function. EDP, particularly when it gets into MIS, is a relatively new discipline and there has not been adequate time to explain and relate the functions properly to users and potential users. The interviews showed that operating department personnel, several key managers included, had beliefs about the computer and the EDP department that were not based on fact. It is similar to the mother who blames the new math which she can't understand on the advent of computers. It is a case of a misunderstanding accentuated by a bit of mistrust.

Track Record of EDP

Some users have been burnt with EDP themselves or have talked to colleagues who were. There is no question that overzealous system analysts with little experience in estimating how long a job should take have gone out on the limb and have clearly missed dates. Furthermore, they have not given the user what he thought he was getting. This situation is aggravated when the user has gone through a great deal of effort to prepare his department for the system cut-over that is late in occurring. A simple example is allowing the stock of a particular paper form to be depleted in anticipation of the use of a new form in conjunction with the new system. When the new system is delayed, it is too late to reorder the old form. As in this instance, the track record of EDP has not been good. An overestimation of ability and an underestimation of resources are common. It was a little different in the case of Paul Foster because he met the scheduled target date for installing the new forecasting and purchasing system. However, he rushed the completion date without having done a good communication or selling job to the prospective users of the system. In this case, it would probably have been better to postpone the conversion date until the users were more knowledgeable and receptive to the new approach.

Motivation and Aspirations

This was a key area that was evident in the interviews. The tendency is to explain the conflict between EDP people and users as being one of lack of communication, or misunderstanding of charters, or lack of education and knowledge. However, one should not overlook the fact that some important and basic personality and aptitude differences exist between the staff people in the EDP department and the line people of the operating departments. Although one runs the risk of generalization, EDP people for the most part are younger, better educated, more individualistic, more selfish, less business oriented, more impatient, more motivated by job content than money, and, in general, less people oriented. They differ from their line department counterparts, and often this factor can accentuate the problems of installing a new system. EDP people can become overenthusiastic about the sophistication of a system, gaining their satisfaction in this way instead of seeing that a less-sophisticated system is being properly utilized. System people cannot understand why operating people fail to comprehend the new approach and see the benefits that are obvious to them. There is no question that this difference in motivation and aspiration has helped build barriers that have all but scuttled systems that had great potential for a company.

Language and Communications

This category ties in with several of the preceding points. The picture of the system analyst as a kind of esoteric technocrat who talks in terms that only other system analysts understand still exists. The EDP terminology and acronymism that have grown up in the industry have been imposing to say the least. Every new specialty or profession has its jargon and EDP is no exception; however, computerese, as some have called it, has made other terminologies look mild. Interviews pointed out that this was a problem in that EDP system analysts made no effort to speak the language of the operating people but assumed terms like COBOL, core dumps, regression analysis, octal patches, and multiprogramming were familiar to everyone.

EDP—Immune to Control

The interviews demonstrated the belief (not entirely unjustified) that the EDP department is like an island apart from the company, not controlled or governed by the same regulations and procedures that govern the other departments. The EDP department was seen as having different budgetary rules, different salary structures, different job performance criteria, and different measures of effectiveness. The line departments were even somewhat bitter about a suspected difference in working hours. This picture tied in with the feeling of the vagueness and broadness of the EDP charter. Although the operating people, particularly the managers, are aware that EDP is a fairly new discipline and cannot have the stability in organization and structure of the older, more-established departments, they feel that there is no need to treat the EDP people as prima donnas, species apart from the remainder of the organization. They also question, in certain cases, the physical separation of the department into a type of ivory tower arrangement. This factor was mentioned by those companies who had a separate computer or EDP facility. The word was that they do not see much of the EDP people; the latter seem to inbreed and remain in their own environment.

ALLEVIATING THE CONFLICT

The preceding discussion presents eight areas of conflict as seen by the personnel of companies using EDP. There is truth as well as misconception in their beliefs, but the fact remains that this is the way people feel; it must be dealt with as such. The following five considerations are presented as a means to alleviate the conflict and move toward a more positive and constructive EDP-user relationship, a relationship that is so important to the successful implementation of management information systems. Adherence to such a list undoubtedly would have aided Paul Foster in the implementation of his system at Brown Manufacturing.

Establish Consistent Performance and Work Criteria for EDP

EDP should be measured by the same criteria that are used throughout the business. If the organization utilizes MBO (Management by Objective) or has a particular "results" orientation, those same principles should be applied to EDP. The same return on investment or profit standards should be applied. Cost accounting reports and other management reports should be incorporated for EDP as they are for other areas of the operation. As the EDP department begins to adopt the procedures of the company, so the individuals should as well. Accounting for time spent on jobs and efforts to measure productivity should be incorporated. More and more, the EDP department's mode of operation should be consistent with the rest of the organization. The procedures should be applied fairly and uniformly to avoid a counterreaction from the EDP people. These measures should be instituted in such a way that the individuals regard them as an aid in better managing their time and activity and not as a bridle to their innovation and creativity.

A major problem hindering the adoption of these business procedures is the shortage of skills that exists in the EDP industry. It has been estimated that there is a shortage of upward of 50,000 qualified system analysts and programmers. With this imbalance in supply and demand, management has been reluctant to employ methods that may be construed as restrictive and distasteful to the individuals. They are wary of increasing the already high turnover rate that exists in the industry. EDP people have been attracted to newly formed software firms and computer service operations. The appeal of challenging creative work, plus the promise of participating in profit sharing or stock options, is extremely attractive. Many system people have followed what has been called the path of the "EDP Gypsy," skipping from job to job and opportunity to opportunity at regular 6-month intervals. However, the high turn into failure rate and disillusionment when the challenging new work assignments become routine programming jobs have dampened the enthusiasm of such system people. The industry has matured to the point where applying sound business policies to EDP operations has a positive influence on EDP people.

Rotation of EDP-User Personnel

One of the healthiest situations has been the interchange of people within the EDP and operating areas of a company. It makes good sense to staff the EDP department with personnel from operating departments who show an aptitude and an interest for system work. Similarly, system analysts should receive a tour of duty outside of EDP, in order to appreciate the problems of the actual business world and understand the difficulties of putting an advanced new system into productive operation. This type of rotation can go a long way toward alleviating the type of conflict that Paul Foster inadvertently discovered. He would have been in a far better position had he understood the feelings of the buyers—better yet, if he had held a position in one of the line departments.

It is important that this rotation of people not be a way of dumping the marginal performers within a department. Management should recognize the long-term benefit of transferring proven performers in key support departments like EDP. Many companies have filled key EDP management positions with individuals with records of success in operating departments who possess a system outlook but lack direct computer experience. Transfer of people from EDP to key operating department positions should also be encouraged. This is certainly one way, and a good one, of alleviating the difference in motivation and aspiration referred to earlier.

Education and Training

This area has already been discussed, but it would be remiss not to list it here because education and training are important tools in alleviating many of the conflict areas. One additional point should be made. The case for the education of non-EDP people in computer-related subjects was stressed; also stressed should be the education of EDP people in pertinent operating areas of the business. Thus it would seem practical for a procurement department to present a seminar or a series of sessions exploring the procurement function to systems people like Paul Foster. The rotation of jobs is the best way to achieve this understanding. Since rotation often cannot be accomplished on a wholesale basis, education and training are the next best vehicles.

Plan Interarea Activities

Whenever possible, EDP and operating personnel should be assimilated in everyday business activities. At conferences, work sessions, or business get-togethers, the groups should be encouraged to work together, to take every opportunity to discuss and explore things together. If possible, EDP people and operating people should travel together, engage in social activities together, and develop an awareness of each other's standpoint on business matters. Most people are prone to stay with employees of their own department and to discuss matters with people of similar background. This situation does nothing to facilitate the understanding and resolution of problems; it merely reinforces one's predetermined judgment on the matter. Another opportunity to work together is on special projects that require interdisciplinary participation. Mutual confidence and respect are built up when a task is accomplished by such a group.

Place EDP in Proper Organizational Position

Although there has been criticism of placing the responsibility of the EDP function under the controller, I feel that this can be a workable relationship if the controller has the proper status in the company and understands the potential role of EDP to his company. However, what is happening more and more is that the control of the computer is being taken away from the controller and placed in the hands of a separate department. This department is given corporate status and its head may go by the title of manager of computing services, director of electronic data processing, or vice-president in charge of management information systems. The department is on equal footing with marketing, engineering, and production. The EDP activity is viewed as an information utility serving the information needs of all operating departments, one of which is the accounting department. This approach to computer organization seems more feasible in light of the impact that a computer can have on the operations of a company. Recent studies point out that the main reason for the mediocre results that companies have had with computers is the lack of management perspective on the scope and potential of the device with which they are dealing. However, there is probably good reason for the slow evolution of this type of thinking. The computer has had to earn its way and prove that it indeed holds the promise that the experts have indicated. It had to establish itself as more than a "paper tiger." Until it did, the elevation of the computer activity to full department status would merely downgrade the prestige of other departments.

Another reason why so many computers are still run by the accounting or controller's department is the lack of competent people to cope with the new technology. The lack is a result of management's inability to define the job of the computer manager, which in turn stems from the basic misunderstanding of the device itself. With increasing understanding of the computer, the job of managing is now much more comprehensible. Again, it is not surprising that the accountant or controller was the closest thing that top management could come up with as the individual who best qualified as the keeper of the computer keys.

SUMMARY

This chapter has been concerned with the level of involvement and influence that management should have if a company plans to implement a management information system. The role of general management, as well as the role of EDP management, has been discussed because MIS involves the proper interaction of the two groups. Once the level of involvement is established (and this factor depends on the relative position of a manager within the company), the various methods of obtaining the necessary involvement and EDP awareness were explored. Direct and indirect EDP participation were discussed, the former involving full-time interaction with the EDP department, the latter implying a part-time but crucial role in directing and guiding the system development activity.

Management education and training were emphasized as a means of developing EDP involvement, for education is a cornerstone of understanding any new activity. Three paths were explored, including schools and universities, internal on-site company training, and external off-site company training. An education matrix presented the types of courses desirable to further the EDP education of managers and indicated a relative ranking of their priority to each management level.

The chapter concluded by exploring the conflict that exists between EDP people and the users of EDP services within a company. Five steps were presented, which, if followed by general management and EDP management, should alleviate the conflict areas materially. Chapters 6 and 7 form a most important portion of the book. Unless management understands the potential impact of MIS and, once recognized, takes the necessary steps to become involved in system development, management information systems will remain the myth they have been to many companies. If these two chapters are heeded, companies can implement successful *Management-Oriented Management Information Systems.*

STUDY CASETTES

THREE B's INC.

TO   All Operating Personnel, Three B's, Inc.
FROM   W. W. Barrett, President
SUBJECT   Systems Study

We are in the process of evaluating our current information processing system with the thought that possibly an electronic data processing system might improve certain areas of it. This approach will be a continuing long-range program that could extend over several years. The study is being conducted by the system study group under the leadership of Dexter Johnson. Members of Dexter's department will be calling upon you to discuss your department's operation and your role in existing systems. It is extremely important to gain your input to ensure that an accurate assessment of system needs is made. Your experience will be invaluable to the system study; we solicit your cooperation as well as your participation.

Because most of you are unfamiliar with the computer and electronic data processing, you may wish to learn some basic computer fundamentals. This will place all of us in a better position to see what these types of systems can do for the company. We plan to hold periodic sessions to update your knowledge of the uses of computers in a variety of ways. There will be afternoon orientation courses held once a week for two-hour periods. In addition, you are welcome to take, at company expense, various courses offered by outside agencies. (You should check with your supervisor.) Dexter Johnson will also hold informal discussion groups with individual departments.

The important thing is that the development of a successful automated data processing system can be accomplished only with your assistance. Despite the wondrous things that computer systems are accomplishing today, we fully recognize that machines work while people think—we need your thinking power.

(Signed)

W. W. Barrett

WWB/c

Study Questions

1. What does this memo indicate concerning W. W. Barrett's involvement in EDP?

2. What will be the reaction of Three B's personnel to the memo?

3. What should Dexter Johnson do as a follow-up to the memo?

4. What additional steps might Barrett take to ensure an orderly transition to EDP?

5. Do you approve of Barrett's action?

DELCON APPAREL

Bob Harris, systems manager for Delcon Apparel, had tried every technique he could think of to get Burt Rutherford interested in the system they were installing in his department. Rutherford had been negative on computers from the start and was quite upset when one of the first major applications selected was computerized inventory control, an operation which had a major impact on how Rutherford's department performed.

Harris had met with Rutherford at the outset of the system design and had asked for Rutherford's opinion on the system requirements as he saw them. Rutherford promised to get back to Harris, but never did. Next, Harris scheduled a three day management overview and personally invited Rutherford to attend. Again a promise, but Rutherford declined the day before the session because of a pressing meeting. Rutherford received copies of the monthly status reports on the inventory control application, but Harris felt certain Rutherford never looked at them.

The application was scheduled to go into production in two weeks. Harris carefully considered what his next move should be.

Study Questions

1. Did Harris do all he could in the situation?

2. What do you think of Rutherford's actions?

3. Do you think it's wise to go ahead with the system introduction?

4. Are there any other ways to get Rutherford involved in the system? Is it really necessary to do so?

DASHMAN COMPANY

The Dashman Company was a large concern making many types of equipment for the armed forces of the United States. It had over 20 plants, located in the central part of the country, whose purchasing procedures had never been completely coordinated. In fact, the head office of the company had encouraged each of the plant managers to operate with their staffs as separate independent units in most matters. Late in 1970, when it began to appear that the company would face increasing difficulty in securing certain essential raw materials, Mr. Manson, the company's president, appointed an experienced purchasing executive from another company, Mr. Post, as vice-president in charge of purchasing, a position especially created for him. Mr. Manson gave Mr. Post wide latitude in organizing his job, and he assigned Mr. Larson as Mr. Post's assistant. Mr. Larson had served the company in a variety of capacities for many years, and knew most of the plant executives personally. Mr. Post's appointment was announced through the formal channels usual in the company, including a notice in the house organ published by the company.

One of Mr. Post's first decisions was to begin immediately to centralize the company's purchasing procedure in conjunction with a new computer-based purchasing system. As a first step he decided that he would require each of the executives who handled purchasing in the individual plants to clear with the head office all purchase contracts which they made in excess of $10,000. He felt that if the head office was to do any coordinating in a way that would be helpful to each plant and to the company as a whole, he must be notified of contracts that were being prepared at least a week before they were to be signed. These purchase contracts would be evaluated by a computer program which analyzed orders for similar products or from the same vendor. Based on quantity discounts, a trend analysis of key commodity indicators and a balancing of the cost to carry inventory with the cost of purchasing, the proper order would be placed with the vendor automatically. He talked this proposal over with Mr. Manson, who presented it to his board of directors. They approved the plan.

Although the company made purchases throughout the year, the beginning of its peak buying season was only three weeks away at the time this new plan was adopted. During this period, contracts totaling millions of dollars would be placed. Mr. Post prepared a letter to be sent to the 20 purchasing executives of the company. The letter follows.

Dear _____:

The board of directors of our company has recently authorized a change in our purchasing procedures. Hereafter, each of the purchasing executives in the several plants of the company will notify the vice-president in charge of purchasing of all contracts in excess of $10,000 which they are negotiating at least a week in advance of the date on which they are to be signed. A new computer program will use a purchasing algorithm to analyze and place the order automatically to take advantage of quantity discounts.

I am sure that you will understand that this step is necessary to coordinate the purchasing requirements of the company in these times when we are facing increasing difficulty in securing essential supplies. This procedure should give us in the central office the information we need to see that each plant secures the optimum supply of materials at the best possible price. In this way the interests of each plant and of the company as a whole will best be served.

Yours very truly,

Mr. Post showed the letter to Mr. Larson and invited his comments. Mr. Larson said that he thought the letter an excellent one, but suggested that since Mr. Post had not met more than a few of the purchasing executives, he might like to visit all of them and take the matter up with each of them personally. Mr. Post dismissed the idea because, he said, he had so many things to do at the head office that he could not get away for a trip. Consequently, he had the letters sent out over his signature.

During the two following weeks, replies came in from all except a few plants. Although a few executives wrote at greater length, the following reply was typical:

Dear Mr. Post:

Your recent communication in regard to notifying the head office a week in advance of our intention to sign contracts has been received. This suggestion seems a most practical one. We want to assure that you can count on our cooperation.

Yours very truly,

During the next six weeks the head office received no notices from any plant that contracts were being negotiated. Executives in other departments who made frequent trips to the plants reported that the plants were busy, and the usual routines for that time of year were being followed.

Study Questions

1. Why did Mr. Post fail to achieve what he set out to accomplish?

2. Was Mr. Post's entire proposal a sound one?

3. What should be his next move?

4. Are the chances of success being materially lowered by the initial experience?

BIBLIOGRAPHY

BEMER, R., *Computers and Crisis* (ed.) Association for Computing Machinery, Inc. (The edited sessions of ACM 70, a conference of the Association for Computing Machinery held September 1–3, 1970, New York.)

Bibliography on Computers and Education. Simulation Associates, Inc., 1970, 115 pp.

CANNING, R. G., Management Training in Data Processing. *EDP Analyzer,* Vol. 6, #5, May, 1968.

GREEN, R. S., W. A. MARTIN, D. N. NESS, and G. A. MOULTON, Computer Education in a Graduate School of Management. *Communications of the ACM,* Vol. 13, #2, February, 1970.

HAROLD, F., *Handbook for Orienting the Manager to the Computer.* Auerbach, Princeton, New Jersey, 1971, 247 pp.

KANTER, J., *The Computer and the Executive.* Prentice-Hall, Inc., Englewood Cliffs, New Jersey, 1967.

MURDICK, R. G., and J. E. ROSS, *Management Information Systems: Training for Businessmen.* McGraw-Hill, New York, 1970.

MYERS, E. A., *Computers in Knowledge-Based Field.* The MIT Press, Cambridge, Mass., 1970, 136 pp.

OETTINGER, A. G., *Run, Computer, Run.* Harvard University Press, Cambridge, Massachusetts, 1969, 302 pp.

RAPPAPORT, A. (ed.), *Information for Decision Making.* Prentice-Hall, Inc., Englewood Cliffs, New Jersey, 1970, 447 pp.

SCHRIBER, T. J., Computer Use in the Business School Curriculum. *Michigan Business Review,* March, 1970.

SCHULTZ, G. P., and T. L. WHISLER, *Management Organization and the Computer.* University of Chicago, Graduate School of Business, 1960.

TRICKER, R. I., Teaching MIS at a British University. *Datamation,* September, 1969.

Chapter 8

THE FUTURE OF COMPUTERIZED

INFORMATION SYSTEMS—

THE GENERATION BEYOND

Chapter 2 indicated the quantitative trends in computer usage, pointing out the growth in numbers and dollar value of installed equipment. The major trends, such as communication, the allocation of computer expenditures to hardware, software, and services, and general application usage, were also touched on. This chapter will explore more of the qualitative changes that can be expected—the manner in which users over the next decade will be utilizing the increased capabilities of tomorrow's computers. Many of the specific subjects to be discussed have been mentioned throughout the book. They will be summarized here and placed in proper perspective.

Although Chapter 2 indicated that the fourth generation of computers can be expected sometime about 1973 or 1974, the 1970s usher in only the second generation of management information systems. The sixties provided the testing ground of the hardware and software components of MIS. EDP was relegated to the technocrats, and it was only in the latter part of the decade and in the beginning of the seventies that management became a major component of MIS. This is the reason why the chapter heading refers to the next generation and not to the fourth generation.

A capsule picture of a management information system of the future will open the chapter. Then it will lead into a discussion of the general qualitative environment of the next generation, including the hardware, software, application, business, and EDP industry trends that will characterize the period of the later seventies. The chapter will then focus on a discussion of the planning process required of the EDP industry to ensure that users have the information-processing tools they need in the 1970s. Finally, we will take a look at some of the sociological and psychological considerations that are becoming increasingly relevant in the growing age of automation and computers.

THE NEXT GENERATION'S MANAGEMENT
INFORMATION SYSTEM

Based on the current trends in computer usage and a view of what the leading companies in EDP are accomplishing, it is possible to project what the next generation's MIS will look like. The system will be built around the same general business concepts discussed in Chapter 3. The MIS of the future is built on overall company goals and strategies in the same manner as this generation's MIS. The business information system is based on the integrated concept, the central data base, and aiding management decision making. The future system that will be described goes further and accomplishes more in these crucial areas. It is assumed that the technology and, most important, the experience and know-how will be available to permit the extension of the MIS concept. This system was initially developed by John J. Murphy of Honeywell Information Systems, Inc., and reviewed by me during a period when we worked together very closely on manufacturing systems of the 1970s.

The major functional areas covered by the next generation's MIS system are

Sales Forecasting and Market Analysis

Sales Processing and Distribution

Engineering

Production

Administration

Management Planning

SALES FORECASTING AND MARKET ANALYSIS

The sales forecasting and marketing analysis subsystem consists of a forecasting module and a market opportunities module. The forecasting module has access to the historical movement of all items currently or formerly marketed. In addition, it has access to a competitive sales file to enable the continual monitoring of share-of-market statistics, various competitive trends, and the like. Also available are data files on key economic indicators that affect the sales movement of the product line. The forecasting subsystem module allows the establishment of short-, medium-, and long-range sales forecasts for use in planning, marketing, production, and other major functions of the business. The company's own data base is supplemented by an on-line tie-in to a number of market analysis firms specializing in the accumulation and processing of market data.

The market opportunities subsystem module aids management in recognizing profit potential through the introduction of new items, new product lines, or the utilization of unused plant capacity. This subsystem module has access to both the customer file and the competitive file; in addition to the statistical data, survey information concerning customer and prospect product preferences is captured and updated periodically. This step permits the analysis of new product opportunities. Costs and other economic considerations are also available to assess the profitability of alternate approaches. Actual activity is continually measured against plant capacity to indicate those items that might be promoted or more actively merchandised.

The major system requirements of the sales forecasting and market analysis system are a comprehensive marketing information data base and the necessary statistical application software to analyze and pinpoint trends in the data continually. Since the data base includes extrinsic information (external data, such as competitive statistics and Gross National Product) as well as intrinsic or internal data, access to machine-readable central information services is necessary. On-line inquiry and updating devices are required in order to maintain an accurate and current marketing data base.

SALES ORDER PROCESSING AND DISTRIBUTION

Sales orders may be entered through a number of input devices, to different classes of customers depending on the distribution patterns. The direct call-answer-back device or the cathode ray tube are the generally accepted techniques. Utilizing this system, customers dial the computer directly, place the order, and receive (orally, visually, and/or hard copy) the promised shipping data after the obligation has been posted and their credit established. During the call, the following processing takes place:

- The product record is scanned to determine when the ordered product will be available for shipment.
- The product is priced and the order extended for total price, shipment, and weight.
- The customer's credit is checked and all or part of the obligation is accepted.
- The portion accepted is verbally acknowledged to the customer.
- The customer signifies "accept" or "cancel."
- The data base is updated with the transaction.

High-speed remote-line printers are used to print out invoices at the larger sales centers and to print picking documents at outlying warehouses. Between the receipt and acknowledgement of the order, the production system takes over and monitors the progress and status of the order. When the shipping date is reached, the distribution system is put into operation. Based on preestablished rules, the optimum routing (most economical mode of shipment that meets delivery requirements) is determined. The pertinent tariff tables are queried if an outside hauler is used, or the firm's own internal cost structure if company-owned transportation is used. Customer billing and cash collection follow the final shipment.

The major system requirements of the sales processing and distribution system are fast and reliable remote order taking and inquiry devices operating on-line to a central data base as well as to remote line printers. In-plant inquiry devices are necessary for expediting purposes. Sophisticated distribution routing and dispatching application software are also required.

ENGINEERING

The engineering system supports the functions of research and development, design engineering, and manufacturing engineering. All scientific calculations are handled through computer subroutines. A high-level problem-oriented and conversational language is employed on a remote basis by the various engineering groups. The search for relevant technical papers in support of the research function may be handled through direct communication with a commercial electronic library bank or by inquiry to microfilm records that are digitized and retrievable under computer control.

Preliminary product design is computer assisted. A vector cathode ray tube with light pen input is utilized for this purpose. On-line plotters are also used where appropriate. As created blueprints are filed in the data base, preliminary designs are routed through the numerical control subroutine directly to the production floor for model creation. Numerical control programs are filed for production use when the final design is released.

Industrial engineering calculates standard costs and lead times for new items for incorporation into the product master file. Engineering personnel have direct access to the product master file for inquiry and change purposes.

System requirements in the engineering area include hardware for computer-aided design (vector CRT's and plotters) as well as advanced numerical control capability. Information retrieval techniques also become significant. In addition, a significant application software is needed to accomplish rapid and efficient creation of bills of material with lead times, standard costs, and other operational information.

PRODUCTION

The production system is composed of the scheduler and the controller modules. Scheduler relies on the sales-forecasting and sales-order processing subsystems to determine requirements. Scheduler feeds back schedule availability data to adjust the sales forecast for overload or to activate the market opportunity portion of the forecast to stimulate the sale of available productive time. The module also handles the flow of orders, from their acceptance through the production process into the warehouse where they are ready for shipment.

The feedback loop of controller is closely related to scheduler to ensure that schedules are met. Briefly, the system operates as described below.

1. A requirement from the sales-forecast or sales-order processing subsystem activates the production system. Unpublished schedules are modified to schedule the requirement as follows:

(a) The production record is referenced for bill of material explosion. Requirements are netted.

(b) The numerical control file is checked for design availability for automatic production. The resource file is checked for manpower, machinery, and material availability. Time requirements for each required machine are obtained from the product file.

(c) The requirement is scheduled against available production capacity. The system may interrogate the forecast subsystem to schedule future requirements for other components utilizing similar machine setups. Furthermore, scheduler utilizes a linear programming model to modify production quantities based on forecasted demand, the current production schedule, and machine, manpower, and material availability.

2. Purchased parts and assemblies are ordered according to vendor lead-time requirements and economic-order quantity considerations. In certain cases, a standard magnetic tape or disk strip is delivered to the vendor for direct machine input and processing of orders.

3. Scheduler assigns work through the production controller system. When controller receives the start job signal from the data collection equipment, signifying that an operation is about to begin, scheduler determines when the job will end and prepares the next job in queue. Numerical control programs are placed on-line, requisitions for inventory are readied, and all job instructions are prepared. Numerical control must be viewed here in its broadest sense. Digital computer programs are written to control (on-line) process control computers. These process control computers govern such operations as mixing, metering, stacker crane movement, and assembly. If production is automatically sensed, documentation will be sent to the shop floor printer when 90 percent of the lot has been completed. If production is not automatically sensed, documentation will be sent to the shop floor printer 30 minutes before estimated time of prior job completion.

4. When work has been completed on any operation (including material handling and inspection operations), the notice of completion is sent to controller through sensing devices on the machine or through operator-activated data-collection equipment. Controller activates scheduler, which

(a) edits data and reports back discrepancies.

(b) adjusts queue by machine to get ready for assembly of "next job" information.

5. Throughout the production process, scheduler and controller monitor the process. Appropriate signals are transferred for visual display in the foreman's office and at the machine for the following reasons:

(a) Setup time is exceeding standard.

(b) Production time is exceeding standard.

(c) Quality is off standard and cannot be corrected by the numerical control program.

(d) Machine stoppage.

Inspection results are sensed and fed to the quality assurance subsystem, which calculates production performance and feeds corrective action to the numerical control program. Maintenance is called if the process cannot be corrected electronically to meet quality assurance requirements. Selectively sensed information is fed to the business data processing system for cost accounting, material replenishment, and inventory recording. Production performance data is continually updated for management interrogation.

In addition to sophisticated production-scheduling and control (including quality control) application software, numerical control is important, as is the ability of a digital computer to interface with process control computers. Production-sensing and data collection equipment are needed to complete the control loop, feedback information to measure actual results against plan, and take the necessary corrective action.

ADMINISTRATION

The administration system provides a wide variety of management support services, including personnel reporting and administration, payroll processing, building and equipment maintenance, cost accounting, general ledger accounting, profit-and-loss reporting, various statistical reports and analyses, and auditing.

MANAGEMENT PLANNING

The important top-management functions of profit planning, budgeting, return-on-investment analysis, merchandising innovation, factory utilization and loading, and business model simulation are part of the management planning system. Although most of the decisions are long range and strategic in nature and do not need on-line, real-time response, the use of computerized graphic display is significant to management planning. Thus it is most useful to be able to show past operating statistics in a graphic form (CRT's or vector display) and to have the flexibility to see different relationships as they are desired—sometimes requesting a particular graphic display in the boardroom as a meeting is in progress. Sophisticated general-purpose simulators are also a requirement in setting up business models and ascertaining the effect of different operating policies before they are tried in a live environment.

The reader should recognize that the system described here is an extension of the concept of integration. The next-generation system integrates the physical production process with the information system. A digial computer provides the instructions, which automatically operate a variety of machine tools. As the items are automatically machined, electronic sensors feed back the results through analog computers to the digital computer. The digital computer produces cost accounting reports, product variance analyses, and other control information. Thus the physical and information systems are integrated; the feedback loop extends from top management through middle management to operating management and directly to the workers who turn out the product. This degree of MIS exists today to a limited extent in a few companies. The greater the degree of integration, the greater the risk of conflict between EDP personnel and management, as described in the previous chapter. However, the benefits of such a system (we might call it a total feedback MIS) provide the incentive to tackle these obstacles with greater energy. An increasing number of companies will, in the 1970s, be successfully implementing next-generation systems of the type described in this chapter.

I do not underestimate the myriad of technical, people-related, and organizational problems in achieving a high degree of system integration. I do not suggest that a high degree of integration is desirable or that it will prove beneficial to every company: what I do say is that some degree (an increasing degree) is essential. Whether it reaches the stage described in the preceding example will depend on company objectives, resources, and willingness to pay the cost to develop such a system. I think that one can say that the greater the degree of integration, the greater the risk of system failure; but is this any different than other business venture?

The manufacturing industry is a natural for the integrated system concept because of the need to combine many interlocking subsystems in order to optimize decision making, but integration is also significant to other industries. Retailing and distribution are in reality subsets of the total manufacturing-distribution process, and an integrated system for these industries would follow the same general pattern as manufacturing; however, emphasis on particular subsystems would differ.

Banking, insurance, and financial institutions have more in common with manufacturing in regard to information systems than at first seems apparent. Although an oversimplification, the main inventory item of banks, insurance companies, and financial institutions consists of customers in the form of depositors, clients, or policyholders. Just as transactions in a manufacturing company affect finished goods, in-process and raw material items, so transactions in a bank or insurance company affect depositors and policyholders. It is important to integrate these transactions; for example, many banks are moving toward the concept of the central information file where the deposit, savings, and loan accounts of an individual are consolidated into one and can be cross-indexed and accessed for credit extension, collatoral needs, and so on. The concept of the cashless or checkless society, if it is to occur, must be built around an integrated system concept.

Education and hospitals are also built around customers as inventory items, students in the former case and patients in the latter. Integrated subsystems, as they apply to students and patients, are vital for efficient and effective operation. By-products of administrative data processing, such as student guidance or patient statistics and diagnosis, can result if the system design is properly integrated. Integration will play a key role in future systems ranging over the entire industry spectrum.

TRENDS IN INFORMATION PROCESSING

There are many ways to categorize and view the trends that are occurring in information processing. These trends are the foundation of the MIS described above. Figure 8.1 gives an outline for discussing these trends under four general headings.

1. **Advanced applications**

   User environment

   . Results-oriented
   . Aid in decision making
   . Integration of functions
   . Geographical diversification

   System needs

   . Management information systems
   . Communication
   . Data management
   . Management science

2. **Systematic, logical growth**

   User environment

   . Business growth (volume and complexity)
   . Rapidly changing technology
   . Fragmented service structure

   System needs

   . Hardware modularity
   . Software modularity
   . Standardization
   . Meaningful conversion

3. **Reduced system implementation cycle**

   User environment

   . Skills shortage
   . Turnover problem
   . Programmer productivity
   . Application backlog

   System needs

   . Application packages
   . Higher level languages
   . Documentation
   . Education

4. **Economical, efficient operation**

   User environment

   . Rising cost of EDP
   . Increasing uptime demand
   . Throughput and turn-around time requirements

   System needs

   . Reliability
   . Simpler operating systems
   . Multiprogramming/multiprocessing

Fig. 8.1 Trends in information processing

The trends are considered from the computer user's point of view. These headings are (a) advanced applications, (b) systematic, logical growth, (c) reduced systems implementation cycle, and (d) economical, efficient operation. Each of the four categories covers the user environment that is responsible for the trend and the system needs that are outgrowths of the environment. Most of these trends have been discussed or at least mentioned in previous chapters. The intent here is to summarize and place the trends in proper perspective.

1. Advanced Applications

First and foremost, computer users are impatient at not seeing the type of advanced applications in operation that they thought were promised years ago. It is true that computer expectations have exceeded computer performance and that a good percentage of computer time is still devoted to basic administrative applications. The management of computer users would like to see the computer assist in areas like planning and decision making. However, advanced applications are not desired merely because they are advanced. I often ask an EDP manager what, in his opinion, is the most significant attribute of his computer installation. Invariably the answer is the degree of sophistication built into his application systems. An advanced system may utilize the most simple hardware and software in basic batch mode. Its advanced stage comes from *what* it accomplishes, not *how* it accomplishes it. This is an important concept to keep in mind.

The user environment that will produce the advanced systems are management's continued concern with computer results and a desire to see greater EDP impact on the decision-making process. Top management realizes that the so-called management information systems are not greatly impacting top and middle management; they are directed at lower levels of management. Management's growing involvement has opened their eyes to the still-unrealized potential that resides in today's computer systems.

Another part of the user environment is the functions integration that is required in business operation. The emergence of the top computer executive indicates management's desire to combine the coordination and control of EDP systems. It is a recognition that a good deal of duplication and redundancy exist under a split-control arrangement. Furthermore, it indicates management awareness that information subsystems cannot be built in isolation of other subsystems. This point was demonstrated in the discussion of the integrated system concept, where it was seen, for example, that the order processing system affects the inventory, productive control, and purchasing subsystems.

Geographical diversification has become a way of life even to small companies. Mergers, establishment of new branches and divisions, and other forms of national and international growth place considerable demand on system design and development. The source of data is remote from the processing of the data, and the results of the processing must be distributed to remote spots. This situation must be considered carefully in system planning.

The system needs that are an outgrowth of this environment include the concept of the management information system that has been emphasized throughout the book. There is no question that MIS represents one of the most powerful trends in the use of computers in the coming decade.

The other three trends—communication, data management, and management science—were discussed in Chapter 5. Communication systems are direct outgrowths of the geographical diversification that is taking place. Systems must be able to incorporate a variety of remote devices on-line to a central computer. In addition, systems must ensure that the response time is consistent with user requirements. Although communication networks are not a necessary part of MIS, more and more the response-time requirements necessitate their employment. The on-line data collection and production monitoring system described in the previous section requires communication links. Similarly, the tie-in of digital and process control computers also requires communication even if the computers are located in the same facility. Communication equipment already accounts for almost a third of the dollar value of computer systems and is expected to reach 50 percent by 1975. There is no question that communication processing is a major trend and represents the fastest-growing hardware segment of the EDP industry.

Data management techniques provide the foundation on which management information systems are built. These techniques facilitate the gathering, updating, organization, and retrieval of an information data base, a necessary prerequisite to the development of the MIS concept. Data base systems were explained in detail in

Chapter 5. The central data base files of a company employing MIS require an effective hierarchical storage system utilizing bulk memory, disk, tape, drum, and other media as the situation warrants. The next 5 to 10 years will see major breakthroughs in providing users with economical, large-capacity, improved-performance, random access storage devices.

Management sciences will also show increased usage. As brought out in Chapter 5, these techniques are important tools to aid management decision making. The discussion of the next-generation MIS in the previous section points out the significance of techniques from statistical forecasting to financial modeling.

2. Systematic, Logical Growth

It is a business fact that most companies are expanding and growing with the increase in Gross National Product and the population expansion. Keeping pace with the growth in volume is the increasing complexity of a company's products and services. As a company adds products and people, the information flow between them is greatly increased and the need for application growth is accentuated.

Businesses are facing a rapidly changing technology, particularly with the growing application of automation to manual tasks. This situation has occurred in both the factory and the office. It is probably most evident in the computer field, where three generations of hardware (each one making the previous one completely obsolete) have appeared in less than 20 years. Many companies have passed through the three generations in a time span of less than 10 years, although not without serious repercussions.

Another complication is the fact that the computer user is operating within a fragmented service structure. The separate pricing policy for software, education, and support services adapted in part by most of the major computer manufacturers has added new impetus to the already expanding EDP service field. As a result, the EDP user now faces a more difficult job in selecting the right combination of products and services to accomplish his data processing job. If he is successful, he will obtain more beneficial results, quite possibly at a lower overall price; however, there is greater risk that parts of the total offering may not dovetail with other parts.

System needs to satisfy the environment are first of all hardware and software modularity. The EDP user does not want to be forced into purchasing hardware or software that is not consistent with his growth plans. This point emphasizes the value of the family concept within a computer manufacturer's line. The user wants to add computing power with minimum inconvenience and with little, if any, rework of existing programs.

One of the major design problems of computer systems is the fact that the hardware and software are designed by different departments within the computer manufacturer's organization. The result is complicated software that tries to offset the hardware weaknesses and vice versa. One of the major architectural advances in computer design in the next decade will be the closer relationship of hardware and software; indeed, many functions now performed by software will be put into hardware. The concept is to make transparent to the user the hardware and software complexities; to develop firmware and make it effective, make it reliable, make it work, and put it "under the hood" where the user need not be concerned or bothered by it. However, the blending of the hardware and software must be modularized so that users can use what they need at the moment and so that they can easily add additional elements with minimum reprogramming or rework as they grow.

Standardization is also significant as a requirement for logical and systematic growth. A company may have more than one computer, thus necessitating the interchange of program and data. Program and data compatibility do not occur by chance. They must be planned and the planning requires some form of standardization. The media on which data is stored as well as the device that reads the data are considerations in a standardization program. Internal work standards, such as tape labeling and programming conventions, must also be observed by the EDP user.

Conversion is defined as replacing a computer system, either with one of another manufacturer's line or with a new line offered by the user's current vendor. The natural growth in business activity and the development of advanced applications can cause a company to reach a stage where a change to a new line of computers becomes increasingly attractive. The constantly improving performance-price ratio and the advanced features of newer equipment add further impetus for change. A negative influence is the bad experience that many users have had in converting. This is a result of a combination of inadequate conversion aids on the part of the vendor and unpreparedness on the part of the user because of ineffective or nonexistent internal standards.

3. Reduced System Implementation Cycle

An often-heard complaint in the EDP business (probably the most common of all) is: Why does it take so long to get an application up and running? The user environment causing such a statement is a shortage of skills existing in the industry. The turnover rate accentuates the seriousness of the situation. The current education and training facilities do not ensure that there will be an adequate number of system analysts and programmers to satisfy the increasing business demands. Many in the industry feel that the gap is widening. As has been stated, the implementation cycle for a computer application lengthens without competent personnel.

Another factor affecting the system implementation cycle is programmer productivity. It is temping to hide subpar productivity and weak supervision behind the personnel shortage. Programmer productivity is an area that must be recognized and improved.

The result of the three conditions listed is a sizable application backlog experienced by most users. Various surveys estimate this backlog to be between 15 and 20 percent of operating programs. It is obvious that the saturation of computer applications is still a long way off.

System needs as a result of this user environment include application packages, higher–level languages, documentation, and education. Although an application package to produce a complete turnkey solution to a payroll job or an inventory control application has yet to be developed, pieces of the application (subroutines) are available, and additional improvements will make it possible to approach the turnkey soluiton. The use of these packages can assist a company in obtaining more mileage from its own system and programming staff.

Higher–level languages or enhancements to existing languages like COBOL and Fortran can move the computer programmer still farther away from the painstaking and tedious job of computer programming and thus reduce the system implementation cycle. It may even be feasible for managers to write their own instructions, which can be interpreted directly by the computer. According to one line of thinking, doing so will be common in the future. As indicated previously, I feel that there still will be the need for information middlemen between management and the computer, although the development of higher–level languages will help reduce the communication barrier between management and the system analyst. One aid in this area is the use of data management languages, as mentioned in Chapter 5.

Improved documentation and educational techniques also play a part in enabling system analysts and programmers to be more productive in a shorter time period. Advances in automated documentation methods—for example, where the computer actually produces a flow chart—permit the programmer to concentrate on the main-line job of getting the program in operation while the necessary documentation is produced automatically as a by-product. Improved educational methods, such as programmed instruction texts and improved audio-visual facilities, will greatly improve the educational process and accelerate the learning curve.

4. Economical, Efficient Operation

Computer users spend more for EDP each passing year. This is a statistical fact of life. Figures show that the average hardware upgrade for a company is between 12 and 15 percent per year, whereas non hardware costs are rising at a slightly higher rate. A key consideration, in light of this rising cost curve, is that the EDP staff make the most efficient use of the computer facility.

Another environmental element is the increasing demand for uptime. Communication and real-time information needs emphasize the fail-safe concept. A batch operation in which reports are produced and distributed at the end of each day can tolerate downtime to a greater extent than a system that processes an inquiry from a sales office and returns the status of an inventory item within seconds.

Coupled with the uptime demand are the requirements for throughput and turnaround time. These two concepts have been described earlier; throughput is the measure of the total output of a system and turnaround time is the interval between the initiation of a particular job and the completion of it. The two concepts usually conflict, so that efficiency and economical operation are reached where throughput and turnaround time requirements are placed in proper balance.

One of the system needs brought on by the environment is reliability of operation. Mechanical or electromechanical devices, because of the number of moving parts, are not as reliable as electronic devices. Therefore there is more concern with peripheral devices than with central processors. System planning should take this factor into account and provide suitable backup facilities for those devices that have the highest downtime expectation and/or operate in a fast turn-around mode.

Today's computer users require operating systems for advance multiprogramming and communication processing. Operating systems have tended to be complex, difficult to understand and execute, and often inefficient as well. Users facetiously refer to operating systems as "egotistical" software systems—that is, software that is so complicated that it pays more attention to its own needs than it does to the user's needs. Users seek improvement that they reason may emanate from incorporating functions currently performed by the software into the hardware. The hope is that this firmware concept will produce easier-to-use and more efficient operating systems.

Multiprogramming and multiprocessing are the significant elements in achieving a higher performance-to-price ratio. As has been stated earlier, there is a considerable imbalance between the slow peripheral devices and the high-speed memory and arithmetic units of a computer. Multiprogramming and multiprocessing enable jobs to run concurrently, thus reducing this imbalance and achieving the most efficient use of the total facilities.

The performance-to-price ratio has been increasing notably in each succeeding generation of equipment. Mass-produced electronic components and batch fabrication methods have enabled the manufacturer to offer greater power per dollar of cost. The key measurement of performance to price has been the number of instructions that can be executed in a specified time period. However, because of the firmware concept and the power of multiprogramming and multiprocessing, instruction execution time is no longer a meaningful performance indicator. The overall execution time of the total application library of a user becomes the significant measurement.

Four major trends in EDP usage have been explored. The changing user environment from which emanated the system requirements were presented first in each case. This is a pertinent point to lead us into the next section—planning for tomorrow's computers. A common feeling within the EDP community is that the manufacturer has not properly reflected what the user really needs in designing succeeding generations of computer equipment. I will be quoting several EDP spokesmen throughout the remainder of this chapter. Their statements were made at a conference held in April 1969 at the UCLA campus on the subject of "setitng the specifications for the fourth generation of computing equipment." Total proceedings can be found in the book entitled *Fourth Generation Computers: User Requirements and Transition* by F. Gruenberger, Prentice-Hall, Englewood Cliffs, N.J., 1970.

THE PLANNING PROCESS FOR TOMORROW'S COMPUTER SYSTEMS

No one will question that the 20-year history of the EDP industry has been characterized by rapid growth and constant change. In the 1950s quite a few companies entered the computer field and folded. Those that survived went through violent reorganizations as their product lines changed and matured and the personnel transferred from company to company. I believe that most who have gone through this change will agree that there has been no parallel to the EDP industry.

It was a brand new industry in 1950, with no precedent. The product was highly complex, highly technical, and not very well understood. The product was marketed by a new breed of salesman and system representative who were very aggressive, very positive, very cocky, and very young. The company's products were planned, designed, and developed exclusively by engineers and mathematicians who wanted to use them to solve their own problems. This was a desirable situation because it ensured that the users had a major role in the planning process. However, as the industry broadened to focus on general business and data processing uses, the planning process did not broaden with it. Engineers and mathematicians were still the planners, designers, and developers of equipment.

The general consensus of the professionals at the UCLA conference, most of them users of computing equipment, was that the problems of the industry can be traced to a lack of valid user participation in the planning process. I can only strongly support that feeling, based on my experience both as a computer user and as a product planner with a computer manufacturer. There have been many abortive design efforts, some of which the public is aware, some of which they are not. These efforts have been major ones and, in some cases, multimillion dollar investments. Some of these products were aborted immediately after announcement or aborted at some stage prior to announcement. Every major manufacturer has gone through this harmful experience. The major cause of these expensive failures is the lack of a sound product planning effort that properly reflects user requirements as well as the internal economical and technological resources of the manufacturer.

As H. R. J. Grosch said at the UCLA Conference, "The thing that gives us strength and that also makes us dangerous is to mistake the ability to do something for the advisability of doing something." This has been so true in the EDP industry. The engineers have frequently developed products that work and work well but that are still in search of a marketplace. In some cases, a high–powered marketing force has found a marketplace, but not to the best interests of the user. Although the manufacturer's interests and the user's interests are not identical on every point, the growing competition in the industry makes it impossible for the manufacturer to ignore the user's needs for long.

Gerrit A. Blaauw started his talk at UCLA with an interesting note. He said

> The place of this discussion of hardware requirements for the fourth generation toward the end of the symposium is an indication of the maturity which the art of computer design has achieved. While the first-generation question was "Will it work?" the questions for subsequent generations have changed from "How should it work?" and "How do I tell it to work?" to the current question "What kind of work should it do?"

This is a most provocative way of putting the issue because it is true that the industry has been busy developing machines and making them work without a real appreciation of what work the user wants to put them to.

However, I believe that the industry is awakening to the general consensus that was established at UCLA. The users are realizing their responsibility, as was effectively stated by Dr. Cloy J. Walter:

The specifications of future generations of computers are not merely matters of speed, or efficiency, or technicalities; users need to clarify and declare their objectives. The lack of user feedback is growing more significant as we move from the off-scene use of computers for routine calculating or accounting into the intimate moment-to-moment use of them in our working lives. As users, we must participate in the design process in order to assure that people are influencing computers, or suffer the consequences of the converse.

Manufacturers are also aware and reacting to the importance of reflecting user needs in product planning functions. I headed up a computer product planning group whose stated charter was to ensure that new products and new product lines meet user needs, thus enabling the company to market and install computer products and services and thereby reach the financial goals established for the division. The group looked at product planning in the following manner. I think that this view is typical of the change in thinking that is taking place in the industry as manufacturers add user backgrounds, marketing backgrounds, and product planning backgrounds to their planning staffs.

The planning process requires the answer to three basic questions:

1. Who do we want to do business with?

2. What should we sell them?

3. Why should they buy from us?

The answer to the first question necessitates a thorough understanding of the marketplace with all its ramifications now and in the future. The first question leads naturally into the second and involves an analysis of the vast array of product offerings, including hardware, software, applications, and support services. The third question leads into the competitive real world and is a logical extension of the other two; it states: "now that we have defined the market and have specified the products, how do we make those products and offer them in such a way that the users are motivated to purchase and use our products?"

The product planning function can be viewed as the application of system analysis to the EDP marketplace. A company investigates, analyzes, and determines the economic and operational feasibility of a computer system to improve company operations, increase profits, and improve its return on investment. In effect, a computer manufacturer should design, produce, and market a computer system that does that very thing, albeit the task is far broader and complex in scope. The computer system in question is one that must satisfy a broad spectrum of the EDP marketplace and result in a satisfactory return on investment for the manufacturer.

Just as the single company's feasibility study begins with user requirements, so the task of a computer company's product planning function also begins there. The needs and requirements of the marketplace must be thoroughly understood and analyzed. The marketplace must be defined and segmented in a meaningful and comprehensive manner. Trends and growth patterns must be carefully assessed. Projections of the market and its dimensions for the next 5-to 10-year time frame must be made. Stemming from this analysis are basic product and market objectives, which must be consistent with the overal financial goals of the corporation. Based on these factors, specific product strategies are developed and translated into specific product requirements. The product is then specified, designed, tested, and manufactured.

Just as system analysis breaks down into three general areas of (a) *analysis* (establishing user requirements and feasibility of a system to satisfy these requirements), (b) *synthesis* (determining the system that best satisfies these requirements), and (c) *implementation* (developing the system and putting it into operation), so the job of introducing a new computer line takes the same form.

I believe that the application of the systems approach to planning for new products is a major step forward. For many years it has been a case of the shoemaker's children going barefoot: the manufacturers have sold the systems approach; they have not used it themselves. The result has had severe economic repercussions on both the user and the manufacturer. The theme is that the next generation of computers should be focused on the kind of work that users want to accomplish. It is important that users be able to express their needs clearly and definitively, without trying to design hardware. If the latter step takes place, we might have as serious a situation as when designers were interpreting user requirements. Murray Laver, Director of National Data Processing Service in London, said it very well at the UCLA conference. He stated:

> There is danger that users may be led into thinking of their needs in terms of improved machine performance. That they need faster, fiercer, smaller, cheaper computers is axiomatic but trivial, and when the computer users focus on fascinating technicalities, whether of hardware or software, they become like those hi-fi enthusiasts who, dazzled by decibels, tantalized by tracking errors, and intrigued by intermodulation, hate music.

SOCIOLOGICAL CONSIDERATIONS

As national attention is drawn to the sociological and psychological implications of technological events these days, it seems appropriate to conclude with several comments in this area. Sometimes these considerations are taken for granted, but both the computer professional and the non-EDP person who works with computers are remiss if they neglect this area, particularly when many of society's ills are blamed on automation. Sociological factors are not unique to MIS development; they are pertinent to the broad spectrum of computerization. As in any area of automation, I believe that these factors should be heeded.

The feasibility of computer applications was discussed in Chapter 4 under the headings of economic, technological, and operational feasibility. These three categories consider whether an application is profitable, whether it can be accomplished, and whether it can be effectively installed. An additional feasibility consideration might be whether it is socially useful or acceptable. H. R. J. Grosch stated it as follows:

I gave the keynote speech for the one-day technical symposium of the Washington ACM chapter some months ago. *Computers and Automation* incorrectly quoted some things I said there. They quoted me as saying that I thought ACM should direct its members into socially significant problem areas. What I had tried to say was that every person who calls himself a professional, and who shows it by joining ACM, should think for himself whether or not he should redirect his efforts from aerospace or defense work into something of a more socially valuable nature. There are, of course, people who regard passive or active defense work as socially valuable; I have no quarrel with them. I simply urge anyone who is concerned with a vital technological tool, before exerting himself to use it, to first ask himself "Am I using this tool for something that I think is valuable and right?" If, for several days in a row, you find that the answer is "no," then do something about it.

I think many of today's managers would view the preceding statement as interesting but a bit naive in the competitive business world. A statement on a recent résumé I received indicated that the individual's objective was to pursue a challenging, rewarding, and socially acceptable job in the computer industry. As businessmen, we expect an individual to be interested in challenging and rewarding work; we are a little surprised to see socially acceptable in a résumé. It raises a valid question, one that we should all give more thought to.

Another social objective is to strive continually to make computers more understandable to the layman, for man has the tendency to fear and feel insecure about things he does not fully comprehend. Every professional should attempt to remove the mystery and semantic barrier that exists between the layman and the professional. The insecurity and fear of others have a tendency to build our own sense of security and well being. Thus it is comforting to hide behind the technical jargon and esoteric appeal of the computing profession. This fear and lack of understanding have added to the general public reaction to the so-called faceless, impersonalized computer society. Students have physically destroyed computer centers and magnetic storage media just as they have burned their draft cards, forcefully occupied buildings, and taken over property belonging to those known as the Establishment. The computer professional is regarded as a prime destroyer of individualism by the radical groups of the left and as an impersonal efficiency expert by the more moderate. The computer professional has the obligation to counter this impression lest the social good afforded by computers in fields like medicine and education, as well as those in general business use, is swept away by the negative reaction. The computer must be placed in proper perspective; those of us who have been involved in designing and using the machines are in the best position to do so.

There is a social difference between using computers in the aerospace industry and in the medical industry. We have learned the system and calculations for sending men into space, but we have not developed the calculations for diagnosing and curing illness. There are obvious reasons why it is easier to use computers in aerospace than in medicine; however, there is an imbalance in the amount of money devoted to each. There is more profit in developing computers for aerospace and for industry. It is reasonable to assume that profit was necessary when the companies were getting established. But the industry is maturing, and manufacturers and users should be expected to dedicate a greater portion of their resources to the more socially oriented industries even if the profit is less assured.

I would like to add a word as to where I think the application emphasis should be in industries like medicine. I believe that there are things that men can do better (and probably always will) and things that machines can do better. The EDP industry has wasted a good deal of money trying to tackle applications that were not technologically or operationally feasible. A computer can aid the medical profession in record keeping and in the business end of operations; hopefully, it can help reduce the spiraling medical costs. It can aid in scheduling scarce facilities and in assisting nurses and doctors in the administrative aspects of their jobs. The computer can maintain historical information about patients and act as an extension of the doctor's recall system to uncover similar cases. It can maintain an index and retrieval system for medical articles, books, and journals. The computer can aid in the initial testing and screening of patients who are either ill or are undergoing routine checkups. I do not think the computer can accomplish surgery or develop the final diagnosis for a patient with neurological disease. I do not think a computer can replace a doctor or the major part of his job, which requires judgment, wisdom, experience, compassion, and manual dexterity.

The June 1970 issue of *Computers and Automation,* which was devoted to medical applications, demonstrated the point I am making. An article on electrocardiograms by computer is a case where a computer is capable of measuring, calculating, and analyzing medical data quicker, more accurately, and perhaps more economically than a doctor. It is an area that deserves attention and investment. It is an area where the computer can be superior to man. This is the way the system as developed by the TELEMED Corporation works.

> A mobile electrocardiograph unit is installed at the location (hospital, clinic, nursing home, doctor's office, etc.) where the ECG is to be taken. The electrocardiograph unit is an automatic three-channel data acquisition unit. It utilizes the 10 inputs of the classical 4-limb and 6-chest electrodes. A patient is wired with leads on both arms and legs (the lead on the right leg is ground), and leads on the chest. Switching circuits in the electrocardiograph unit make appropriate combinations, 12 in total, for sequential recording on three channels.
>
> The first three combinations include the 3 possible pair combinations of the active limb electrodes. The next three combinations include the same pair combinations as the first three, except each combined signal is attenuated and mixed with the remaining unattenuated limb electrode signal. Finally, the six chest electrodes are each mixed with the attenuated signals from all three limb electrodes combined. While the resultant signals are being used to drive a conventional chart recorder, they are also used to frequency modulate carrier signals. These are in turn transmitted to the computer center over normal voice-grade telephone lines. The mobile cart includes the oscillator and mixer circuits as well as a built-in Touch-Tone Pad for entering location and patient code information. Telephone lines transmit ECGs to the computer with no clinical distortion, and noise in the lines can be readily filtered out.
>
> At the computer center, the analog telephone signal is converted back into its original analog form, then converted into digital form and entered

into the computer system for analysis. The computer will then perform an analysis which will: (1) measure all pertinent ECG amplitudes and duration; (2) characterize the wave forms from each of the twelve leads of the scalar electrocardiogram; (3) calculate such factors as rate and electrical axis; and (4) produce an interpretation of the status of the electrical function of the heart based upon these parameters. The resultant interpretation is then teletyped back to the location at which the ECG has been taken, in digital matrix format with a summary set of correspondent interpretive statements.

["Real-Time Analysis of Electrocardiograms by Computer" by Dr. G. A. Kein, T. V. Balacek, L. L. Linka and W. V. Murphy. *Computers and Automation,* June 1970.]

Extending this type of computer application to other types of diagnostic tests is a sound and feasible social usage of technology. It promises major advances in preventive medicine.

Another article later in the journal illustrates, in my opinion, the potential misuse of computer resources and is a classical case of working on the wrong problem. The title of the article is "In the Year 2001: Surgery by Computer." I would like to think the article is science fiction, but I believe that the author is more serious than that. He refers to a patient who receives a kidney transplant from a robot doctor using laser beams after his problem had been diagnosed and the size of the artificial kidney calculated by determining his weight and body volume, the latter by a system of photo-sensing devices. The computer even calculated the patient's survival chances without the operation, versus his chances while undergoing the operation, versus his survival chances as a result of having had the operation, and then mathematically selected the best statistical course of action. The article concludes by stating:

> At the end of 180 seconds, Mr. Bright has a freshly tested, newly installed, artificial kidney that will outlast him, and he is passing on the conveyor belt out to the back door, where his timed recovery will enable him to get a post-hypnotic cue to "Sit up! You are all better again—and healthier and happier for your visit to Compu Hospital." And so, Mrs. Bright accompanies him home in their car, less than five minutes from the time that Mr. Bright walked in the front door of Compu Hospital, an ailing man, in need of a serious operation!

["In the year 2001. Surgery by Computer" by Robert Fondiller. Computers and Automation, June 1970.]

I think investment of computer resources for computerized operations or for full computerized diagnosis is rather absurd. Although both the electrocardiogram application and operation by computer are socially useful, we must use intelligence and our knowledge of machines to direct their use to those applications that are technologically, operationally, and economically feasible. I intended that "socially useful" be a fourth feasibility consideration and not be used *in lieu of* the other three.

Like other technological breakthroughs (atomic energy, for example), computers can have positive or negative social use. Computers with communication links can make possible the reversing of the trend toward concentration of workers in the large urban centers. On the other hand, they can facilitate the centralization of business and political power. I have often thought of the potential impact of having a voting machine in each home, linked over a communication line to a central computer where, in a matter of minutes, a public referendum could be conducted Computers can replace people and cause unemployment or they can open up new business opportunities and provide more challenging and satisfying jobs. Computers can take away freedom by maintaining personnel data banks and dossiers on each individual's public and personal life from birth, or it can give us more freedom if those same personal data banks are used to point out opportunities for underprivileged people who would not otherwise know of them. Computers can be impersonal by dunning us for erroneous bills or by sending us "junk mail" for vacation homes in Florida, while adding our name to burgeoning computerized mailing lists, or they can be personal by culling out our backgrounds and interests and matching us with job opportunities that would have been impossible to find on a conventional basis.

The message is quite simple to state, yet complex to carry out. The message is that technology always places power in our hands to use for good or bad, wisely or foolishly. The EDP industry has made costly mistakes during its maturation process, but these mistakes have not been damaging on a social basis. The social errors have been of omission rather than commission. However, as the computing profession matures, the potential for social good and social evil becomes much more real. The computer professional must accept this added responsibility and must add the social dimension to his thinking. Thus the message is simple. How he carries out this responsibility is the complex part of the job. It must remain an individual consideration. This thought was stated extremely well by Murray Laver.

> The falling cost and rising speed of computation could mislead us into substituting computing for thinking, but an ounce of insight remains worth a ton of processing. That we can type faster than he could pen, offers no assurance that we will write better plays than Shakespeare. There is a rather early limit to the substitution of good computers for bad mathematics. Computing mirrors the simplification of science; but in dealing with the real world we do well to heed Whitehead's warning "Seek simplicity and distrust it"; nothing can be safely left out. Progress in applying computing has so far been rapid; we have been advancing quickly over the open plain. Now we are reaching thickly-wooded foothills, and our progress will depend more on genius and less on honest journeymen; more on good ideas, less on hard work. People can be paid to work harder, but good ideas cannot be forced, and above all else it is in the efficient application of ill-conceived ideas that computers could have their most troublesome effects in influencing people.

SUMMARY

Chapter 8 has taken a look at the future of computers and management information systems. The discussion of the fourth-generation MIS for a manufacturing company led to the analysis of EDP trends under the headings of (a) advanced application, (b) systematic logical growth, (c) reduced system implementation cycle, and (d) economical, efficient operation. A plea was emphasized throughout for user involvement and proper reflection of user needs in planning for future computer products and product lines. The importance of management information systems was stressed as a cornerstone of user requirements. Whether the company is large or small, management seeks the real payoff from computers and that payoff means aiding them in making better decisions and in giving them more analytical information to control costs, increase sales, and thereby improve the rate of return on investment. This is the promise of MIS in general and management-oriented MIS in particular.

Finally, the social and psychological values of computer automation were discussed. Although the major focus of the book has been on the economic, technologic, and operational feasibility of computerized information systems, it is appropriate to include the social feasibility criterion.

Although computers can do wondrous things and can materially aid management in conducting its business, I think we must retain the perspective to realize that the discipline of management still remains part art, part science. There are still things man can do better than machine, and still things that only man can do. It will always be that way. I think this point is made clear by a book called *The Analytical Engine,* in which the science writer Jeremy Bernstein recalled the career of Charles Babbage, the nineteenth-century English mathematician who invented the analytical engine that was the forerunner of modern computers. Bernstein mentions the time that Babbage wrote to Lord Tennyson as follows (from "The Assault on Privacy" *Newsweek,* July 27, 1970):

> "Sir, in your otherwise beautiful poem 'The Vision of Sin' there is a verse which reads
>
> > Every moment dies a man
> >
> > Every moment one is born.
>
> It must be manifest that if this were true, the population of the world would be at a standstill. In truth, the rate of birth is slightly in excess of that of death. I would suggest that in the next edition of your poem you have it read—
>
> > Every moment dies a man
> >
> > Every moment $1\frac{1}{16}$ is born . . . .
>
> I am, Sir, yours etc."

STUDY CASETTES

BARTON MANUFACTURING, INC.

Sam Jones is the Vice-President and General Manager of Barton Manufacturing, a producer of lawnmowers, garden tools, and lawn furniture. Barton has warehouses and manufacturing plants throughout the midwestern 22 states in which the company operates. Jones has been a forceful proponent of computerized information systems and has thought for a long time that Barton could and should be tying in all warehouses and plants into a single computer network. This network would allow centralized buying economies, improved manufacturing control, better customer service and inventory control. There would be computer terminals in each sales office, each warehouse, and each plant enabling departments to instantaneously inquire into the status of an item or a plant order. Jones brought home his point by recalling the big order that they had recently lost because they couldn't ship for 30 days. The problem was that because the operating decisions of the company were so autonomous, the Salina warehouse actually had inventory of the item that was required to fill the order which was placed on the Brownsville warehouse. If a central system maintaining inventory records of all warehouses could have spotted this problem, it could have saved a key order for the company.

Jones called in Wallace Barnstone, data processing director, and indicated his desire to move toward a network approach. He was aware of the trend toward communication oriented systems which accessed central data bases and could spew out operating information in millisecond time to outlying plants.

Barnstone was a little chagrined because he knew that with the rather basic system currently in operation, it would take a complete new design and approach to get anywhere near what Jones was demanding. He had been through an attempt to completely resystematize and develop a communication-based integrated system and the effort had been disastrous. This was one of the reasons he took the Barton job—their EDP operations seemed straightforward, uncomplicated, and built on a solid foundation.

Jones went on to indicate he was dead serious in his request—that he knew it would be expensive and would take time, but he intuitively knew the benefits were there to justify the added cost. The Barton company was profitable and had the required cash to invest in this type of venture. It was for this reason that Jones wanted to move on the system now, while things were going well, not when they were in a weak, defensive position. He could see competition moving toward centralized information systems and he wanted Barton to retain its competitive edge.

After discussing the philosophy and general benefits of developing such a system for about an hour, Jones turned to Barnstone and said he wanted an initial report on the proposed new system to be presented to his monthly staff meeting in three weeks. He wanted Barnstone to take personal charge of this project, at least at this stage, and to give him weekly updates of the direction he was taking prior to the staff session. Jones indicated they were embarking on what could be the most significant step in Barton's long history and that he, Jones, would want to be involved personally in designing and developing the new approach.

Barnstone's head was whirling as he left Jones' office. He knew the general manager was a forceful man and meant what he said, but he wondered whether Jones had any idea of the scope of what he was proposing. Barnstone thought of his previous experience and wondered whether he could go through it again—and he must admit to himself that there was a growing doubt that this centralized, communication-based approach was the way to proceed. He knew he had some deep reflection ahead of him before he would meet again with Jones.

Study Questions

1. Do you think Barton should go to such a system?

2. Is Barnstone the man to lead the development effort?

3. How practical and realistic is Jones' approach?

4. What should be Barnstone's next steps?

5. How much can be done prior to the staff meeting?

6. Outline the contents of what you think Barnstone's report and presentation should be.

COMPUTERIZED DATA BANKS AND PRIVACY

[Excerpts from Senate testimony given by Robert P. Henderson, Vice-President and Assistant General Manager of Honeywell's Information Systems North American Operations, March, 1971]

In history there is no real precedent, legal or otherwise, for the situation today. The Constitution does not even mention privacy by name.

Thus I think that some new legislation is needed to protect this right. The legislation should give the right to privacy the same status as the rights to life, liberty and property—rights guaranteed by the various amendments to the Constitution. And of course, such legislation must be consistent with those other provisions in our Bill of Rights.

I think the best way to accomplish this now is to make some provision that would allow everyone to examine his own file, wherever it may be kept, and to challenge its contents if he feels the file is inaccurate. Everyone should have the right to know to whom and under what circumstances this data can be released; and in some cases the individual's permission should be required before the information is released. I think that a keeper of personal data banks would be deterred from irresponsible actions if he knew that the people referred to in his files could view and challenge those files.

Some concerned individuals have urged strict controls on the technology of data banks. I think that such action, at this time, would not be in our best interests. Because new developments occur every day, any legislation controlling today's technology would quickly be outdated by tomorrow's breakthroughs. Thus I believe that any legislation that would seek to control the data bank itself would be premature and I am against such federal regulation.

Beyond legal action, I think there is a great deal that can be done by the users of computers, including federal agencies.

In conjunction with the manufacturers, I think some form of standards for security devices and systems should be set to ensure their effectiveness. As a convenience to the user, security devices such as locks for terminals should be interchangeable between different computers.

I recommend that users conduct periodic audits of their data files to determine what information they have. One aim of this would be to erase information that is plainly outdated and irrelevant. If, for instance, a person received a speeding ticket 10 years ago, I see no reasonable excuse for keeping that data in the file.

Users should exercise a special sensitivity in selecting the personnel who have access to the data banks for no matter how secure the system, there is always the danger of people being compromised. Trained, dependable people are an absolute necessity.

Perhaps most important, I would urge upon every user who maintains a data base that he exercise concern over the matter of privacy and security at the very beginning of the system design stage. Building concern for the problem into the system from the very first is much more effective, and more economical, than adding devices or altering the system after it has been installed.

Finally, I feel that public education is imperative. As Ralph Nader has said, "The problem of doing something constructive is that there aren't enough people who care." The first step to the solution of any problem is recognition that the problem exists. If concerned individuals, businessmen, and others do not act soon, it may be too late. For control of information is power, and absolute control of information is technically just around the corner."

Study Questions

1. Do you think the government should control the technology of data base development to ensure that an individual's privacy and security are not compromised?

2. Do you agree that the type of safeguards described are adequate to ensure the right of privacy?

3. What role in information security should be taken in a company by top management, middle management, operating management, and EDP management? Whose problem is it?

4. How can we overcome the image of the computer as the symbol of the fully automated, depersonalized society?

BIBLIOGRAPHY

DIEBOLD, J., *Business Decisions and Technological Change*. Praeger Publications, New York, New York, 1970, 268 pp.

DIEBOLD, J., *Man and the Computer—Agent of Social Change*. Praeger Publications, New York, New York, 1969, 157 pp.

FREED, ROY, *Computer and Law*. Freed Publishing, New York, 1971, 663 pp.

GRUENBERGER, F., *Expanding Use of Computers in the 70's*. Prentice-Hall, Inc., Englewood Cliffs, New Jersey, 1971, 120 pp.

GRUENBERGER, F., *Fourth Generation Computers: User Requirements and Transition*. Prentice-Hall, Inc., Englewood Cliffs, New Jersey, 1970.

HAMMING, R., *Computers and Society*. McGraw-Hill Book Company, New York, 1972, 284 pp.

HITCHCOCK, R., and E. WILLE, *The Computer and Business Unity*. American Elsevier, New York, New York, 1969, 229 pp.

MARTIN, JAMES & ADRIAN, and R. D. NORMAN. *The Computerized Society*, Prentice-Hall, Inc., Englewood Cliffs, New Jersey, 1970, 560 pp.

MILLER, A. R., *The Assault on Privacy*. The University of Michigan Press, Ann Arbor, Michigan, 1971.

INDEX